D1337023

The Glovemen

The incumbent Australian keeper Ian Healy, designer of the splendid suits worn by the 1993 Australians on their arrival in England, is a model of concentration behind the stumps against the West Indies at Kingston, Jamaica. By scoring 102 not out in the first Test at Manchester against England in 1993 during his record stand of 180 unbeaten with Steve Waugh, Ian Healy became only the second Australian wicket-keeper to score an Ashes century (Rod Marsh was the first).

The Glovemen

THE WORLD'S BEST WICKET-KEEPERS

Jack Pollard

Foreword by

Rodney Marsh

ROBERT HALE • LONDON

ACKNOWLEDGMENTS

The photographs in this book came from the *Sydney Morning Herald*, the Melbourne *Herald-Sun*, the *Adelaide Advertiser*, the *West Australian* and the Sport And General agency (London), the personal albums of the wicket-keepers discussed, or are the work of the outstanding English cricket photographers Ken Kelly, Patrick Eagar and Adrian Murrell of All Sports. Kersi Meher-Homji provided the statistics on Indian keepers, Tony Cozier assisted with material on West Indian players, and Phillip Bailey, of the Association of Cricket Statisticians, with the statistics on English keepers. The bulk of the statistical material in the book, however, came from Ross Dundas, official statistician to the Australian Cricket Board and operator of the Sydney Cricket Ground's electronic scoreboard. Statistics in the book are current to the start of Australia's 1993 English tour. The front cover photograph of Rodney Marsh in action came from Ken Piesse's *Australian Cricketer* magazine. The back cover illustration of the 19th-century wicket-keeping star Tom Box was generously supplied by Stephen Green, curator of the museum and library at Lord's. The author and publisher would like to sincerely thank all of these people, and offer their special thanks to Rodney Marsh for his Foreword.

Front cover: Ken Piesse's shot shows Rod Marsh completing a rare stumping.
Back cover: Thomas Box, who made 397 dismissals between 1826 and 1856, when he was the finest keeper in England.

© Jack Pollard 1993

First published in Great Britain 1994

ISBN-0-7090-5371-1

Robert Hale Limited
Clerkenwell House
Clerkenwell Green
London EC1R OHT

Printed in Singapore

Contents

Foreword *Rodney Marsh*   7
 1 Prince of Stumpers   9
 2 Aunt Sallys   21
 3 Billy the Lawman   31
 4 Barndoor Men   43
 5 Warwickshire Duo   55
 6 A Trick with Steak   62
 7 Cricket Courtier   73
 8 The Ben and Charlie Show   83
 9 The Bundaberg Kid   92
10 Godfrey the Showman   102
11 The Griz   111
12 Wollongong's Finest   122
13 Old Iron Gloves   131
14 The Health Advocate   142
15 The Packer Influence   155
Appendix I   Test Wicket-keeping
             Records   164
Appendix II English Wicket-keeping
             Records   172
Index   176

Foreword

Rodney Marsh

It's generally thought you have to be mad to be a fast bowler or a wicket-keeper. I've tried both and would say that running any further than a few paces to deliver a cricket ball is an absolute waste of time and energy. Keeping wickets is for the adventurous, those who bore easily and, on reflection, for those with just a touch of stupidity.

There have been times when I would have given my eye teeth (had they not been knocked out while keeping) to have been a tearaway fast bowler. It would have been nice to intimidate a few of the fast bowlers who constantly terrorised myself and team-mates. Often, however, a well-chosen word can do more damage than a rearing bouncer.

Fortunately most of the glovemen I've known have had the ability to give more than they get and consequently are universally recognised as the characters of the game.

Jack Pollard has captured this aspect of the keeper in his well-researched book. It's essential reading for wicket-keepers young and old, but also absorbing reading for all cricket fans and all those interested in human nature.

Jack hasn't spared Old Iron Gloves. He's given him a fearful going-over regarding the early part of his career. Nevertheless it's a pleasure to write the foreword to a book on the sometimes forgotten men of cricket, the glovemen. May the keepers of the world continue to congregate after a day's play and talk to each other about the craft about which even the finest students of the game know little—that is, unless they've kept wickets.

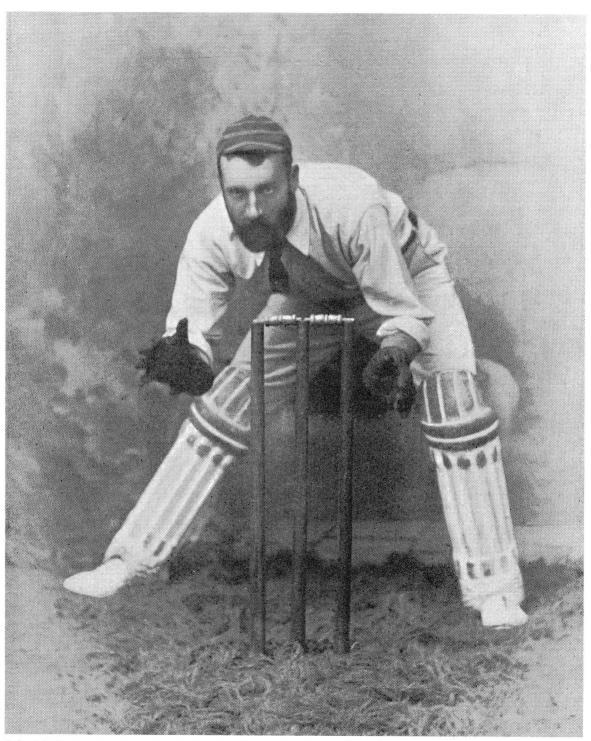

John McCarthy Blackham, Australia's first Test wicket-keeper, set standards which all those who followed have had trouble matching. W.G. Grace said he was the greatest of all glovemen.

1

Prince of Stumpers

John McCarthy Blackham appeared at a crucial period in the development of wicket-keeping as the toughest, most unrewarding job in cricket, a freakish player who single-handedly took the evolution of his job to a stage that gave Australia a decided advantage in the initial international matches. His role involved painful knocks, cracked ribs, the occasional loss of a tooth to balls that smashed into his face and frequent torment off the field. He had virtually no coaching but built an imposing record with fast, dexterous hands that dramatically exposed batsmen's momentary mistakes.

Wicket-keeping had evolved from the need of 18th-century bowlers to take a rest between overs. The most accessible spot was just behind, but to one side, of the two-stump wicket. Now and then a ball popped or flicked from the edge of the bat, then shaped like a hockey stick. Instead of allowing these deliveries to go down to the long-stop fieldsmen, the resting bowler intercepted them and in so doing showed the need for a fieldsman just behind the stumps.

On 22 May 1775, in a match at the Artillery Ground in London, the fiendishly clever bowler, 'Lumpy' Stevens, sent three deliveries between the stumps in a match which his team lost. The unfairness of this result caused the introduction of a third stump. The Marylebone Cricket Club, in its revised laws of the game, issued in 1830, said: 'The wicket-keeper must remain silent at a reasonable space behind the wicket, and not stir until the bowler has delivered the ball', and cautioned wicket-keepers against annoying the strikers with uncalled-for remarks.

Blackham was born 24 years later, on 11 May 1854, the son of a Melbourne printer who worked for *The Age* newspaper and lived in North Fitzroy. Frederick Blackham, also a wicket-keeper, gave his son the second name McCarthy because it was his wife Lucinda's maiden name and sent the boy to Bell Street school in Fitzroy, where Irish-born Tom Horan, later a Test team-mate, joined in playground matches. Young Blackham's talent for intercepting bouncing balls with bare hands was first spotted in a park match between Romsey and a Melbourne Press XI.

'I was a little fellow then, attending school and playing with Carlton Seconds,' Blackham told *The Referee* newspaper years later. 'I stood up to the wicket with a long-stop, and impressed John Conway, captain of South Melbourne, a crack footballer, who was to become manager of the first Australian team to England. Jack told my dad I could play for South Melbourne and the next season I became a team-mate of Conway, Frank Allan and Billy Midwinter, all of them Test players. In the final that year against East Melbourne, Lou Woolf, the well-known barrister, was our long-stop, a position in which he was a champion. He said, "I'm getting nothing to do, Jack", and suggested he should field at fine leg, which he did. At first I did not like being deprived of this safety valve but it gave the fielding side an extra man.'

Before wicket-keepers adopted the bent-knees crouch, Blackham stooped close to the stumps, legs straight but wide apart, back stiff, a slight figure with a gleaming black beard and generous moustache, hands in mittens like gardening gloves, and an unshakeable air of confidence that hid his highly strung make-up. He shrugged off the heavy blows that over the years took a big toll on his fitness, and fully lived up to John Nyren's instructions in his book, *The Young Cricketer*, published in 1833:

'The wicket-keeper may be considered the fugleman to a regiment. His position should be that of a man prepared to spar, so that he may in an instant move any way he pleases. His legs should be extended from each other. He should feel easy in his position, with the legs of the utmost importance in this situation. The upper part of the arms, to the elbow, should hang down easily to the body. From the elbow they should incline upwards towards the chest, both hands being open.'

Blackham's major contribution to his team's triumphs confirmed public acceptance of wicket-keeping as a specialist position. John Conway, who had played for Eighteen of Victoria against Heathfield Harman Stephenson's English touring side in 1862, in Australia's first international match, played a major role in his rise to fame. Blackham was working as a clerk in a bank when he won selection in the Victorian Colts XI at 16, but he was unable to win a place in Carlton's first team. Conway persuaded him to switch to South Melbourne on a promise of a first XI spot.

In Australia a lot of the early keepers captained their teams, but in England the majority of them were professionals and captaincy was left to the amateurs. In February 1851, banker John Marshall led Tasmania to an unexpected victory over Victoria in Australia's first intercolonial match from the wicket-keeping position. Three seasons later Marshall, believed to have been born in 1795 before registration of births became compulsory, was Australia's oldest first-class cricketer when he played for Tasmania against Victoria aged 58.

Blackham made his first-class debut at 20 when he played for the Victorian team which New South Wales defeated by six wickets on Melbourne Cricket Ground between 26 and 30 December 1874. He was one of the few Victorian successes in a rain-affected match when teams used a fresh strip for each innings, scoring 32 out of 149 in Victoria's first innings and dismissing five New South Wales batsmen. Two summers later

Blackham performed brilliantly for the Victorian Fifteen that defeated James Lillywhite's fourth England touring team by 31 runs. A fortnight later Fifteen of New South Wales beat England by 13 wickets in Sydney.

A return England v. New South Wales match on level terms ended in a draw when England had to catch their ship to New Zealand. Although England, 270, only needed to take four wickets for 47 to win that match outright over New South Wales (82 and 6 for 140), the performance of the Australians convinced Conway, who acted as England's agent for the tour, that the time had come for a test of strength on level terms between England and a combination of the best Australians.

Conway suggested that a match between 'All England' and 'All Australia' be added to the tour program. Lillywhite agreed that such a match had big money-making potential and took his players off to New Zealand, leaving Conway with instructions to arrange what became the first cricket Test.

Conway took advice from a selection committee chaired by showbusiness entrepreneur George Coppin, a generous donor of trophies for cricket competitions, but bypassed both the Victorian Cricketers' Association and the New South Wales Cricket Association by individually contacting selected players. The associations were not impressed. The NSWCA passed a resolution disclosing the match had been arranged without its sanction. Despite this, Sydney heroes Dave Gregory and his father, Ned, Nat Thompson, Charles Bannerman and Tom Garrett agreed to play.

Fast bowler Fred Spofforth, whose skills were a major reason for the Australian cricketers daring to challenge the English tourists, initially accepted but withdrew in protest when he found that his close friend Billy Murdoch would not keep wicket. Spofforth and Murdoch had spent much of their childhood together playing cricket on the old Pigeon Ground, later Gladstone Park, in the Balmain district of Sydney.

Conway stuck with his choice of Blackham as wicket-keeper, despite jibes from Sydney that he was showing home-town bias for a match to be played in Melbourne. Sydney fans argued that Murdoch's batting was enough to ensure him of

Billy Murdoch, Australia's second Test captain. Demon bowler Fred Spofforth refused to play in the first Test because Blackham was preferred to Murdoch as Australian keeper.

a place in the team and pointed out that Blackham had been unable to win a place in Carlton club's first XI. *The Australasian* made this scathing comment: 'Spofforth, apparently believing his success was due to his wicket-keeper and not to his own merit, and fearing he would be shorn of his lustre if another "who knew not Joseph" were behind the sticks, declined to play unless his own special wicket-keeper was picked. As this could not be arranged, this modest gentleman had to be left behind.'

Blackham was virtually self-taught when he made his Test debut in only his fourth first-class match. He had not seen the wicket-keepers in the three English touring teams which had visited Australia to that time. None of the keepers in those teams—Surrey's Heathfield Stephenson and Edwin Stephenson (1861–62), Surrey's Tom

Lockyer (1863–64) and Gloucestershire's James Bush (1873–74)—demonstrated more than journeyman talent. Their main concern was judging where balls from their lob bowlers would descend. Underarm expert, Cris Tinley took 171 wickets on the second English tour, with hauls of 27, 23, 26 and 22, or 98 victims, in four games against the odds (that is, against teams with more than the normal 11 players).

The selection row intensified when Spofforth's replacement, lanky left-arm pace bowler Frank Allan, sent a telegram from his home in Victoria, saying he could not spare the time for the Test match. Allan said he would prefer to go to the Warrnambool Show, held at the same time. Then Edwin Evans withdrew because, as an inspector of selections (government land grants), he would have to neglect his official duties to play. Conway patched up the gaps by bringing in Billy Midwinter and John Hodges, who had been unable to win selection in the Victorian team after a trial with Richmond.

Despite the immense pressure all this generated for himself and for Conway, Blackham remained unchallenged as the finest keeper in world cricket, from the time he took the field as one of the five Australian-born players in the first Test team until he retired from first-class cricket 17 years later. He quit with 455 first-class dismissals (181 stumped, 274 caught) to his credit. He not only transformed the entire concept of the wicket-keeper's role wherever he played, forcing captains to rethink field placements, but he gave the wicket-keeping art a special status. All over the cricket world selectors started to favour keepers for captaincy of their teams, aware that, even if only a part of Blackham's skill in detecting the opposition's weaknesses rubbed off on their man, they had an advantage.

Conway's judgment in preferring Blackham behind the stumps was accepted by all Australia after that first Test, when Blackham dismissed four batsmen and first displayed his amazing courage. He never made a Test century, but had 27 scores over 50 and an even 100 against New South Wales in his 6,395 first-class runs. He made his highest score for Australia, 96 against Warwickshire at Birmingham in 1888, and his highest Test score, 74, in his eighth and last Test as Australia's captain.

Blackham remains the only wicket-keeper from any country to tour England eight times and the only full-time wicket-keeper to captain Australia on an English tour. The first wicket-keeper to lead England in overseas Tests was Ronald Thomas Stanyforth, who had yet to play county cricket when he kept wicket in four of the five Tests against South Africa in 1927–28.

All bowlers found Blackham calm and unceasingly confident. The only bowler he regularly stood back for was the former labourer and miner Ernie Jones, who was given to wildly erratic spells and was one of the fastest bowlers ever, though he did stand back occasionally when Spofforth signalled that he wanted to bowl at his fastest.

England went into the first Test at Melbourne in 1877 without their only specialist wicket-keeper, Ted Pooley, who had been arrested in New Zealand on a charge of causing a malicious demonstration after a pub brawl. Pooley bet a local cricket enthusiast, Ralph Donkin, that he could forecast each Christchurch player's score against England. They agreed Pooley should receive a pound for every correct prediction and forfeit one shilling for every incorrect score. Pooley wrote '0' against every batsman's name and when nine of the Christchurch team were dismissed for ducks made a tidy profit. But the magistrate who heard the case held Pooley responsible for the disturbance that followed after Donkin realised he had been duped. When the first Test was played between 15 and 19 March Pooley was in a New Zealand police cell.

Charles Bannerman opened the batting for Australia in the Test, his seventh first-class match. Before he reached 10 he spooned a possible catch to Tom Armitage, but the ball rebounded off Armitage's stomach before he got his hands to it. Bannerman went on to 165 before he retired hurt, his finger split by a ball from George Ulyett. Blackham, who made a plucky 17, always argued that none of the great batsmen who followed, like Harry Graham, Jack Lyons, Clem Hill, Joe Darling and Victor Trumper, ever matched Bannerman's batting in the first Test.

When England batted, Blackham pressured the batsmen by taking all five Australian bowlers used by Dave Gregory from just behind the stumps, catching Charlwood and Armitage off Midwinter.

England keeper Edward Pooley, a fearless gloveman who was in a New Zealand cell when the first Test was played.

Leading by 49 runs on the first innings, Australia made only 104 in their second knock. Left to score 154 to win in the final innings, England were all out for 108, thanks to slow–medium left-arm spinner Tom Kendall, who provided Blackham with a catch and a stumping. Bowling off a two-step approach run, Kendall took 7 for 55. Blackham allowed only four byes in the match. England tried two keepers in the match as substitutes for Pooley, Henry Jupp and John Selby, who between them conceded only five byes in the second innings. A whip-round among MCG spectators realised £83 7s. 6d. for Bannerman and £23 5s. 0d. each for Kendall and Blackham.

Pooley was still fighting the charges against him in a Christchurch court when the second Test was played a fortnight later. He was again missed for he was the best English keeper of his time, the man who had taken over from the great Tom

Tom Lockyer, the great Surrey keeper who toured Australia as a member of George Parr's England team in 1863–64.

Lockyer when Lockyer's hands became too badly damaged for him to continue. From 1866, Pooley had a wonderful partnership with James Southerton. No other keeper could take Southerton's sharp off-breaks like Pooley, who was always sure and often brilliant when stumping. In 1868, Pooley dismissed 12 batsmen for Surrey at The Oval, stumping four and catching eight Sussex batsmen in a world record that still survives.

Pooley had exceptional charm and when the Christchurch Supreme Court finally cleared him of all charges local residents took up a subscription for him that brought in £50, more than enough to pay his fare back to England. Despite his acquittal, the case proved the start of a decline that often forced him to seek shelter in London workhouses. Pooley's brilliance as a keeper was shown in his career total of 854 dismissals, 496

of them caught, 358 stumped. He also made 9,345 first-class runs, batting right-handed in the middle of the order—highest score 125, average 15.86—but he never appeared in a Test.

Lillywhite tried to fill the gap left by Pooley's absence by giving John Selby special coaching to keep wicket for the second Test. Murdoch strengthened the Australian team's batting but Blackham remained wicket-keeper and was promoted to number three in the batting order in the first innings. He made 5 and 26. Spofforth and Thomas Joseph Dart Kelly made their Test debuts with Murdoch. Kelly, who owned the most dazzling multi-coloured blazer seen at an Australian cricket field, hit eight successive balls for four in Australia's second innings but his 35 could not prevent an English win by four wickets. Selby allowed 18 byes in the match.

Dour batting by the Yorkshiremen in England's team produced 329 of the 383 runs conceded by Australia. Blackham stifled Murdoch supporters by brilliantly stumping Alfred Shaw off Spofforth's bowling. Standing right up on the stumps, he whipped off the bails as Shaw moved forward fractionally to drive and at 2 for 4 had England reeling. He scorned the risk of conceding fours by keeping his nose close to the bails with Spofforth and allowed 13 byes (out of 27 sundries) in the two innings, compared to the 31 extras on the England scorecards.

Despite the lack of protection from his flimsy mittens, Blackham wore no inner gloves and seldom used his skimpy, slatted pads to stop a ball. He was 5 feet 10 inches tall (175 cm), and rarely weighed more than 11 stone (70 kg). He grew a heavy black beard and moustache soon after his initial Test appearances and kept them for the rest of his life. His stumpings in each of his first two Tests were the first in Test history, and were not emulated by an English keeper for five years, when Richard Pilling stumped Hugh Massie off Billy Midwinter's bowling at Melbourne in 1882 in Test number five.

Throughout his long career, Blackham was always among the first in the Australian XI to spot opposing batsmen's weaknesses. His captains soon learned to seek his advice, consulting him about fielding placements, bowling changes, one-off ideas to end long partnerships and the best ways of blocking opponents' favourite shots.

Blackham's habit of absorbing nasty knocks without the slightest emotion quickly made him popular with crowds, and in his native Melbourne they revered him. He had been taught at Bell Street school to honour the highest ethics of the game and tantrums were abhorrent to him. He seldom raised his voice in appealing and simply raised the index finger of his right hand to ask the question. Very few of these hushed appeals were rejected. English batsmen simply walked off when he lifted his finger, often still shocked by the speed with which he had stumped them down the leg side or punished them for lifting a boot out of the crease. When Blackham called 'Howzat?' in a Victorian country match after a legside stumping, the umpire answered: 'Bloody wonderful!'

The bald-headed Melbourne leg-spinner William Cooper told how he enticed the legendary English batsman Dr W.G. Grace down the pitch, only to have the resultant stumping denied. The umpire had noticed that Blackham did not appeal. At the end of the over Cooper demanded to know why Blackham had not supported the appeal. 'I was so excited over the chance to stump the old man I grabbed the ball in front of the stumps,' said Blackham. 'It was my mistake, but in the circumstances I could not appeal.'

Blackham only allowed fieldsmen to be positioned behind him on particularly bad wickets or when bowlers generated exceptional pace. The first Australian team to tour England played on some very rough fields in 1878, with pitches that received little preparation, but after the second tour in 1880 the Australians' high standard put them on to well-prepared strips on grounds built specially for cricket. More and more batsmen used the hook and pull shots in the 1880s, so the fieldsmen Blackham freed from duty at long-stop became very useful for their captains.

The first white Australian team to England played a vital role in pioneering international cricket. They were a sturdy, well-behaved lot, eight of the 12 heavily bearded. Only the Bannerman brothers, Alick and Charles, Billy Murdoch and Billy Midwinter shaved. They were splendidly drilled thanks to expatriate English coaches Charles Lawrence and William Caffyn, who had remained in Australia after touring in 1862 and 1864. The tourists were watchful for captain Dave Gregory's signals, and Blackham's excellence

behind the stumps lifted their fielding in 33 of their 41 matches. His understanding with all nine bowlers Gregory used on the tour gave them confidence and, even during long opposition partnerships, he always had encouraging words for the bowlers.

Blackham usually only rested to allow bruises to heal, with Murdoch going behind the stumps, but Murdoch was preferred for the big match at Lord's against MCC, the only selection setback Blackham ever suffered. Australia defeated the cream of English cricketers in only 3 hours 40 minutes, a victory that established its reputation in international cricket, but when Tests became a regular part of tour itineraries Murdoch never seriously challenged Blackham for the keeping spot.

Blackham became an amiable, courteous tourist, keen to mix with rival keepers and discuss mutual problems. 'His enthusiasm was boundless, his dexterity remarkable, and his fairness unquestionable,' the English keeper Arthur Lilley wrote in his book, *Twenty-Four Years of Cricket*. 'It was a perfect education for me to watch the perfect movements of this great player. There was no straining after effect nor any suggestion of the acrobat, which is occasionally an unfortunate feature with some wicket-keepers. His judgment was so perfect in estimating the behaviour of a ball after delivery, he could stop the most difficult delivery with the maximum of ease. I learned more by closely observing Mr Blackham and his methods than by anything I had been taught before or since.'

Blackham was the only player in the first Australian team with any musical flair, a compelling singer of black American spirituals, but was sometimes too shy to perform despite pleas from team-mates. For passengers on the ships and trains on which the team travelled, Blackham's rendition of 'Genevieve' and 'See that My Grave's Kept Green' tugged at the emotions.

Some English writers suggested that Blackham brought wicket-keeping to such undreamed-of perfection spectators watching him for the first time were disappointed his displays did not include juggling tricks. He was bemused by the knowledge that several early English keepers had dispensed with long-stops but he was given credit for pioneeering the move. English clergymen grumbled that Blackham deprived them of their traditional position at long-stop in village matches by showing keepers did not need support behind them.

Test colleague George Giffen wrote that Blackham was peerless for all the 275 first-class matches in a career that stretched from 1874 to 1894. 'One could not help admiring him as he stood behind the stumps at a crucial stage of a game,' said Giffen. 'With eyes as keen as a hawk and regardless of knocks, he could take the fastest bowling with marvellous dexterity and woe betide the batsman who lifted the heel of his back foot.'

Blackham finished second on the Australian batting averages to Charles Bannerman on the first Australian tour in 1878. He averaged 19.60, Bannerman 24.10, never surrendering their wickets without a fight. Nobody who caught even a brief glimpse of Blackham's talent behind the bails was surprised when he caught four and stumped six against Eighteen of Longsight. Six years later, when Australia beat the Gentlemen at Lord's, Blackham stumped the last three batsmen to give Australia victory by 46 runs. In 1878, his close association with Spofforth helped the bowler to a remarkable haul of 764 tour wickets, 281 on the preliminary tour around Australia, 326 in England, 69 in America and Canada, and 88 after the team returned home.

On subsequent English tours Blackham executed stumpings from the off-breaks of Joey Palmer and George Giffen just as easily as he took catches off the edge with Spofforth bowling on the first trip. His coolness showed in the Ashes Test at The Oval in 1882, when the excitement was so intense a spectator died and another nibbled through the handle of his umbrella. After Spofforth took 14 wickets for 90 runs, including a spell of four for two off 11 deliveries to give Australia victory by seven runs, Blackham calmly pocketed the ball that had been used. When the crowd in front of the pavilion shouted his name, he had the ball in his hand as he went forward to acknowledge the applause. In the summer of 1915–16 that ball went for £617 in an auction of cricket memorabilia at Melbourne Cricket Club in aid of a wounded soldiers' fund.

Playing for Victoria against New South Wales at Sydney Cricket Ground in January 1893, Blackham noticed that Frank Iredale lifted his heel when he turned balls to leg. He told medium-pacer Bob McLeod, who then bowled a yorker down the legside. Iredale missed it and was stumped. Iredale went off convinced the only way Blackham could have stumped him in the fraction of time his foot was out of the crease was to have caught the ball in his left hand and knocked the bails off with his right. The square-leg umpire and Victorian fieldsmen had to convince him Blackham's stumping was legitimate and had been executed with both hands on the ball.

Blackham's historic sequence of appearances in the first 17 Tests ended in the second Test at Melbourne in January 1885, at his own volition. He chose to join team-mates who refused to play unless they received 50 per cent of the gate takings. There was no national control authority at the time, with the Board of Control still 20 years away, but the Victorian Cricketers' Association suspended Victorian members of the Test XI for this action and blamed the gate-money row on John Conway, who pioneered Test cricket in Australia and overseas tours, and never let a money-making opportunity pass him by.

The gate-money dispute had simmered from the time the fourth Australian team arrived home in 1884. Thrown into the first Test in Adelaide in mid-December, the Australians demanded half the gate money and the match was only played when the South Australian Cricket Association compromised and paid each team £450. The Victorian Cricketers' Association immediately suspended the Victorians who appeared in Adelaide—Boyle, Blackham, Palmer and Scott. Spofforth, who did not play in Adelaide, expressed disgust at the money-grabbing demands of his team-mates. The upshot of it all was that Australia fielded a completely new team for the second Test in Melbourne in which only the captain, Tom Horan, and Sam Jones had Test experience. The Adelaide coachbuilder Arthur Jarvis took Blackham's place as wicket-keeper and one of the nine players making their Test debuts. England won by 10 wickets.

Banker Hugh Massie took over the Australian captaincy for the third Test in Sydney, with Blackham still under suspension. Jarvis kept wicket again, and Australia won by six runs, the smallest margin in Tests until Australia beat England by three runs in 1902. All the suspended

Arthur Jarvis, who replaced Blackham in the Australian team when Blackham joined team-mates demanding more money. Jarvis was destined to spend years as Blackham's understudy.

players returned for the fourth Test when Blackham became Australia's fourth captain in as many matches. Australia won by eight wickets after the giant George Bonnor, 6 feet 6 inches (195 cm) tall, 16 stone 6 pounds (104 kg) reached 100 in 100 minutes on his way to 128, which included four fives (awarded then for hits out of the ground) and 14 fours.

The dispute over gate receipts flared again before the fifth Test and Blackham was again suspended. Horan resumed the captaincy, Jarvis returned as keeper. Arthur Shrewsbury won the match and the series for England with a superb 105 not out. England won by an innings and 98

runs. Jarvis failed to make a dismissal in England's innings of 386 but caught team-mate Spofforth when he fielded as a substitute for England.

The top players' grievance that they were not paid enough for home matches sent Australian cricket into decline. Victorian officials suggested dropping one of the two annual matches against New South Wales but the association's arch rivals, the Melbourne Cricket Club, prevented this by taking financial responsibility for both intercolonial matches. Blackham, who had transferred from South Melbourne to the Melbourne club, was at the centre of the dispute.

The players were clearly too greedy in refusing to allow some of the profits from Test cricket and overseas tours to flow back to district clubs. Robbed of a share of income won by players they helped develop, the district clubs could not challenge the Melbourne club's resources. Many Australians were convinced that, given the Melbourne club's record for making correct decisions, it should take over administration of Australian cricket just as the Marylebone Cricket Club controlled English cricket, but the district clubs held out for their independence, determined not to allow one club to become their boss.

Blackham's selection as colonial captain had a marked influence on a revival in Victorian playing standards. Victoria had a history of wicket-keeper captains dating back to George Marshall, their first captain. Marshall, born in Nottingham on 20 December 1829, led Victoria for 11 matches from the start of intercolonial matches with New South Wales in 1856–57 to his retirement in 1863 because of a row in Sydney when he refused to finish a match. This stemmed from an on-the-field dispute that began when John Conway hit a Sydney player named Syd Jones with a nasty round-armer. Jones staggered about in pain, leaving his crease, and Marshall, a temperamental character, took the chance to stump him. The umpire at square leg upheld the Victorians' appeal but the umpire at the bowler's end refused it, saying he had already called for the end of the over. Spectators stoned Marshall as he left the field in protest and when further angry protestors gathered at his hotel Marshall left for Melbourne with team-mate William Greaves, who was also English-born.

The match finally was awarded to New South Wales after eight Victorians were dismissed in their second innings and the remaining two batsmen failed to appear. Curiously, New South Wales did not use a wicket-keeper in either innings. It all set the stage for a century or more of bitter New South Wales v. Victoria clashes.

Billy Murdoch dodged taking sides in the pay dispute by marrying a buxom amateur actress and retiring to his country law practice. Percy McDonnell could not get leave from the Victorian Education Department. Harry Boyle wanted to concentrate on developing his sports goods business. Yet it remained a major shock when the Melbourne Cricket Club invited Dr Henry ('Tup') Scott to captain the fifth Australian team to England in 1886 despite Blackham's superior credentials. Scott had no knowledge of the players or conditions the team would encounter and had to be introduced to several of his team.

George Marshall, the keeper who captained Victoria in her first 11 inter-Colonial matches, hailed from Nottingham. He was a keen advocate of cricket ethics.

There was friction among the Australians throughout the tour. Scott and Major Ben Wardill, who managed the team, spent much of that English summer adjudicating in arguments between the players. Australia won only nine of their 31 matches, but the tour was a financial triumph, with the Australians out-drawing county cricket. Not the least of Australia's attractions was Blackham, who was frequently applauded simply on taking the field.

The regular cheques for his share of English tour profits enabled Blackham to leave the bank where he worked as a clerk when he began in international cricket. He invested in a variety of shares and concentrated on his career in cricket, but despite the obvious appeal of his light, athletic frame topped by that shimmering black beard, he never married. Behind the stumps he retained a calm exterior as he matured, but inwardly he became more and more agitated as years of tense finishes caught up with him. Unknown to team-mates, financial woes wounded him deeply.

He took to pacing up and down the dressing room as he waited his turn to go out and bat. He hardly slept in matches in which he was captain, especially Test matches, and when Australia was in trouble he sometimes threw a towel over his head. Team-mates spoke of him vomiting in tight finishes and during a Test in which fortunes ebbed and flowed through the last afternoon he took a hansom cab ride for half an hour to get away from the tension.

Blackham made his eighth and last tour of England in 1893 as Australian captain. He had just won the rubber in Australia against the English team captained by Dr W.G. Grace and sponsored by Lord Sheffield. Tossing with Grace before the Melbourne Test, Blackham won the vital right to bat first in Australia's first six-ball-over match. Grace objected to the coin Blackham used. 'When that coin is tossed you have to take it into the light to see if it's man or woman,' said Grace. 'Don't use it any more.'

Grace and Blackham were involved in dozens of incidents but always showed great respect for each other. Blackham was not afraid to crowd the overweight Grace by pushing fieldsmen in close to the bat, but strongly defended Grace against charges of gamesmanship or unsportsman-like behaviour. This time fortune favoured Grace, whose team won the only Test decided in 1893 by an innings and 43 runs, with Lancashire left-arm spinner Johnny Briggs taking nine wickets.

George Giffen argued with Blackham on this tour whenever he thought Blackham delayed his entry into the attack too long. One clash almost came to blows but lanky Hugh Trumble stepped between them and pulled down their fists. Arthur Coningham, a notorious eccentric whose behaviour had no place in Blackham's strait-laced script, had so little to do he absented himself from the team for long periods. At Blackpool Blackham kept Coningham fielding out on the boundary for so long Coningham lit a small fire at the fall of a wicket to keep warm.

The Australian manager Vic Cohen was so unhappy with the team's behaviour he introduced a system of fines for misdemeanours. They lost their effect when they were not enforced. Cohen said he had to defend himself against more than one assault by drunken players. Factions within the team fought it out in punch-ups, and Blackham had more spiteful altercations with George Giffen. At Scarborough in the festival match they were reported to have 'tweaked each other's nose'. Lower gate money reduced tour profits and the players received £190 instead of the customary £500 or more.

Constant feuding drained six kilograms from Blackham. A kicking delivery staved in a rib and left him with a cavity he carried permanently. He had to ask two team-mates to stay with him in the dressing-room before Giffen went out to bat in one close finish. They were trying to pacify Blackham, whose hands were trembling, when Giffen burst through the door. With Blackham fearing a fresh disaster, Giffen reached into his kit. 'Took the wrong hat,' he said, returning to the crease.

At Sydney in 1894 Blackham took the field for his eighth Test as Australia's captain and his 35th over all, aged 39. He batted with stubbornness for 74, his stand of 154 in 76 minutes with Syd Gregory setting up Australia's total of 586. When England batted, Ernie Jones' pace forced Blackham to retreat from the stumps, a procedure he hated. Then a ball from part-time bowler Jack Lyons forced a thumb back, injuring the top joint of Blackham's hand and re-opening an old wound. For the rest of the match Blackham fielded at mid-off and Charles McLeod kept

A relaxed study of Blackham in his prime, showing the healthy black beard but not his highly emotional temperament.

wicket. When McLeod bowled, Jack Reedman kept wicket.

Blackham enforced the follow-on when England fell 261 short on the first inning, but Stoddart's Englishmen kept the Australians in the field from Saturday afternoon until Wednesday morning in a notable fightback, taking a 176-run lead. On the sixth morning Australia wanted only 64 to win with eight wickets left, but had to bat on a rain-soaked pitch. After nursing his injured thumb through sleepless nights, Blackham scored only 2 before he became Bobby Peel's sixth victim. England won by 10 runs. Blackham immediately retired.

When Blackham went broke in his old age, friends organised a benefit that brought in £1,359, but he had to dip into the Victorian Cricket Association's Distressed Cricketers' Fund. The Melbourne Cricket Club helped with a small annuity and friends paid for him to go to Sydney to watch the Tests. After his death in 1932 at 78, the VCA paid £125 towards his funeral expenses, shared with the Melbourne CC.

In big cricket's most difficult job, and on rough, bumpy pitches, Blackham set standards that all who followed have had trouble matching.

His hands had the magic in them that sets great wicket-keepers apart, providing Australia with skills that established her international reputation. An amazing 40 per cent of his victims were stumped, 24 out of 60 in 35 Tests, a percentage he sustained over 19 years. A few English and Australian keepers have enjoyed similar longevity, but very few from India, Pakistan, South Africa or the West Indies have lasted as long.

Luke Greenwood, who played 51 matches for Yorkshire between 1861 and 1874 and later became a famous umpire, said: 'If all the English keepers could be rolled into one they would not make another Blackham. At every point Blackham was smarter than our super specialists—offside, legside, catching, stumping or running men out.'

Newspapers announcing the death of the 'Prince of Stumpers' needed no interpretation. Their obituaries coupled him with the immortal racehorse Carbine, with whom he shared the nickname 'Old Jack'. Both were synonymous with courage. Dr W.G. Grace, asked to nominate the best wicket-keepers he had encountered in his 38-year career (1870–1908) said, 'There was only one, Jack Blackham. He was in a class by himself.'

Tom Box, prince of keepers in the 1790s, played 24 seasons for Sussex without missing a match. He held his spot in the All England XI solely as a specialist keeper.

2

Aunt Sallys

First evidence of wicket-keeping as a specialist position on the cricket field came in a painting by Francis Hayman in 1740 showing an underarm bowler aiming at a two-stump wicket with a player crouched behind, ready to gather the ball in bare hands. A year later, when cricket's first laws were drawn up, they said the wicket-keeper should stand a reasonable distance from the wicket and not move until the ball left the bowler's hand. The keeper had to refrain from making any noise 'that would incommode' the batsman and if the ball hit the wicket with the keeper's hands, feet, knees or head in front of the stumps the batsman was not out.

In *The Young Cricketer's Tutor*, published in 1833, John Nyren defined all the fielding positions, with advice to keepers to exploit to the full their view of the whole field. 'He is the general and is deputed to direct all movements of fieldsmen,' Nyren said, 'not by word of command but simply by motion of the hand.'

Stumpings were regularly recorded from the time of the first scorecards and Thomas Box, of Sussex, made himself famous as keeper for the All England XI by holding his place solely through his keeping skills. All of his predecessors had also been bowlers. The All England XI and other strong travelling teams flourished from 1847 until the 1870s, and then, as they disappeared, country house cricket enjoyed some popularity with teams that included guests of the gentry who owned the pitch and the adjoining house. The introduction of regular county competition in 1873 produced a new breed of English

professional cricketers, cautious men who had to deal with the carefree amateurs in their teams, attracted from the mines, potters' wheels and weaving looms by the emergence of cricket as a viable public entertainment.

Box became so famous for his wicket-keeping in the 1830s and '40s William Lillywhite wrote: 'Have me to bowl, Box to keep wicket and Fuller Pilch to bat—and then you'll see cricket'. Box frequently appeared for Players v. Gentlemen, and apart from his service to the All England team, gave Sussex 24 seasons without missing a match. Charles Brown, known as 'Mad Charlie', followed Box as England's leading keeper. Brown could flick off a bail with his finger when the ball narrowly missed the stumps with a speed that convinced batsmen and onlookers they were bowled.

Throughout the 19th century rough pitches were common. Sheep kept the grass down at Lord's but lots of ankles were sprained in the holes they left. Batsmen wore billycock hats as rudimentary helmets and protection against kicking deliveries. Wicket-keepers prone to dirty tricks were just as big a hazard, it seems, and each revision of the laws of cricket warned them to be silent. In *The Valiant Stumper* G.D. Martineau said William Yalden, Surrey and England, was one of the most talkative of the late-18th-century keepers. Nyren went so far as to say Yalden was not to be trusted when he put a batsman out, as he often resorted to tricks of low cunning.

Yalden's great rival was the smooth-talking Hambledon keeper Tom Sueter, of whom Nyren

The first known illustration of wicket-keeping, Francis Hayman's 1740 painting of an under-arm bowler in action with a barehanded man behind the stumps. –*MCC Library*

wrote: 'For coolness and nerve in this trying and responsible post, I never saw Sueter's equal'. Neither Yalden nor Sueter attempted to stop every delivery the batsman missed, only those that might bring stumpings or had been mishit. The others they left to long-stops. The ethics of the job were high among keepers apart from Yalden, speculative appeals were taboo and removal of the bails while batsmen were still within their ground was the work of 'nasty sneaks'.

John Hammond, from Pullborough in Sussex, also won Nyren's admiration. 'Neither Sueter nor Hammond ever put down a wicket without a genuine chance of putting the batsman out,' said Nyren, 'and they did it without fuss or flourish.' Both Hammond and Sueter realised the value of speed in stumping as more and more players advanced down the pitch to hit. In the 1806 match

at Lord's, Hammond caught the Hon. E. Bligh and stumped William Lambert for the Players against the Gentlemen and stumped J. Willes in the second innings. In between he had a bowl and dismissed the notorious gambler Lord Frederick Beauclerk, who had the intriguing habit of hanging his gold watch on the stumps while he batted.

Swiftness in stumping had become an important part of a keeper's attributes by the time Edward Wenman of Kent took over the job for the Players in 1829. He stood without pads or gloves, eyes on the batsmen's feet, ready to break the wicket. His judgment of mistakes was so good his appeals were seldom rejected. Wenman and his contemporaries had to be prepared to absorb a battering on uneven pitches and be rewarded by occasional stumpings. They took most balls one-handed, swinging their arm back to diffuse the pace of the delivery. Keepers' hands were so badly mauled they often found bowling a relief.

In a remarkable 17-year span as the Players' keeper that ended in 1846, Wenman's biggest challenge came in the 1829 match against the Gentlemen when he took the wickets of Budd, Jenner and Potter in the second innings. The Gentlemen's keeper Herbert Jenner responded by claiming four victims, restricting the Players to scores of 24 and 37. Jenner, often rated the best keeper ever produced by Cambridge University, became president of the Marylebone Cricket Club in 1833, aged 27.

David Lemmon, in *The Great Wicket-Keepers*, described how Jenner took up a position two or three strides behind the stumps and moved forward to meet each ball. 'His actions were electric,' wrote Lemmon. 'At the lift of a heel, he would skim off the bails. Active, athletic, with a quick eye and unbounding energy, he relished stumping chances above all else, but was always moving eagerly about in search of work.'

Lemmon agreed with Pelham Warner, Harry Altham and other cricket historians that Tom Box, who made his debut two years before Jenner retired, was the first Englishman to win his place in a first-class match only because of his keeping. Box began his career with an upright stance, but as bowlers' delivery styles changed he adopted a bent-kneed position and took to wearing pads and gloves. When Box retired with 247 first-class appearances behind him he had dismissed 397 batsmen, 235 caught and 162 stumped. He became the groundsman at Prince's, scene of many of his triumphs, and died of a heart attack in 1876 while changing numbers on the Prince's scoreboard.

After Box's departure, a new generation of English keepers contended for the number one position as bowlers went from underarm to roundarm and finally to overarm. Tom Lockyer, of Surrey, was given top rating because of his high standard on rough and damaged pitches. Sussex's Henry Phillips and Northamptonshire's Tom Plumb enjoyed outstanding success, but it was Lockyer who went to America in 1859 when England made its first overseas tour.

The most admired English keeper when tours to Australia became popular in the 1860s was

Harry Phillips, of Sussex, made a big contribution to the development of keeping in England when he dispensed with a long stop in the 1873 match against Gloucestershire.

Edward Pooley, whose courage was legendary. Pooley endured nasty knocks without complaint, breaking bones in his hands that eventually made it difficult for him to effectively grip the bat. His hands became 'mere lumps of deformity' with every finger broken and both his thumbs. One day at Lord's Pooley staggered into the pavilion with three teeth knocked out and Jem Mace, the famous prize-fighter, asked to be introduced to him. 'Pooley,' said Mace, gazing at Pooley's face in awe, 'I would rather stand up to any man in England for an hour than take your place behind the stumps for five minutes.'

Pooley was unhappily confined to a cell in New Zealand when Test cricket began. On Lord Harris' tour of 1878–79 there was no recognised wicket-keeper but the Irishman Leland Hone kept wickets in the only Test, which Australia won by 10 wickets. The first player to appear for England without first representing a first-class county, Hone was an old Rugbeian whom Lord Harris asked to join his team in Australia when Harris was without a keeper. Hone acquitted himself admirably in the Test by holding smart catches, but failed with the bat, scoring 7 and 6. He later made invaluable contributions to All Ireland scorecards.

His brother Nathaniel Hone followed him to Rugby and was showing rare promise for Cambridge University as a keeper when he went into a chemist shop in Limerick. Feeling unwell, he asked for a draught and by mistake was given a dose of carbolic acid. He died within a few hours. Two other members of the family played for All Ireland but generations later it was Nathaniel's skill that lingered in the memory.

Pads to protect keepers' shins were flimsy. Bandaged hands were common among keepers who shoved towels down their trousers to safeguard themselves against groin injuries facing bowlers allowed to throw without rebuke. In 1864, when over-arm bowling became legal, keepers started using raw meat inside their gloves.

The Rt Hon. Alfred Lyttelton followed Leland Hone as England's Test keeper in the only match in 1880. Lyttelton's brother Charles had scored the only century against Dave Gregory's pioneer Australian touring team in 1878. Six Lyttelton brothers played first-class cricket, with Alfred ranked the best of them. He survived the traditional path for affluent gentlemen into the English team, graduating from the Eton XI to the Cambridge University XI, both of which he captained, and appeared in four of the first five Tests played in England at a time when he was regarded as the foremost amateur keeper in England. At The Oval in 1884 when Australia's batsmen mastered all 10 bowlers, he took off the pads and gloves and took 4 for 19 with his lobs. Only two of his career total of 204 keeping dismissals (134 caught, 70 stumped) came in Tests.

Alfred Lyttelton was also England's leading Real Tennis player, a skilled rackets player, an English international soccer player, a lawyer and, from 1895, a member of parliament. He was always too busy to tour Australia and in 1881–82 the Lancashire professional Richard Pilling took the keeping spot for the Melbourne Test.

Pilling created a sensation by stumping Hugh Massie off Midwinter's bowling with only nine runs on the board, and he followed this by catching Joey Palmer and stumping William Cooper. But he flopped with the bat, adding only 5 and 3. He went without a dismissal in the second Test in Sydney, but made three splendid catches

Lancashire professional Richard Pilling, who caused a sensation by stumping Australia's Hugh Massie in 1881–82, the first Test stumping by an Englishman. He died of TB at 36.

in the third Test on the same ground. At Melbourne in the fourth Test he dismissed Blackham with a fine catch off Midwinter, but found himself replaced by Lyttelton for the sole Test in England in 1882 when Australia's seven-run win inspired the Ashes legend.

The Hon. Ivo Bligh picked Edward Ferdinando Sutton Tylecote, his team-mate in the Kent side, as the tourists' keeper when he assembled a team to regain the Ashes in Australia in 1882–83. Tylecote had distinguished himself in a house match at Clifton College in 1868 by scoring 404 not out for Classical v. Modern. He captained Oxford to victory in the 1872 Varsity match by eight wickets.

Tylecote hit 66 in the Sydney Test for Bligh's team, but managed only five dismissals in the four Tests, each side winning two. Thereafter Tylecote's touring was restricted by his appointment as mathematics master at the Royal Military Academy, but he distinguished himself by scoring

100 not out for Kent against the 1882 Australians at a time when Joey Palmer and Tom Garrett were overwhelming county batsmen.

Pilling regained the Test keeping role for the first Test in 1884 but was replaced for the last two by Alfred Lyttelton. The second Test in that series was the first ever played at Lord's and Lyttelton impressed by allowing only six byes on a deteriorating pitch and scoring 31. The third Test was the match in which Lyttelton handed the gloves to W.G. Grace and became the 11th English bowler in an Australian innings of 551. Five of Lyttelton's 12 overs were maidens and he finished with 4 for 19.

Yorkshire stonemason Joe Hunter, who had taken over in the county team from George Pinder, accompanied Shaw and Shrewsbury's English team to Australia in 1884–85. He was a regular member of the Yorkshire team for 143 matches between 1878 and 1888, making 217 catches and 113 stumpings before ill health forced his retirement and his job was taken over by his brother David. Joe Hunter died in 1891, aged 35. He had dismissed 11 batsmen in his five Tests and enjoyed some exciting triumphs for the Players against the Gentlemen.

David Hunter was without a superior in England in many of the summers he devoted to Yorkshire. Between 1888 and 1909 he caught 914 batsmen and stumped 351 for a career bag of 1,265. At Sheffield in 1891 against Surrey he sent back six batsmen, five caught and one stumped, and against Surrey at Bradford seven years later he caught two and stumped six. He appeared for the Players many times in the 18 years from 1891 to 1909 and, although he did not score a lot of

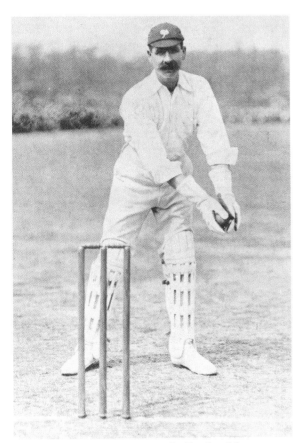

David Hunter, without peer in England in a career in which he dismissed 1272 batsmen. With the bat, he figured in lots of big stands for Yorkshire.

Mordecai Sherwin, a 17-stone Notts powerhouse, who fancied his stumping ability. He played in two Sydney Tests in 1886–87. He was probably the heaviest Test keeper of all time.

runs, he could be very difficult to dislodge. For Yorkshire David Hunter figured in numerous century partnerships without reaching 50. His successor as Yorkshire's keeper was Arthur Dolphin.

For the 1886–87 Australian tour, organisers Alfred Shaw, James Lillywhite and Arthur Shrewsbury decided to take Mordecai Sherwin as the keeper. Sherwin was the Nottinghamshire keeper, noted for his powerful, iron-muscled physique and sharp tongue. He was a remarkably nimble player for his bulk and his fleshy hands were seldom injured. 'Oi'm not much with moi pen, but oi'm ready to bung moi fist into face of any who says aught be wrong with moi stumping', said Sherwin, who usually spent his winters keeping goal for Notts County soccer team.

He made his Test debut at Sydney in January 1887, and scored 21 not out on a rain-soaked pitch in the second innings that had a big bearing on England's 13-run win. Left to score 111 to win, Australia were dismissed for 97. Australia brought in the virtually unknown Fred Burton to keep wicket in the second Test in place of Blackham, who was among the Australians suspended for demanding more pay. Sherwin stumped two and caught two in Australia's second innings to help England to a 71-run win.

At 17 stone (108 kg) one of the heaviest keepers of all time but extremely agile Sherwin captained the Players to victory over the Gentlemen by an innings in 1892, with four Notts team-mates in his side. But he played only one Test for England in England—in 1888 when Turner and Ferris gave Australia victory on a rain-affected pitch by dismissing England for 53 and 62. He was on Lord's ground staff for 25 years (1877–1902 and captained Notts in 1877 and 1888). In 20 years of first-class cricket, Sherwin dismissed 836 batsmen, 611 caught and 225 stumped. He was a genuine tailender, scoring only 2,339 runs at 7.61.

Sherwin's successor in the England team, genial, painstaking Harry Wood had successfully taken over from Tom Lockyer and Edward Pooley in the Surrey line-up when he was invited to play in the second Test of the 1882 rubber. He justified his selection by stumping Harry Trott and catching George Bonnor and figured in a last-wicket stand of 58, but he was not asked to play again for England at home. Wood did, however,

Fred Burton, who kept wicket in Blackham's place in 1887 in Sydney when Mordecai Sherwin was England's hero. Burton later settled in New Zealand.

make two tours of South Africa with English teams, in 1888–89 in the side led by C.A. Smith and in 1891–92 in Walter Read's team. He made 134 not out for England against South Africa in the Cape Town Test on the second tour.

English critics gave Wood a place among their finest keepers because of his consistency over 16 years with Surrey, for whom he took the bowling of speedsters Tom Bowley, John Beaumont, John Sharpe, George Lohmann, Tom Richardson and William Lockwood. His hands were badly mutilated by this battery. Strangely enough, when his hands became too sore for keeping he could often bowl a few overs of very useful right-hand round-armers.

Wood survived in the Surrey XI until 1900 and finished with a Test batting average of 68.00. In all first-class matches he made 5,523 runs at 16.94 and dismissed 674 batsmen, 556 caught and 118 stumped. He became a prominent umpire when his playing career ended.

Clapham-born Frederick Henry Huish attributed the fame he won as Kent's keeper to the coaching he received from Harry Wood. Between 1895 and 1914 Huish kept wicket for Kent in 469 matches and dismissed 1,262 batsmen, 906 caught and 356 stumped. Huish and Wood were on opposing sides in some epic matches, the tenseness of the play never interfering with their exchange of ideas on technique.

Cricket historian Haygarth found that Huish had an astonishing ability to recall precise dismissals from his amazing total. Huish twice dismissed 100 batsmen in an English season, in 1911 when he made 38 stumpings and in 1902 when he had 32 stumpings in his 102 victims. Australians remembered him for his run out of Reggie Duff on their 1902 English tour. Duff edged a ball behind the stumps. Huish did not try to pick it up but kicked it at the stumps. The ball missed the nearest wicket but hit the stumps at the far end before Duff completed his run. Huish was one of the few wicket-keepers to figure in a hat-trick by stumping batsmen off three successive balls.

Huish's failure to win Test selection was due to the high standard achieved by his rivals for the job. Best known of these was Gregor MacGregor, the Edinburgh-born keeper who was seldom out of the headlines for 20 summers. He was a brilliant Rugby player for Cambridge University and Scotland and played in his first cricket Test at Lord's in 1890 when still a month off his 21st birthday. He was lucky at Cambridge to have the fiery Australian pace bowler Sammy Woods provide him with regular catches. Like Woods, MacGregor rode to hounds, boxed with champions and regularly made 100 breaks at billiards.

From the moment he took his stance behind the stumps MacGregor's class was obvious to onlookers. *Wisden's Cricketers' Almanack* said: 'To see Woods and MacGregor in the University match was never to be forgotten. Putting on all his great pace Woods was apt to be a little erratic but MacGregor was quite imperturbable and equal to any emergency.'

Woods captained Cambridge in 1890 but in 1891 played under MacGregor. After graduation Woods went to Somerset and MacGregor to Middlesex, but for many years their partnership resumed in the Gentlemen's XI against the Players. Only Pilling came close to MacGregor on his best days, and MacGregor's inclusion in the English team discounted the advantage Australia had through Blackham's presence.

MacGregor invariably kept wicket wearing a tie and his Cambridge University cap. While the leading keepers of the period favoured bushy moustaches, his was pencil-thin and always trimmed. His hands were small but his timing was so smooth only unexpected bounces from rough patches hurt his fingers. He played in only eight Tests, sending back 17 batsmen, 14 caught and three stumped. His first-class bag reached 559 (411 caught, 148 stumped). With the bat, he made 6,381 runs at 18.02.

MacGregor's brilliance prevented Hylton ('Punch') Philipson improving on his record of five Test appearances. Philipson took the ball with easy grace and confidence from a position close to the stumps, with a ball sense befitting an accomplished tennis and rackets player and soccer fullback. He was an old Etonian who won blues at Oxford in four sports, a keeper who sometimes opened the batting and had a top score of 150 for Oxford against Middlesex in 1887.

Philipson played for the Gentlemen in 1887 and in 1889 went to India with G.F. Vernon's English team. He toured Australia twice, in 1891–92 as a member of the team sponsored by Lord Sheffield and captained by W.G. Grace, and in 1894–95 with Stoddart's side. MacGregor kept him out of the major matches on his first Australian visit but on the second trip he played in four of the five Tests, winning selection over Leslie Hewitt Gay, the England soccer goalkeeper who played cricket for Hampshire, Somerset, Cambridge University and the Gentlemen. Gay lost the Test berth after dismissing four batsmen and scoring 33 in the first Test because of his sloppiness in taking Walter Humphreys' lobs. Humphreys had taken 150 wickets at an average of 17.32 with his lobs in the previous English season.

Harry Rigden Butt was another highly proficient keeper who only got his chance to play for England by joining an overseas touring team. Butt kept for Sussex from 1890 to 1912, dismissing 1,228 batsmen with 953 catches and 275 stumpings. Despite damaged hands he sent back six batsmen in an innings several times and in 1903

Gregor MacGregor, who had a famous partnership at Cambridge University with Australian Sammy Woods. The only England keeper to compare with Blackham, he was a superb stumper who played in 13 rugby internationals for Scotland.

Harry Butt claimed more than a thousand victims, and carried on for 23 years with Sussex despite damaged hands. He kept in three Tests and later umpired six Tests.

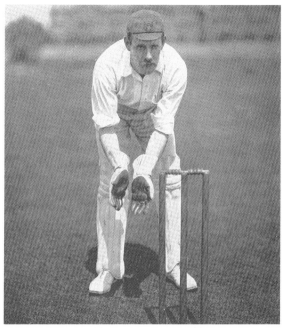

Derbyshire's William Storer, who missed a great chance to depose Dick Lilley as England's keeper when he dropped a simple catch from Australia's Joe Kelly.

against Hampshire at Hove caught six and stumped two. In four matches for Sussex at Hove in 1895 he allowed only six byes while 1,938 runs were scored. Butt had six seasons under Australian Billy Murdoch's captaincy. His sole venture into international cricket came when he toured South Africa in 1895–96 with Lord Hawke's team. He helped England to handsome victories in his three Tests, though he made only one catch and one stumping.

Arthur Frederick Augustus Lilley, widely known as 'Dick', made his debut for England in the first Test at Lord's in the 1896 series against Australia and continued for 35 Tests spread over 13 years. Other keepers only got a chance to appear for England when Lilley declined overseas tours.

William Storer, a polished keeper from Derbyshire, was one. Storer was responsible for 431 dismissals in first-class matches between 1887 and 1905, he played for the Players against the Gentlemen, and he was particularly admired for his coolness in standing up to the fearsome pace of Charles Kortright for MCC against Australia.

Storer also was a competent batsman with 12,966 runs at 28.87 and 17 centuries, but neither this nor his 376 catches and 55 stumpings could gain him preference over Lilley.

Storer's batting won him a chance to dispose of Lilley in the first Test of the 1899 series against Australia at Trent Bridge. But he missed a simple catch from Joe Kelly with Australia on 5 for 167. Kelly stayed to score 26 and add 62 runs with Clem Hill, a stand that proved the turning point of the match. Storer scored only seven runs in two innings and was replaced by Lilley for the four Tests that followed.

Storer toured Australia in 1897–98 as the number-one wicket-keeper for Stoddart's team, but failed to produce the big scores expected of him. He showed his versatility, however, by taking 22 wickets from 124 overs of leg-breaks at an average cost of 21.59. When Lilley continued to dominate the keeping scene in England, Storer began to bowl more. He ended his career with 232 wickets at 33.89 and in among his 12,966 runs was a double century, 216 not out for Derbyshire v. Leicestershire in 1899 at Chesterfield.

John Board, another fine keeper kept out of the England team by Lilley, toured Australia in 1897–98 but found Storer preferred in Tests. Board played all his six Tests in South Africa.

Lilley's high standards also restricted the opportunities of John Henry Board, a fine, fearless and untiring keeper for Gloucestershire for 23 years. Board succeeded J.A. Bush in the Gloucestershire XI and between them they handled the keeping chores for 40 years. Board toured Australia with Stoddart's team in 1897–98 but could not displace Storer in the important matches. His six Test appearances all came on his two trips to South Africa. He played two Tests there in 1898–99 and four in 1905–06, with Lilley declining both tours.

Board dismissed 11 batsmen in Tests, eight caught and three stumped, and scored 108 Test runs at 10.80. After his retirement from county cricket he coached at Hawkes Bay in New Zealand for several years. He had innings of 214, 195 and 134 in his 15,674 first-class runs, average 19.37, and scored more than 1,000 runs in an English season six times. Behind the stumps he accounted for a total of 1,207 batsmen (852 caught, 355 stumped).

All of these men set standards for craftsmanship and reliability that helped lift wicket-keeping to a cricket art form, opening up the opportunities for the keepers who followed. They gave their job an importance it has never lost and from the early years of the 20th century keeping has been regarded as a specialist position vital to any team's success. Some with little hope of scoring runs held their team spots entirely because of their keeping skill. Herbert Strudwick was an automatic number 11 from the time he first played for Surrey and England. Richard Lewis, the Oxford University and Middlesex keeper who toured the West Indies in 1896–97, made only 134 runs at 3.62 in 58 first-class innings. One keeper who could really bat, however, was the colourful Australian Billy Murdoch.

3

Billy the Lawman

William Lloyd Murdoch was a fun-loving lawyer who filled in as a comedian in shipboard minstrel shows on his five tours to England with Australian teams. He had the gift of conveying enjoyment to team-mates and opponents and through his diplomacy helped international cricket overcome problems that threatened the establishment of Tests. He remains the only player to captain Australia in six series against England, and the only man to keep wicket for both countries.

Nothing about Murdoch was commonplace. He ate, drank, smoked, talked and wore a hat in a style all his own and followed no fashions. A burly man of medium height, with clever hands and fast, twinkling feet that enabled him to play superbly on wet pitches, he was one of the few regular exponents of the 'dog' shot or leg glance between the legs. The great English games exponent C.B. Fry wrote that Murdoch was as at home at a Mansion House dinner with London's lord mayor as he was with Klondike miners.

As Australia's first high-scoring batsman, he was forced to safeguard his hands like a surgeon, and on the rough pitches of his period he could not afford to keep wicket frequently for fear of endangering his batting contributions. This became an easy decision with Blackham in such commanding form and superior to the array of keepers who had blossomed for English counties.

Murdoch's parents Susannah and Gilbert Murdoch came from Tasmania to settle in the Victorian mining town of Sandhurst not long before Will was born on 18 October 1854. The Murdochs moved to Sydney before Sandhurst

changed its name to Bendigo in 1891. Will learned to play cricket on an open paddock in King Street, Balmain, on a primitive grassless pitch with his elder brother Gilbert and a lanky, knobbly-kneed kid named Fred Spofforth.

The threesome were far superior to other Balmain kids and Spofforth attributed this to Murdoch's ability to keep wicket to his bowling. Will followed Gilbert to Sydney University, where they both graduated in law. The Murdochs joined the Albert club, Spofforth the Warwick club. Will made his debut for New South Wales against Victoria at the Melbourne Cricket Ground on 27 December 1875, taking over as keeper at Spofforth's suggestion when Nat Thompson injured his hand trying to catch Bransby Cooper. Will immediately caught Blackham and maintained a high standard while Edwin Evans won the match for New South Wales with 11 wickets, including 7 for 16 in Victoria's second innings of 34.

Murdoch retained the New South Wales keeping job in the match against Victoria in February 1876, but handed the gloves back to Thompson the following season, when James Lillywhite's English team were 6 for 185 at the Albert Ground in January 1877. He missed selection in the first ever Test, much to Spofforth's disgust, but went to England later that year with the first Australian team as Blackham's deputy. He had had a brief spell with the gloves when sunstroke incapacitated Blackham on the final day of the second test—Murdoch's debut—in Melbourne in March 1877.

Billy Murdoch playing his famous dog shot in which he lifted his front leg and leg-glanced to fine leg between his legs. He was the first wicket-keeper to captain Australia.

The closeness of the first two Tests convinced entrepreneur John Conway that the time had come for a white Australian team to follow the Aboriginal team that had visited England successfully in 1868. Conway picked the players to tour, bypassing the colonial administrative bodies. Murdoch, who at 23 had just qualified as a solicitor, was among those who agreed to put up £50 towards tour expenses, help raise money for fares by appearing in preliminary matches around Australia and in New Zealand, and to share all profits with team-mates when they got home.

Some of the players chosen thought so little of the team's prospects of making money they paid their return fares before they sailed from Sydney for America to ensure they would not eventually be stranded in England. James Lilly-white, the Australians' advance agent, was unable to fill all the available dates and occasionally the tourists found themselves in remote villages facing teams of 14 or 18 players. In a wet English summer they played in the rain to make certain they collected their agreed gate money.

Although he had not scored a lot of runs, Murdoch was preferred to Blackham in the celebrated match at Lord's on 27 May 1878, when Australia defeated a strong MCC XI in only 3 hours and 40 minutes. The great Dr W.G. Grace hit the first ball of the match for four and spectators settled down to the run-scoring they believed would follow, but Midwinter caught Grace off the second ball and MCC collapsed for 33, which included six ducks. Australia responded with a first inning of 41, Murdoch batting pluckily for what was described as a priceless 9.

Harry Boyle and Spofforth repeated their first-inning rout of MCC by dismissing them for only 19 in their second knock. Nine of the MCC batsmen were bowled. Murdoch, having stumped Alfred Shaw and G.F. Vernon in the first innings, did not concede a bye and Australia lost only one batsman in scoring the 12 runs needed for victory.

London newspapers were intrigued by Murdoch's understanding with Spofforth. The London *Home News* said: 'Spofforth's delivery is quite appalling; the balls thunder in like cannon shot; yet he has the guile when on a signal from Murdoch he drops in a slow one when seemingly about to bowl at his fastest, which is generally fatal to the batsman'.

Murdoch sent back four batsmen when he took over from Blackham against Eighteen of Hunslet on that tour, and also was behind the stumps against Twenty-Two of Buxton. In his only other wicket-keeping appearance on the tour, Murdoch took the gloves against C.I. Thornton's XI when Blackham was hurt.

Murdoch's tour statistics failed to show his dramatic development with the bat. In 39 innings in all games he had a top score of 73 and 49 in 28 first-class games. He averaged 13.98 in scoring 755 runs in all. The figures could not show the fun-loving nature, good fellowship and bonhomie he brought to a tour that lasted for 13 months. The team had a boisterous reception when they sailed up Sydney Harbour on the return home. In stark contrast to the lack of interest when they left, dozens of small boats went out to meet their ship. Crowds lined the shores and hundreds joined with a band to give them a spirited salute on the wharf.

Murdoch threw himself into legal work that had been neglected, familiarising himself with cattle theft, breaches of contract and a large amount of rural litigation. He sometimes appeared in court five times a day. Magistrates often irked him and he told his brother Gilbert: 'They are a lot of fossils, and when I've been here a spell I'll warm their tails for them.'

In February 1879 Murdoch found himself at the centre of the celebrated England v. New South Wales match in which spectators invaded the field on the second day. The English captain, Lord Harris, was struck across his back with a stick and A.N. Hornby had his shirt torn from his body. Harris had been so impressed with the umpiring of Australian football hero George Coulthard in the first Test, won by Australia in Melbourne, he took Coulthard with him to Sydney. New South Wales beat England by five wickets in their first match, in which Murdoch made 70 and 49. In the second match Murdoch made 82 not out in the first innings but England forced the follow-on. Fighting hard, the local team were 34 without loss when Coulthard gave Murdoch run out. Disgruntled punters who had heavily backed New South Wales were among the hundreds who jumped the fence to protest at Coulthard's decision. All attempts to clear the ground failed to end the demonstration, which captain Dave Gregory worsened by refusing to send in another batsman.

Some of the rioters spent the weekend in the cells and they were in court receiving £2 fines for common assault when England won the match by an innings and 41 runs on Monday morning. Immediately play ended Lord Harris took his team off, refusing to stay for the scheduled second Test in Sydney. England beat Victoria by two wickets and six wickets, with Coulthard umpiring in the two matches that followed before Lord Harris took his side back to England.

Murdoch's batting had improved so dramatically he was unchallenged as Australia's premier batsmen when the team for Australia's second English tour in 1880 was named. He confirmed his supremacy with a brilliant innings of 153 for the Australian XI v. Fifteen of Victoria, a display described as without equal on the Melbourne ground. His continued success as New South Wales captain led to his election by his fellow players as captain of the 1880 team to England.

The Australians always knew this would be a difficult assignment, given Lord Harris' outbursts on the behaviour of his opponents in Australia. They arrived to find they faced only five first-class matches. No Tests had been arranged. They paid the price for the Sydney riot by being forced to advertise for matches. Murdoch and manager George Alexander retained their friendly, outgoing demeanour as the team played their way through matches against fifteens and eighteens in isolated villages. Finally they were rescued by W.G. Grace, who arranged a meeting for them at Lord's that turned the tour from a disaster to a resounding success.

Initially, Lord Harris objected to the idea of a Test, claiming all the best English players were out enjoying the shooting season on the moors, but he finally was persuaded to stage the first Test on English soil at The Oval from 6 to 8 September 1880, the dates originally set for Australia's match against Sussex.

Spofforth was unfit to play after breaking a finger at Scarborough and manager Alexander had to play for Australia. The English team included three Graces, W.G. and his brothers Edward and Fred. The Hon. Alfred Lyttelton kept wicket for England, with Lord Harris captain. Lord Harris said he had only been able to complete the England team by writing to A.G. Steel and begging him to give up his grouse shooting in Scotland. The Australians joked that the match had only been arranged to settle a bet between W.G. Grace and Murdoch over who would make most runs.

When W.G. opened England's innings with his brother Edward before 20,814 spectators, Murdoch whispered to Joey Palmer to try a yorker first ball as it might get through before W.G. was set. Palmer pitched the ball in precisely the right spot and it passed under W.G.'s bat and grazed the stumps without dislodging a bail. The Graces' opening stand of 91 allowed England to reach 420,

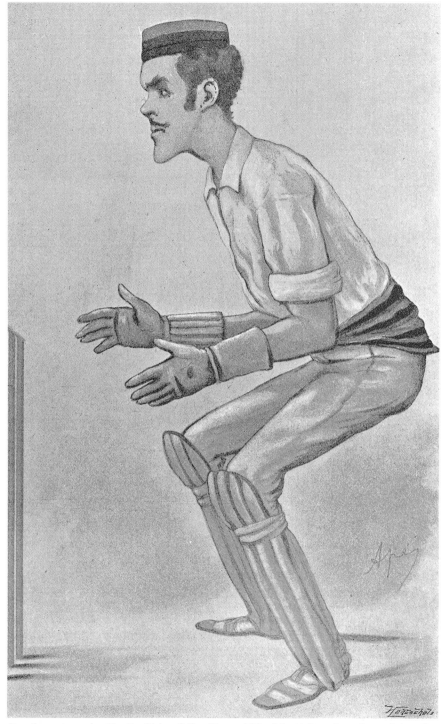

Spry's cartoon in *Vanity Fair* of the Hon. Alfred Lyttelton keeping wicket for the home side in the first Test on English soil in September 1880. England won by five wickets, but Lyttelton did not dismiss a single batsman.

with W.G. scoring 152. Murdoch was out for a duck in Australia's first innings of 149, but then played one of his finest innings in the follow-on against the best England bowling ever assembled to that time.

Murdoch and Percy McDonnell took the score from 3 for 14 to 97 before McDonnell went for 43, and later George Alexander and Bill Moule, the Melbourne barrister, stayed with Murdoch in valuable stands. Alexander contributed 33, and Moule 34 in a last-wicket partnership of 88. The innings ended at 327, with Murdoch 153 not out, one run ahead of W.G.

Murdoch's was the sole century by an Australian on that tour but failed to prevent England winning by five wickets. The Australians forced England to fight for every run in the 57 needed to win, but at 5 for 31, with G.F. Grace and E.M. Grace both out for ducks, W.G. strode to the crease. Without Spofforth to bowl, Murdoch could not prevent W.G. adding the winning runs. Australia's great recovery brought new interest to their tour, however, and in the last month they played six first-class matches.

The gold sovereign W.G. gave him in settlement of their bet never left Murdoch's watch chain. Australians living in London presented Murdoch with a giant silver loving cup to commemorate his innings. His aggregate for the tour of 2,405 runs included 339 in first-class matches at an average of 24.21.

The Australians received £1,100 as their share of the Test receipts but the important thing was that international cricket had been saved and Australia's high status in world cricket established. After 37 matches in England and 10 in New Zealand on the way home, each man in Murdoch's team, three of them only 19, received a handsome dividend. At a time when batsmen who made 50 were venerated, Murdoch's feat in becoming the first Australian to bat through an innings was regarded as miraculous.

Murdoch set up a law practice in Cootamundra on his return home, captaining the local team in matches against towns like Grenfell, Junee, Temora and Yass. His marksmanship on bush shooting trips was awesome and he was a consistent winner at billiards and a man who could handle a beer in any company.

In the summer of 1881–82 he was the leading Australian batsman in a program of 11 matches, scoring 679 runs at 61.72. He kept wicket for New South Wales against Alfred Shaw's visiting English team and against Victoria, and at the end of the summer helped Harry Boyle pick the team to tour England in 1882. In between he captained Australia to win the Test series two–nil, scoring a brilliant 85 in the drawn fourth Test.

At Sydney Cricket Ground in mid-February 1882, Murdoch became the first batsman to score more than 300 runs in Australia. He went to the crease after New South Wales lost their first wicket at 21 and hammered the Victorian bowling for 495 minutes in scoring 321, with 38 fours, 9 threes, and 41 twos. He gave only one chance, at 120. The match had been scheduled for three days but after New South Wales reached 775, then the world's highest first-class total, and Victoria had replied with 6 for 206, the captains agreed to add extra days. Murdoch missed the fourth day because of a Cootamundra court commitment, but returned to Sydney late at night in the milk train to resume wicket-keeping duties on the fifth day, when Victoria lost by an innings and 138 runs.

Murdoch's 321 remained the highest score in Australia until Clem Hill's 365 not out in 1900–01 and was recognised by a collection that reached £200, the presentation of a gold watch, and a trophy in the form of a Maltese cross. Three weeks later Murdoch took over when Blackham was injured in the drawn fourth Test against England in Melbourne. This match was advertised and it proved a promoter's nightmare.

Play began on 10 March but neither side had gained an advantage after three days. The fourth day, 14 March, was washed out, which forced the captains to leave the match an unfinished draw. England were scheduled to play Twenty-Two of Dunolly on 15 and 16 March and Twenty-Two of Ballarat on 17 and 18 March. The Australians had to board their ship for England at Williamstown on 17 March. The organisers deservedly were bitterly criticised for their choice of Test dates for what proved to be the last Test drawn in Australia until 1946–47. Murdoch's 85 enabled Australia to put on 110 for the first wicket—the first century opening stand in Australia. Alick Bannerman made 37.

Murdoch was on the field for all of the Australians' 37 matches in England. Blackham played in 31 matches, but Murdoch had to substitute for him when he was hurt or needed a rest. Despite his heavy workload, Murdoch showed no loss of form, scoring 1,582 runs at 31.64, with a highest score of 286 not out against Sussex in the second match. Critics rated his 107 not out against the New Orleans club in difficult batting conditions a superior knock. He also made some clever stumpings and held his catches.

The only Test of the tour proved a thriller, with Murdoch's shrewd captaincy the decisive factor. Murdoch won the toss on 28 August 1882, but his side were bundled out for 63, Australia's lowest total in England. Only three Australians reached double figures. Six were bowled on a turning Oval pitch. Spofforth put Australia back in contention by taking 7 for 46 and restricting England's lead to 38.

Heavy overnight rain soaked the pitch and here Murdoch made the winning move by instructing opener Hugh Massie to go after the bowling before the sun dried the pitch enough to make batting perilous. Massie made 55 of the first 66 runs at one a minute, vindicating his reputation for big hitting. Murdoch, 29, was the only other batsman to get a start and Australia were all out for 122.

W.G. Grace angered the Australians by running out 21-year-old Sam Jones when Jones left his crease to pat down a bump in the pitch. Jones had completed his run but technically the ball was still alive and W.G. saw that Jones had left the sanctuary of his crease. Murdoch protested that the dismissal was unethical but umpire George Thoms refused to change his run-out decision.

The Australians' resentment over the Jones decision stirred them to an inspired exhibition of fielding when England set out for the 85 runs needed to win. So many wonderful saves were made that even scoring singles became difficult. Spofforth and Boyle joined in with masterly bowling displays, but England appeared certain to win when W.G. and Ulyett took the score from 2 for 15 to 51. Then Blackham took a magnificent catch low down on the leg side to send back Ulyett. England still had eight batsmen left with only 34 required.

W.G. hit an off-drive off Boyle into Bannerman's hands at mid-off and was out for 32. England were then 4 for 53. Murdoch switched

his bowlers to bring Spofforth on with the dark background of the pavilion behind him. Spofforth and Boyle sent down 12 successive overs without conceding a run until Murdoch suggested Bannerman deliberately misfield to give Spofforth a bowl at Lyttelton. Four maidens later Spofforth bowled him. At 5 for 66, and only 19 needed, the Englishmen completely lost hope in getting a ball past a fieldsman.

Spofforth bowled 10 maidens in his last 11 overs and took four wickets as Australia went on to a celebrated victory. Spofforth finished with 7 for 44, Boyle 3 for 19. Horan wrote that after Grace left, incoming batsmen went to the crease ashen-faced, mouths dry, bats shaking as they took guard. The bowlers took most credit for Australia's seven-run success but Murdoch's uncanny field placements in blocking the strokes of England's finest batsmen won high praise. The pressure the Australians mounted reduced C.T. Studd, who had hit two centuries against them earlier on the tour, to a state of helplessness in his half-hour in the middle.

Australia's triumph created the legend of the Ashes when the *Sporting Times* published a mock obituary after the match, indicating that the ashes of English cricket would be sent to Australia. Twenty years went by before another Australian team was rated strong enough to compare with Murdoch's team, and over the years the legends of the Ashes match gained in colour. Spectators had had heart attacks in the excitement, one man had eaten through the handle of his umbrella. The cold fact was that Spofforth allowed only one scoring stroke while taking four wickets in England's first innings from his last 11 overs, and finished with 33 maidens in his 64.3 overs.

Only days after they arrived home from that tour Alick Bannerman (78 and 101 not out) and Murdoch (71 and 67) steered New South Wales to victory over Victoria in Melbourne. Yet when the Hon. Ivo Bligh's English team won two of the first three Tests and claimed the Ashes back critics said Murdoch's men had become stale, gross and careless, and accused Murdoch of drinking too much champagne. The criticisms were forgotten when Australian won the fourth Test to leave honours even.

Next season Murdoch made 158 against Victoria, with Richard Hall keeping wicket for

New South Wales. Early in January 1884, Murdoch scored 279 in Melbourne in the first of nine matches arranged for the players named in the 1884 Australian team for England against a Combined XI. This time South Australia's Affie Jarvis relieved him of the wicket-keeping duties. These innings gave him 567 runs for the 1883–84 season at an average of 113.40.

The 1884 Australians played three Tests in England for the first time and all their 32 matches were against teams of 11. They lost three of their first six matches in a bad start but won the only Test completed and had by far the better of the two draws. With Blackham and Jarvis handling the wicket-keeping duties, Murdoch was able to concentrate on his batting and in the third Test scored 211 out of Australia's total of 551. He headed the batting averages for the third successive tour, with 1,381 runs at 30.68 in a team that won 18 matches, lost seven and left seven unfinished.

The Surrey secretary Charles Alcock reported in *Cricket* magazine that during this fourth Australian tour of England Fred Spofforth and Billy Murdoch had become engaged to Derbyshire girls, but on the 48-day voyage home in the *Mirzapore* Murdoch fell in love with Jemima Watson, daughter of a Bendigo mining magnate and an actress prominent in shipboard theatricals. They were married a few weeks after they arrived home. Murdoch took Jemima to Adelaide for the first Test against Arthur Shrewsbury's English team but after 16 successive Tests, 13 as captain, he withdrew from the next 15 Tests, retiring to his legal practice in Cootamundra.

He left the Australian team in a state of deep-seated unrest, with the players determined to get a share of the gate money from international matches played in Australia. The colonial administrators objected strongly to this, claiming the money was needed for development of club teams and the Test players were already well paid from their English tours.

Colourful Newcastle saddler Dicky Bryant succeeded Murdoch as New South Wales' keeper. The Melbourne *Age* said of Bryant: 'The best wicket-keeper brought to light since Blackham has been discovered. He is neat, easy and remarkably quick, and unlike most youngsters stands up to his work with perfect confidence.'

Bryant first attracted attention in December 1882, when he stumped Ivo Bligh playing for Eighteen of Newcastle and Maitland. He had taken over the keeping duties when the selected player was injured. In his first match for New South Wales in Sydney in February 1883, Bryant sent back the first two Victorian batsmen, catching one and running the other out. His selection followed months of dissatisfaction among Sydney fans about Murdoch's apparently casual approach to keeping. 'Censor' noted in the *Sydney Mail* on 6 January 1883 that the side would be strengthened by the inclusion of Bryant, whom he said was by far the best keeper in the colony: 'Murdoch's inefficiency behind the stumps must have cost his side more runs than this very capable cricketer made off his own bat.'

Bryant kept wicket all day against Victoria without allowing a sundry, effortlessly taking the bowling of Spofforth, Edwin Evans, Tom Garrett and Sam Jones, but he disappeared from the team after only two matches. Just before the 1888 team for England was finalised, Bryant had refused urgent invitations to travel to Sydney to play against some of the selected players. NSWCA secretary Dave Gregory, Australian captain Percy McDonnell and Sam Jones all sent telegrams trying to entice Bryant back to big cricket but he refused to try out and his place was taken in the New South Wales team by W.J. O'Hanlon.

Bryant, born in Maitland in 1847, never got another chance to play representative cricket, though his gifts were widely admired. In his absence O'Hanlon and then the Carlton club's Fred Burton kept wickets for New South Wales.

After six years absence from first-class cricket, Murdoch was persuaded to come out of retirement to captain the seventh Australian team to England in 1890. He received a rousing reception from spectators when he led New South Wales to a nine-wicket win over South Australia. Senior players from Victoria and New South Wales who picked the touring team were divided about who to take as deputy wicket-keeper to Blackham. The Victorians wanted Jack Harry, the ex-miner, while the New South Welshman supported Sid Deane. The team left Sydney with the issue undecided but at a Melbourne conference Blackham suggested Ken Burn and a message was sent to Burn in Tasmania.

At two day's notice Burn accepted and he went to Adelaide to present himself at the wharf saying: 'Here I am—but I've never kept wicket in my life'. Burn's selection remains the worst in a long list of Australian selectors' blunders. Several of the 1890 side were tried as deputies to Blackham, but even in shipboard games Burn refused to put on the gloves. He had a miserable trip, playing in only six of the 21 first-class matches, but his batting was promising enough to win him a place in two Tests. He scored 41 runs in four Test innings and 344 runs at 10.42 on the tour. At Lord's he snapped the handle of his bat taking guard. Given a new bat, he was bowled first ball. Final score: two bats, no runs, no contact.

At 36, Murdoch could not repeat his dazzling batting of earlier trips but he headed the Australian averages for the fifth time, scoring

Tasmanian Ken Burn, picked to go to England as Jack Blackham's deputy, confessed when he joined the team that he had never kept wicket in his life.

1,394 runs at 24.45 in the first-class matches, including 158 against Sussex at Brighton. This prompted Sussex to offer him the county captaincy.

Australia were unlucky not to share the Test series distinguished by the keeping of Blackham and Gregor MacGregor. No byes were allowed by either side in the first Test, England winning by seven wickets. In the other Test, Dr John Barrett had the chance to run out England's last batsman and win the match but his wild throw instead produced overthrows that gave England victory.

This proved to be Murdoch's last appearance for Australia. His captaincy in 16 Tests had produced five wins, seven losses and four draws. The damage done to his reputation by Barrett's wild throw saw selectors drop Murdoch from the Australian team when he returned home on the grounds that he was too old. He made fools of the selectors and all who agreed with this notion by returning to England to take over as Sussex's captain and play for the Gentlemen and for England in South Africa.

Sussex enjoyed Murdoch's captaincy from 1893 to 1899 and the great Indian batsman Ranjitsinhji said he joined Sussex after leaving Cambridge University so he could play under Murdoch. When he wanted a break, Murdoch handed the leadership of a happy team to Ranji. They made a spectacular pair when batting together, Ranji the masterly exponent of the leg glance, Murdoch reviving his celebrated dog shot. Murdoch dismissed Sussex's claim that the birds embroidered on their caps and blazers were martlets and always claimed they were crows.

One of his Sussex team-mates, Charles Fry, wrote: 'Murdoch does not commit puns, of course, nor splutter epigrams; he is simply, genuinely, and unaffectedly amusing. It's the way, not the words. Mark him even now as he leads his adopted sons of Sussex onto the field. He has lost the toss easily; he has suggested to ten sad pals that "Now, boys, the white coats are out". How well they know the sound of that well-fed voice making that remark! And three or four of them were waiting, padded and gloved, jostling to go in first. "Not again, Billy, splendid sunshine, too, and a real treat of a Brighton wicket." But who would have expected so experienced a captain to have had so little control over a shilling.'

Playing for Walter Read's English team in South Africa in 1891–92 Murdoch saw countryman Jacky Ferris take 6 for 53 in the first innings. Wicket-keeper Harry Woods made 134 not out when England batted and in the second South African innings Murdoch allowed Woods to rest by taking the gloves. He made a brilliant legside stumping to send back Clarence Wimble for his second duck of the match. Ferris finished with 13 wickets for 90 runs, and England won by an innings and 189 runs.

South Africa had enormous difficulty finding a reliable wicket-keeper in these early outings in international cricket. For the Test against Major Warton's touring English side in March 1889 they gambled on Frederick W. Smith, a fast-scoring batsman for Kimberley (later Griqualand West), not then a first-class province. Smith was so

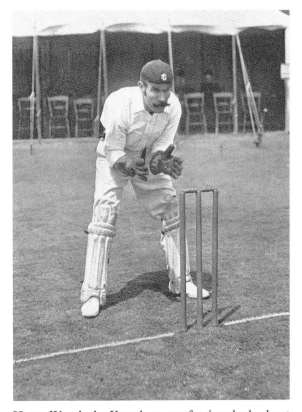

Harry Wood, the Kent-born professional who kept wicket for England in their first-ever Test against South Africa in 1888–89. He had little luck with his native county but was a success with Surrey, with 674 career dismissals.

unimpressive in England's first innings Sir William Milton replaced him behind the stumps in the second. Sir William had played Rugby for England and served as parliamentary secretary to Cecil Rhodes. He allowed seven byes, but kept like a park cricketer.

In the first Test Charles Aubrey Smith, later a famous Hollywood actor, became the first and only player to captain England in his only Test. He was succeeded in the second test by Monty Bowden, who used Harry Woods and himself behind the stumps, while Fred Smith kept wicket throughout for the Springboks, conceding 12 byes in England's innings of 292. South Africa collapsed for 27 and 43 and England won by an innings and 202 runs, Johnny Briggs taking 15 for 28. Bowden stood in as captain for C. Aubrey Smith, who had a fever that mystified doctors.

Fred Smith took over as captain of Transvaal. In 1894 he collided on the field with a team-mate and broke his collarbone. He made his third appearance for South Africa in the second Test at Johannesburg from 2 to 4 March 1896, scoring 4 and 11 not out in another lopsided match in which George Lohmann took 9 for 28 and 3 for 43 for England. Smith played as a batsman as the South Africans by then had discovered the wicket-keeping skills of Ernest Austin Halliwell, born in the London suburb of Ealing in 1864.

'Barbeton' Halliwell, plump, powerfully-framed, with a thick black moustache, toured England three times, in 1894, 1901 and 1904, establishing himself as one of the best keepers of his generation. Halliwell's father, R. Bissett Halliwell, kept wicket for Middlesex and the Gentlemen. Halliwell junior's success ended Fred Smith's Test career.

At the age of 18, Halliwell had migrated from England to the African Gold Coast, afterwards going on to India, where he played a lot of cricket in the north-west provinces before settling at Barbeton in the Transvaal in 1891. At Johannesburg in 1892 in a match between teams labelled the Mother Country and Colonial Born, Halliwell joined Tom Routledge with the Mother Country needing 350 to win in 105 minutes. They put on 289, Halliwell scoring 139 not out and Routledge an undefeated 147 before time ran out after the highest partnership to that time in South Africa.

Ernest Austin Halliwell, known to all cricketers as 'Barberton', the Transvaal town where he settled, returned to England three times as South Africa's number one wicket-keeper.

Praised for his keeping on the first trip to England in 1894, Halliwell found himself called a wicket-keeping maestro seven years later. He stood up to the stumps for the fast bowling of Johannes Jacobus Kotze, a Boer farmer from Western Province considered one of the most penetrative opening bowlers South Africa has produced. At home on matting pitches Halliwell was forced to stand back to take Kotze, who took 104 wickets in 1904 at 20.50.

Halliwell played in eight Tests, five against England and three against Australia in 1902 when Joe Darling's team visited South Africa on the way home from England. Joe Kelly kept wicket for Australia, whose spinners, Bill Howell and Jack Saunders, were responsible for the two-nil win in a three-Test rubber. Halliwell captained South Africa three times and persisted with the habit of placing raw steak inside his gloves in a first-class career that yielded 112 dismissals, 75 caught and 37 stumped. He made 1,702 runs at 19.34 in first-class matches. On the 1901 tour he played as a guest for Middlesex and the Gentlemen. He died of gangrene of the leg in 1919, aged 53.

One of Halliwell's team-mates in the Gentlemen XI was Billy Murdoch, who the following year joined W.G. Grace in the London County side. Murdoch was 46 and had spent seven happy years with Sussex, for whom his top score was 226 in 1895 at Hove against Cambridge University. The sight of him and Grace batting together was for connoisseurs but failed to attract enough spectators to keep London County solvent.

Murdoch signed off with 140 for the Gentlemen against the Players in 1904 at The Oval, his 20th century in a career that produced 16,953 runs at 26.86 and 243 dismissals, 218 of them caught and 25 stumped. He was 49 and with his departure London County went out of existence.

Old photographs of Murdoch at the crease in his mature years show a well-rounded face and a drooping Charlie Chan moustache, with the bat almost perpendicular and held well away from his bulging midriff by powerful wrists. There appears plenty of room between bat and pads for the ball to pass through, but even when threes and sharp singles were taboo, bowlers seldom found gaps in his patient, watchful defence.

In 1906, Billy and Jemima Murdoch heard of the death of his brother Gilbert, Mayor of Balmain, who had just failed in a bid to enter the New South Wales parliament. In 1911, the Murdochs brought their two sons and three daughters back to Australia so Billy could supervise the disposal of his wife's father's estate. At lunch during the South Africa v. Australia Test in Melbourne Bill Murdoch suffered a stroke. Four doctors failed to revive him and that afternoon flags flew at half-mast above the Melbourne Cricket Ground to mourn the death of a great player.

Murdoch died with W.G. Grace's gold sovereign still on his watch chain. He was 56. Jemima had his body shipped back to England and on 18 May 1911, during the funeral at Kensal Green cemetery, all play in English county matches was suspended as a tribute to a much-loved cricketer, a master batsman and guileful captain, if not a great wicket-keeper.

Billy Murdoch and his close friend Dr W.G. Grace together in England after Murdoch became captain of Sussex. Australians considered Murdoch too old for big cricket but he played for England in a Test after his homeland discarded him.

James Joseph Kelly, Melbourne-born but a lifetime Sydneysider, migrated when Blackham blocked his path to Test cricket, but endured to carve out an impressive record.

4

Barndoor Men

Arthur Harwood Jarvis was the first of the barndoor Australian wicket-keepers, large robust figures who gave the impression nothing could get past them. He was the first South Australian chosen for an Australian team, touring England as Blackham's deputy in 1880, 1886, 1888 and 1893, and kept wicket for South Australia from 1877 until 1901. He had the build of an outhouse door and could bat better than most critics recognised. Despite the frustration of a wizard like Blackham barring his inclusion in the Australian team, he remained a valuable, productive tourist.

He was the most distinguished of a family which made a major contribution to South Australian cricket. Three Jarvises played for the State. For most of his first-class career 'Affie' Jarvis kept wicket to two of the greatest bowlers Australia has produced, Ernie Jones and George Giffen. Jones was exceptionally fast but often erratic, but Jarvis was able to get to his wayward balls in a manner other keepers could not match. Jarvis' combination with Giffen brought dozens of catches and stumpings, with Giffen relying on Jarvis the way Dennis Lillee relied on Rod Marsh 70 years later.

Giffen wrote that when he came into first-class cricket Jarvis was the best batsman in South Australia, and it was for his batting that Jarvis played in the colonial team against Tasmania in the initial first-class match on South Australian soil in November 1877. Jarvis, born at Hindmarsh in 1860, was only 16, and he made a duck. But with the teams changing pitches for each innings, he managed four stumpings, two off Giffen and

two off John Bevan, South Australia winning by an innings and 13 runs.

Australia's initial English tour in 1878 showed that Blackham needed a deputy whose presence would allow Murdoch to concentrate on his batting. The selectors looked at all the available talent and picked Jarvis in 1880 for the first of his four trips to England. Unfortunately, Blackham hated missing matches and Jarvis had few opportunities. He had shown great promise on hard Australian batting strips against Lord Harris' English bowlers but on soft, often-wet English pitches his unsophisticated technique was found wanting. He made only 318 runs on the tour at 10.25 per innings.

Jarvis captained South Australia when they achieved their first victory over Victoria in March 1882, on Adelaide Oval. South Australia won by 31 runs after Jarvis scored 33 in each innings, with his second-innings partnership of 94 with John Noel paving the way to victory. He made 91 in February 1884 for South Australia against Victoria in Adelaide. The next season, when Blackham and others refused to play in the second Test against Arthur Shrewsbury's English tourists without a rise in pay, Jarvis was an automatic replacement. He made 82, top score by an Australian, but England won the Test by 10 wickets.

He reached 98 for South Australia v. New South Wales at Adelaide in 1894–95, 96 not out for Australia against Cambridge University in 1886, but in 226 first-class innings never managed a century. His average of 16.83 in 11 Tests was higher than his first-class average of 15.57. Behind the stumps he accounted for 197 batsmen, 114 caught and 83 stumped, 18 of them in Tests (nine catches, nine stumpings).

Playing for the fifth Australian team against Victoria in Melbourne in January 1886, he stumped four and caught two, in an innings. For the same Australian team he caught 12 and stumped five against Eighteen of Canterbury at Christchurch. At Wellington on that tour he scored 27 singles in an innings of 60, a feat that denied fans the big hits his burly frame suggested were within his power.

Unlike Blackham, who scarcely had a sound finger on either hand, Jarvis's hands were unmarked. His batting allowed him to play in 34 of the 1886 team's 39 matches and he gave a vastly improved performance, finishing with 823 runs at 17.93. 'If Blackham had not been around, Jarvis would have made a name for himself second to none,' wrote Giffen, whose off-breaks carried added menace with Jarvis standing right up to the stumps, exchanging signals with him about the next delivery.

Ernie Jones attributed his 19 Tests to the manner in which Jarvis tidied up for him when he let fly with wild deliveries early in his career. Without Jarvis to reduce the byes he conceded, Jones believed he would never have received a Test trial.

Jarvis, a happy, garrulous family man never short of a smile, was a coachbuilder by trade and took his nickname 'Affie' from a lisping nephew who could not master Arthur. His brother Alfred, widely known as Fred, followed him into the South Australian team in 1889–90. Fred Jarvis, eight years 'Affie's' junior, was one of Australia's best cricketers, playing 54 matches for South Australia without Test recognition. Affie's son Harwood played two matches for South Australia in 1905–06, scoring five runs before he was dropped, and returned to keeping for West Torrens.

Midway through Jarvis' career Australian selectors were attracted by Frederick James Burton, born in 1865, who kept for Carlton CC in Sydney. Burton made his Test debut against England in Sydney on 25 February, 1887 when Blackham, Giffen, Bruce, John Trumble and Palmer refused the pay offered. He went in last, did not score in the first innings, stumped J.M.

Read off Ferris in England's second innings, and was 2 not out when England won by 71 runs.

Burton looked impressive in the nets and had a second chance the following season, when he fielded while Blackham kept wicket. He managed only 2 runs and left the Test arena with an average of 2.00 and a career total of 32 dismissals (25 caught, seven stumped). Burton was the ninth keeper used by New South Wales in first-class cricket, following W.L. Murdoch (Albert CC), Dick Hall (Carlton), Richard Bryant (Newcastle), Billy O'Hanlon (Carlton), Jack Callachor (Carlton), Isaac ('Ike') Wales (Warwick) and Jimmy Searle (Sydney). Victoria had a similar high turnover and in the period 1887 to 1909 used 14 keepers, including Tom Hastings who remains the only Sheffield Shield batsman to make a century batting at number 11, a feat he achieved in 1903 with 106 not out in his only innings over 25 in 15 state matches.

Burton settled in New Zealand at the turn of the century and in 1905 umpired an Australia v. New Zealand match when Australia were on route to England. He died at Wanganui during the Depression in 1929, a year after his wife's death, leaving four orphan sons. Despite hardships, all four played for senior school teams and three represented their provinces.

By the mid-1880s George Giffen's all-round brilliance prevailed in his duel with Jarvis for the South Australian captaincy. They remained firm friends and a remarkably successful combination in the final years of intercolonial cricket and the initial years of the Sheffield Shield competition. Giffen often used Jarvis as an opening batsman and in 1887–88 when two English teams toured Australia—one captained by G.F. Vernon, the other by Arthur Shrewsbury—Jarvis and Giffen opened the South Australian innings. Jarvis had the chance to press for Test selection when he opened for an Australian XI against Shrewsbury's team in Sydney, but missed selection in the only Test played that summer, with Blackham keeping wicket.

Percy McDonnell used Jarvis mainly as a batsman on the sixth Australian team's 1888 English tour. Soft pitches again exposed his technical deficiencies and in 52 innings he contributed only 597 runs at 12.18. He played his best innings for the team with a bright 57 against

Combined Victoria and New South Wales on his return home. He missed selection in the 1890 touring team when selectors made their infamous blunder by including Ken Burn as the second keeper, but was back for the 1893 tour when Blackham's presence again restricted his opportunities and he played mainly as a batsman in 15 of the side's 26 matches, scoring 61 runs at 4.98.

Typical of his misfortune on this tour was his appearance at Lord's in the match against MCC. Charles Kortright, rated as the world's fastest bowler at that time, scattered Jarvis' stumps with the first ball in both innings. It was reported that Jarvis could not restrain a chuckle as he disappeared into the pavilion.

Selectors showed their faith in Jarvis when Blackham retired after the first Test in 1894–95 against Andrew Stoddart's Englishmen by inviting him to keep wicket in the four remaining Tests. He made eight stumpings in these four Tests, demonstrating his high calibre in taking turning deliveries from Giffen, C.T.B. Turner and the Trott brothers. For all his bulk, his reflexes were fast and his work polished in an outstanding farewell to international cricket.

When Joe Darling took over as South Australian captain Jarvis frequently cooperated in a ploy to inject extra pace into Ernie Jones' bowling. As Jones wilted in the heat, Jarvis took up his stance just behind the stumps. Affronted, Jones reacted to this slur with a volley of deliveries of awesome speed.

In his 11 Tests, seven in Australia, Jarvis conceded exceptionally few byes, considering the rough pitches used.

James Joseph Kelly, born in Port Melbourne on 10 May 1867, suffered similar frustrations to Jarvis because of Blackham's dominance. He learnt his cricket in Victoria, but migrated to New South Wales when Blackham blocked his progress into first-class cricket, joining the powerful Paddington club where he benefited from the brilliance of team-mates Victor Trumper, Monty Noble, Dan Gee and Alick McKenzie. He made his debut for New South Wales against Stoddart's England XI in November 1894 and remained a colourful figure in Australian first-class cricket for 10 tough seasons, building a record to rival Blackham's, but without Blackham's natural talent.

Kelly was built on similar lines to Jarvis and

Kelly was tough and durable, ready to take nasty knocks as part of his job. He was also prominent among Australian cricketers who carefully cultivated moustaches.

gave the same impression that nothing would get past his wide shoulders and huge hands. He stood up to the stumps for all bar the fastest bowlers and during his career kept wicket to a variety of spinners (Saunders, Howell, McKibbin), medium-pacers (Noble, Trumble, McLeod) and pace bowlers (Jones, Cotter) with equal success. His stamina never faltered and he was as alert for half chances at the end of a day as at the start. His advice was always sought by bowlers eager to break long stands and he had Blackham's tenacity in absorbing nasty knocks without loss of purpose. His success was entirely due to his nerve and pluck, for he was never graceful.

He became the New South Wales keeper in 1894–95 and was virtually unchallenged for the job for ten years. He went to England four times with Australian teams, in 1896, 1899, 1902 and 1905. In his debut at Lord's in 1896 against the MCC he made 8, his side's top score in a total of 18. He began his Test career at Lord's on that tour when England won by six wickets despite a record fourth-wicket stand of 221 in 160 minutes by Harry Trott (143) and Syd Gregory (103).

Kelly and Hugh Trumble won the second Test for Australia at Old Trafford by three wickets by scoring the 25 required for victory, defying the great fast bowler Tom Richardson as they edged closer to the target in singles. Australian captain Harry Trott, with only batting duffers McKibbin and Jones to bat, could not watch and took a ride in a hansom cab to save himself from nervous collapse.

Despite his air of clumsiness Kelly missed very few catches, few byes eluded his vast hands and he was quick to take stumping chances. Opponents respected the fairness of his appeals and he was certainly not one of the dirty-tricks men John Nyren referred to in discussing wicket-keepers. He stooped without bending the knees, legs wide apart, fingers pointing towards the bails, generous moustache conspicuous on his craggy face. George Giffen wrote: 'Joe Kelly was a big-hearted cricketer whom no disaster could appal'.

With the bat, Kelly could defend or hit as his captain ordered. He made 4,108 runs in first-class matches at an average of 19.94, with highest scores of 108 for New South Wales against South Australia in Sydney in 1896–97, 103 for Australia v. Warwickshire at Edgbaston in 1899 and 102 not out for Australia v. the Rest at Sydney in 1898–99. In an innings of 98 for Paddington against Waverley in 1904 Kelly and Victor Trumper (189 not out) put on 219 runs in 90 minutes, including 51 from 18 balls from top-class spinner Tom Howard. In 36 Tests Kelly made 664 runs at 17.02 and sent back 63 batsmen (43 caught and 20 stumped). In the Sydney Test in 1902 he took eight catches.

Team-mates ridiculed Kelly's comment when he returned to the pavilion at Lord's on the 1902 tour, shaking his head in disbelief after facing Bernard Bosanquet. 'There's a bloke out there bowling leg-breaks that turn back from the off,' said Kelly, in an apt description of Bosanquet's revolutionary googly. English keeper Dick Lilley had been so impressed by the delivery he arranged special practice in taking it.

The Australians paid a high price for forgetting that wicket-keepers are keen judges of bowling skills and in 1903–04 Bosanquet took 6 for 51 with his new delivery to win the Sydney Test. At one point he had 6 for 12.

Kelly announced his decision to retire after Australia's 1905 English tour, owing to a damaged finger and a weakness of the heart caused by a blow he received from a ball bowled by Walter Brearley. His benefit match in Sydney in 1906 earned him £1,400. He served as cook to the 28th Australian Infantry Battalion in World War I. Kelly died at 71 on the same day in 1938 as his old team-mate Hugh Trumble.

Alfred Ernest Johns, born on 22 January 1868 in the Melbourne suburb of Hawthorn, went to England with the 1896 and 1899 Australian teams as Kelly's deputy, but was a major disappointment. Most critics agreed with George Giffen's assessment that Johns had a genius for wicket-keeping but his hands were soft and easily knocked about.

Johns first showed promise at Wesley College, Melbourne, and later at Horton College, Tasmania. He had a term with the Richmond club

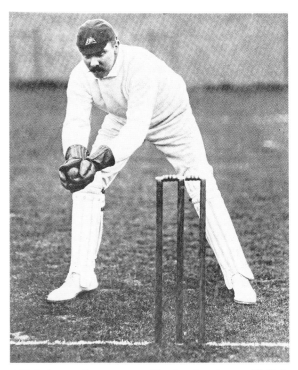

Alf Johns, who went to England twice as Kelly's stand-in, was regarded as a genius by George Giffen but suffered from unusually soft hands.

in Melbourne before becoming captain of the Melbourne University XI while he studied law. He made his debut for Victoria at 26 when Blackham injured a thumb and withdrew from the 1894–95 match against Stoddart's English tourists. Johns impressed with three stumpings and a catch. He was not highly rated as a batsman but in March 1896 he stayed for 90 minutes in scoring 15 not out, which allowed Syd Gregory (75 not out) to pull off a win for the Australian XI v. the Rest. In 1896–97 he put on 136 for the last wicket with Jim O'Halloran (128 not out) for Victoria v. South Australia, finishing with 57.

Blackham and Kelly prevented Johns winning Test selection but in a first-class career that lasted only five summers he accounted for 84 batsmen (58 caught, 26 stumped), dismissing both Sydney stars Harry Donnan and Syd Gregory six times. He scored 429 first-class runs with his left-handed batting at 11.28. His 20 innings for Australian touring teams brought only 134 runs. Johns, a solicitor, gave valuable service as a committeeman to the Melbourne CC.

In the 1904–05 Australian season, word swept round the inner circles of Australian cricket that the next Test keeper would be John Elliott Monfries, born at Gumeracha in South Australia, who had been performing brilliantly for the Melbourne club and in a brief career with Victoria. Monfries appeared to be in a class above his rivals for Jim Kelly's Test spot. Kelly acknowledged this when he took Monfries aside during the Victoria v. New South Wales match in Sydney in March 1904 and suggested they make a deal on the 1905 English tour.

Kelly said that on the previous English tour in 1902 he had become so involved with cricket he had been unable to visit relatives. 'This time you can have the cricket and I'll have the trip,' said Kelly. But it turned out to be Monfries' final appearance in first-class cricket. He missed selection for the 1905 tour when South Australian Phil Newland won the second wicket-keeping spot. Ironically, Monfries had displaced Newland as keeper in the East Torrens first grade side when he played club cricket in Adelaide.

Monfries played club cricket in three states, but always found difficulty in securing leave as a senior executive of the Australian Postal Service, which he helped form. A keeper with exceptional stumping speed, he counted Clem Hill, Victor Trumper, 'Sunny Jim' Mackay, Reggie Duff and Syd Gregory among his victims. His displays for the Melbourne club to the bowling of Warwick Armstrong, Charlie McLeod, Hugh Trumble and Jack Saunders was keeping of the highest class, but the Postal Service virtually ended his career by sending him to run their Tasmanian office.

William ('Barlow') Carkeek, a rough-hewn blacksmith turned wicket-keeper, came into big cricket as Kelly departed. A stumpy, wide-shouldered man with highly developed forearms and vast hands, he was a neat but uninspired

The one-time blacksmith Barlow Carkeek, one of the barndoor-style of keepers, who twice toured England in Australian teams.

keeper. He looked like a prize-fighter, nose bent and scarred, a man who would let nothing get past him, but he failed to match the standards of Blackham, Jarvis and Kelly, despite the air of reliability he created by his presence behind the stumps.

Carkeek was lucky to make two tours with Australian teams as he was clearly inferior to most other Australian keepers. He went to England in 1909 with Monty Noble's side when Hanson Carter was the number-one pick, and in 1912 had a second trip when Carter and five other leading players refused the tour on the Board of Control's terms.

A left-hander born in the famous Victorian mining town Walhalla on 17 October 1878, Carkeek learned his cricket in the Walhalla district where batsmen who could swat the ball over the boundary fence became folk heroes. The Walhalla ground was created when miners blew the top off a small mountain and levelled out what was left. Big hits over the fence rolled down the mountain and the ball could travel for miles before it was retrieved.

After the gold ran out in Walhalla, Carkeek joined the Richmond City club in Melbourne and from there was recruited to play for Hawksburn, a popular Melbourne club, in 1903–04. His solid efficiency impressed in club cricket and in 1904 he went into the Victorian team against Pelham Warner's English tourists.

The English keepers on that tour, Dick Lilley and Herbert Strudwick, were models for ambitious youths, tough but ethical professionals who disciplined their emotions and relished the firm bounce in Australian pitches. Strudwick described how his predecessor in the Surrey XI, Fred Stedman, stuffed railway time-tables inside his shirt for protection on ill-prepared county wickets. When a ball kicked awkwardly and hit him Stedman said: 'Oops, I'll have to get a later train. The 7.30 has been knocked off.'

Strudwick's career total of 1,496 dismissals was the English record for half a century, J.T. Murray lifting it to 1,527 in the 1970s. Strudwick's rate of stumpings—254 or 16.9 per cent of his dismissals—was far below that of his Surrey forerunner Edward Pooley, whose stumpings provided 41.9 per cent of his dismissals (358 out of 854 victims), and was behind his Leicestershire

Dick Lilley, who started learning cricket in a chocolate factory team, sports the tie that made Australians think him a dandy.

contemporary John Whiteside's 22.3 per cent (98 out of 438).

Hanson Carter, New South Wales' keeper, was born in Halifax, Yorkshire, and settled in the Sydney suburb of Waverley where his family ran an undertaking business. He was a smart, alert performer, the last keeper to wear slatted pads and the first to squat, knees bent, on his haunches. Burial services often prevented him practising and he sometimes arrived for matches in a hearse. He was a widely accepted authority on the laws of cricket and saved officials the trouble of writing to Lord's by arbitrating on club disputes. He had only one christian name, Hanson, but was known as 'Sep' or 'Sammy' and Wisden printed his name as 'H.S. Carter'.

Apart from inventing a stance for keepers, Carter—Ray Robinson labelled him the

Herbert Strudwick, much admired by Australians who knew him with affection as 'Struddy', held the English record of 1496 dismissals for half a century until J.T. Murray lifted it to 1527.

Hanson Carter, funeral parlour director, who often arrived for big cricket matches in a hearse, or even a horse-drawn dray, believed keepers should never desert their post.

'Crouching Genius'—introduced a novel style of footwork, standing a metre back from the stumps to give his quick eye a fraction longer to sight the ball. This gave him the appearance of stalking his victims and contributed to the drama of his catching and the fascination of his bird-like footwork.

Carter said he fell into the habit of squatting on his haunches as the bowler made his approach run in 1902 in England because it imposed less strain on his legs, even though he had to rise as the ball arrived. He kept his heels on the turf throughout and insisted that keepers who lifted their heels lacked balance. The Carter crouch quickly became common in keepers of all nationalities, though some rolled on the balls of their feet or lifted their heels.

Australian writer Ray Robinson discovered that

Carter was the last Australian keeper to wear slatted pads. He believed finger stalls and finger tapes reduced sensitivity. He was renowned for his mastery of cricket laws.

after viewing Carter's squat, a nurse at London's St Thomas' Hospital evolved special exercises for expectant mothers. She said they made the spine flexible and expanded the pelvis. 'Though structural limitations prevent keepers from turning this to full benefit, it may explain why so many last so long,' Robinson wrote. Lilley was a grandfather before he quit. Carter played first-class cricket for 24 years, retiring at 47, but returned as a grey-haired Father Christmas to keep for Arthur Mailey's team on its 100-day, 51-match tour of America in 1932. At 54, he was the oldest and smallest in the team.

In taking returns from fieldsmen, Carter disapproved of keepers leaving their post to gather wayward throws in mid-pitch and made it a point of honour not to move more than an arm's reach from the stumps. Denzil Bachelor said batsmen were acutely aware of human mortality when they caught sight of undertaker Carter keeping wicket in a post-bedside manner.

Carter went to England with Australian teams in 1902, 1909 and 1921. Cricketers enjoyed his infallible store of the game's past, but officials often begrudged him his dogmatic views. Despite a nasty blow in the eye that eventually cost him the sight in it, he refused to become a passenger on the U.S. tour, helping to find lost passports and taking over as baggageman.

Fans relished Carter's unorthodox batting, characterised by a 'shovel shot' he lifted over his left shoulder past mid-off. His popularity was so widely admired it was a major shock when slim South Australian solicitor Phillip Newland beat Carter to the spot in the 1905 team to England. Newland, coached by Affie Jarvis, was 30, but virtually unknown in eastern states. He had a disastrous trip.

Playing cricket on the deck of the team's ship just after leaving New Zealand, Newland took a blow from a ball which dislocated his jaw. Team captain Monty Noble, a practising dentist, spent hours with the ship's doctor trying unsuccessfully to get the jaw back into place and in London Newland had to seek specialist treatment.

Newland appeared in only 12 of the Australians' 38 matches and suffered the indignity of London newspapers commenting that he was 'not very robust'. This was the first tour on which wives accompanied players and newlyweds Mrs

Phil Newland, regarded as a gifted keeper, had his jaw broken so badly in Fiji on his way to England it virtually ended his career.

Clem Hill and Mrs Ailsa Newland travelled with the team, Mrs Hill continually griping that scorer Bill Ferguson did not credit her husband with all the runs he scored. The broken jaw ended Newland's career and he retired when the team arrived home, without appearing in a Test. He had dismissed 48 batsmen, 30 caught and 18 stumped.

The retirement of Kelly and Newland left Carter established as Australia's top keeper, with Carkeek and the Queenslander Patrick James ('Paddy') Carew challenging for the spot as his deputy. Carkeek had the honour of scoring the first century for the Prahran CC in 1906–07 but thereafter became a plodder. Carew looked superior, but with Queensland unable to get a place in the Sheffield Shield competition lacked opportunities.

Carter made his Test debut in Sydney in the first of the 1907–08 series against A.O. Jones's

English touring XI. He was very impressive, dismissing batsmen and scoring handy runs throughout that rubber, which Australia won four to one. He won a lifelong admirer in a Waverley woman by building her a special coffin for her dead canary. He played in all five Tests in the 1909 series in England in which Australia retained the Ashes two–one. Carkeek was his deputy on this tour but never seriously threatened Carter's Test spot.

Back in Australia Carter kept wicket in all five Tests against South Africa, Australia winning an inaugural rubber four–one in 1910–11. The morale of the Australian stars then began to disintegrate in persistent clashes with the Australian Board of Control. This intensified in the long fist fight between Australia's captain Clem Hill and selector Percy McAlister. England won an unpleasant series four tests to one.

Australia began the first day of the historic first series against South Africa by scoring 6 for 494, which is still the highest score on the first day of a Test. Percy Sherwell, South Africa's captain, kept wicket stylishly in a rubber dominated by googly bowlers, but watched his batsmen succumb to Australian 'Ranji' Hordern's subtle use of the same delivery. Sherwell enhanced the big reputation he had made in England in 1907. In the 1950s Johnnie Moyes, a fair-minded critic, wrote: 'Whether any keeper to visit Australia has excelled Sherwell is open to doubt, for his neat, unobtrusive and extremely clever work left a lasting memory with those privileged to see it'.

Although occasionally overshadowed by Sherwell, Carter would have been among the first picked for the Triangular series in England in 1912 had he not joined Trumper, Ransford, Cotter, Hill and Armstrong in demanding that the players retain the right to appoint their manager. The demand was refused and all six players withdrew from the tour, bitter that the Australian Board of Control had broken a promise made when it was founded in 1905.

The team that represented Australia in the Triangular competition is generally ranked as the worst Australia ever sent away. The tour lost £1,286, but the board won the challenge to its authority. Carkeek's performance behind the stumps contributed to Australia's sloppy fielding, despite manful bowling efforts by Bill Whitty and

South Africa's first captain in Australia, Percy Sherwell, was a keeper who could score runs. He was outstanding when keeping to googly bowlers whom batsmen had difficulty reading.

Gervys Hazlitt and a dramatic double hat-trick in the Manchester Test by Thomas James Matthews. Carkeek made only 156 runs in 29 tour innings at 9.17.

In his manager's report George Crouch condemned the behaviour of several tourists. The committee appointed to enquire into his charges called several players to account for their actions but its findings were never made public. Carkeek's deputy on this unhappy 1912 tour was the slightly built Harold Wynne ('Darkie') Webster, who had played only six times for South Australia when the tour began. Webster, born in the Sydney suburb of Randwick on 17 February 1889, appeared in 12 of the team's 37 matches and was never asked to play again for his state. There was no polish or style in his work, only frequent clumsiness, and he averaged only 15.9 with the bat, with a top score 26.

Carkeek continued to play for Victoria until the 1913–14 season but found himself in trouble for failing to join up when World War I began. This became a highly emotional issue in Melbourne, with headmasters naming Test players who had not answered the call to arms and contrasting this with the high number of New South Wales players who had joined up. Wesley College headmaster L.A. Adamson openly accused players like Carkeek of cowardice. The VCA had no doubt about his loyalty, however, and made several payments to him from its Distressed Cricketers' Fund, including housing and medical assistance.

Introduction of district competitions conducted within electoral boundaries produced some outstanding keepers in all states. Sid Deane from the Sydney Club, Harold Evers (South Sydney), Walter Loveridge (Central Cumberland), John 'Paddy' Lane (University) and George Harvey (Petersham) were all good enough to play for New South Wales had Carter faltered.

Queensland had Bill 'Poley' Evans from Nundah, Dick Pryke (North Brisbane), Alfred Sims (Rockhampton), John Bolton (Woolloongabba) and Leo O'Connor from the Valley all attracting admirers. South Australia used Claude Jennings (East Adelaide), John 'Bert' Woodford (Sturt), Gordon Campbell (Adelaide) and Charles Moyle (Adelaide) from a pool of sound keepers. Victoria boasted Richard Delves (Fitzroy), Albert 'Allie' Lampard and William Reeves (both Richmond), Tom Hastings (Carlton), Matthew Ellis (Fitzroy) and John Woodford, before he moved to South Australia, in a similar group of skilful keepers.

Through the golden years of Australian cricket just before the First World War these men demonstrated every Saturday how successful Australians had been in learning the art of wicket-keeping. Carkeek continued in the Victorian team until he was 36 and stayed with the Prahran club all his career. His statistics in six Tests were modest, six dismissals from catches and 16 runs with the bat at 5.33. He was named in the Australian team to tour South Africa in 1914–15, but the tour was abandoned when war began. He played in 95 first-class matches, scoring 1388 runs at 12.17, top score 68. Behind the stumps he sent back 159 batsmen (114 caught, 45 stumped). He dismissed Charlie Macartney seven times. He died in 1937, aged 58, the last of the keepers chosen by selectors impressed by physical bulk who regarded men with fast hands as sneaks.

Towards the end of the 1914–15 season the Glebe club in Sydney lifted William Albert Stanley Oldfield, known to clubmates as Bert, from third grade to the first XI for two matches. The first of these was at Wentworth Park and Oldfield made it memorable by catching the celebrated Test batsman Syd Gregory after he had made only 3.

'There are other reasons why I shall never forget that game,' Oldfield wrote years later. 'As I arrived at the ground "Sammy" Carter drove up in a sulky, a two-wheeled vehicle drawn by a pony. It was amusing, but I soon learned that this was his usual means of transport if a hearse was not available. Sammy was like that—full of independence. Little did I dream what would unfold for both of us. He was so far ahead of any other keeper I had seen I knew I had to model my work on his.'

Lilley remained a remarkably consistent keeper in 35 Tests against Australia who often saw his stumping style. Varicose veins forced him out of cricket after 321 matches for Warwickshire.

5

Warwickshire Duo

Arthur Frederick Augustus Lilley was the best-dressed cricketer of his time, a dandy who wore clothes of the highest quality and parted his hair and trimmed his moustache with extreme care. He played right-half for the Warwickshire County soccer team, won trap-shooting ribbons from Monte Carlo to Blackpool and for 10 years reigned supreme as England's Test wicket-keeper. On the field he wore tailored white flannels, a tie or cravat and a straw hat, and was often consulted by captains who valued his judgment of the game.

Ernest James ('Tiger') Smith was a big, tall, robust keeper who taped his fingers to prevent breaks, a bellicose man who enjoyed his end-of-play beer. He had a worn, open face, powerful forearms and hands, and could handle himself impressively in a fist fight. He was considered too tall for a keeper but took the fast bowling of Frank Foster with nonchalant ease, standing up on the stumps.

Lilley and Smith both learned to play cricket in Cadbury Brothers' chocolate factory works team at Bourneville after they left school in Birmingham. Between them they kept wicket for England in 46 Test matches and lifted Warwickshire to the top of the county competition.

Lilley was persuaded to take the gloves when the regular keeper did not turn up for his works team's practice. The only coaching he ever received were the few brief hints on where to stand and how to take the ball from professional coach John Shilton when he first pulled on the gloves. He taught himself the finer points by watching the successful keepers of his teens like Blackham ('The

greatest keeper who ever lived'), Kelly, Gregor MacGregor and Alfred Lyttelton.

Lilley had a close association with Richard Cadbury, who strongly encouraged the works cricketers. The workers called this Cadbury boss 'Gaffer Dick' and young Lilley quoted him so often, starting his comment with 'Gaffer Dick says', that the men began to call him 'Gaffer Dick', too, and finally just 'Dick'.

Shilton, the Yorkshire-born coach hired by Cadbury, recommended to Warwickshire in 1888 that they try Lilley in a trial match. Lilley did so well he was chosen to play for Warwickshire in their next match—against Australia. He studied Blackham carefully, noting the lack of histrionics, the positioning of body and hands for each delivery, the spurning of acrobatics. He listened intently as Blackham advised him never to take unfair advantage of batsmen or umpires, and always to behave ethically.

Lilley had to overcome the handicap of playing for a second-class county, as Warwickshire was until 1894, but was recognised as the best keeper in England. He kept wicket for Warwickshire for 23 years. At Edgbaston in 1889 he caught three and stumped four Yorkshiremen, exploiting the skill of spinner H.J. ('Nack') Pallett, who bowled leg-breaks and off-breaks with equal accuracy. He was responsible for a healthy percentage of the 305 wickets Pallett took for his county.

Although he had to wear thin gloves made of felt that offered little protection against fast bowling, Lilley sought to position himself to take the most difficult bowlers without strain. He wore no box, an appliance unknown before 1910, but there was no safer catcher of the ball. *Wisden* called him 'a marvel of consistency'.

He began his career standing up to all bowlers as he had seen Blackham do, but in one of his first big matches W.G. Grace warned him that there was only one Blackham and that he would do better standing back to fast bowling. 'I thought I was correct standing up to Richardson but when Grace suggested I move back I accepted the doctor's advice, and undoubtedly it was the wiser policy to pursue,' said Lilley. 'I succeeded in catching three batsmen. By standing back one is able to cover so much more ground to make catches, and there are very few opportunities of stumping off fast bowling, so I am sure it is the right thing for me.'

Lilley played frequently for the Players after his debut for them in 1895 and he was an automatic choice for England against Australia after his outstanding first appearance at Lord's in 1896 against Harry Trott's touring team. He took two important catches in each innings. He failed with the bat but made amends in the following Test at Manchester with a solid 65 not out. This was the Test in which he handed the gloves to J.T. Brown and sent down five overs of leg-breaks in which he broke a long stand beween Frank Iredale (108) and Harry Trott (53).

Blackham saw Lilley develop from a nervous youngster lacking control in his long legs into a seasoned Test player who exploited his exceptionally long reach. Blackham was stumped by Lilley in only their second match against each other and paid Lilley a rare compliment by presenting him with a pair of his gloves.

Lilley's consistency as a batsman improved markedly after Arthur Shrewsbury altered his stance and showed him how to position his feet in playing forward. His batting grew in confidence and he made more than 1,000 runs in a season three times, with 16 centuries in his career total of 15,597 runs, average 26.30.

He toured Australia twice, in 1901–02 under Archie MacLaren's captaincy, and in 1903–04 when Pelham Warner captained England. Warner highly praised the value of his frequent consultations with Lilley, who also appeared in all five Tests in England against Australia in 1902, 1905 and 1909, each time setting a standard

Lilley with his close friend and advisor Jack Blackham at Lord's. Blackham saw him develop from a nervous youngster into an automatic Test selection for England.

behind the stumps which lifted England's overall fielding displays.

Traditionalists complained Lilley lacked brilliance, but there were plenty of exciting incidents in his 35-Test career. In the 1896 match against Australia at Old Trafford Lilley dropped Joe Kelly when Australia wanted nine runs with three wickets left. He took the ball cleanly but struck his thighs with his arms and the impact dislodged the ball from his hands. Six years later England were within eight runs of scoring the 124 needed for victory on the same ground when Lilley hit a skier into the outfield. Most spectators thought it would be a six, but the ball held up in the wind and Clem Hill, sprinting hard for 40 metres, dived full length to bring off a miraculous catch. Rain then delayed play for 45 minutes and on the resumption Trumble bowled Lockwood and Saunders bowled Fred Tate to give Australia a win by three runs.

Lilley's biggest triumph came at Sydney in 1903–04 when Warner gambled by bringing on Bosanquet, the man they called the 'best bad bowler in England'. Lilley had taught himself to read Bosanquet's googlies and in the celebrated introduction of this delivery to Tests, Australian batsmen kept playing for leg-breaks. Lilley knew this was a misjudgment and helped himself to three stumpings and a catch. Bosanquet dismissed two other batsmen through a catch by Foster and an lbw in a 6 for 12 spell that Noble and Trumble extended to 6 for 51. England won by 157 runs and regained the Ashes.

Cricket historians have argued that it was ridiculous for Warner to have given Bosanquet a bowl, considering his past performance. Warner counteracted this by saying he knew all along that Bosanquet would prove a match-winner on a day when he found a persistent length. Lilley's four dismissals have never been given credit for making Warner's gamble work and establishing the googly.

On his first trip to Australia in 1901–02 Lilley had also formed a deadly combination with the great bowler Sidney Barnes, who provided him with most of the 20 catches he took on the tour. He also made six stumpings. At Sydney in the match against New South Wales he made 80 in the second innings but saw England beaten by 53 runs. He continued in top form in the first Test on the same ground, scoring 84 and stumping both Noble and Frank Laver off leg-spinner Len Braund. He also held three catches and England won by an innings and 124 runs. He had four more victims in the second Test in Melbourne, which Australia won by 229 runs thanks to Noble's 13 wickets for 77 runs. MacLaren had him batting at number five in the third Test at Adelaide, but with Barnes out of the series through injury the other bowlers gave him few chances. MacLaren increasingly consulted him, but they could find no inspiration to halt a grand Australian recovery to win the rubber four–one.

On his second trip to Australia in 1903–04 with the team captained by 'Plum' Warner, Lilley made 91 not out in the first match against South Australia in Adelaide and 59 in Launceston against Tasmania. Both matches were drawn, after England appeared in danger before Lilley batted. He ended the tour with 29 dismissals, 16 caught and 13 stumped. Five of these dismissals came in the first Test, which England won by five wickets, and five more in the fourth Test— 'Bosanquet's match'. In the fifth Test Lilley was the third batsman sent back in Hugh Trumble's hat-trick.

His high percentage of stumpings—194 out of 911 dismissals—was achieved at a time when England fielded left-arm bowlers who offered frequent legside chances. For Warwickshire against Yorkshire in 1899, Lilley caught three batsmen and stumped four at Edgbaston. For Warwickshire against the MCC at Lord's in 1896, all his eight victims were caught.

Lilley's generosity towards his opponents was as well known as his coolness at the gaming tables when he visited Monte Carlo to compete in trap-shooting competitions. He had the bearing and grooming of an affluent amateur, but the lowly social status generally accorded professionals. Even when he brilliantly stumped 'Plum' Warner for the Players against the Gentlemen at Lord's when Warner, scoring freely on 59, missed a fast ball on the leg side from Arnold, Warner refused him the courtesy of including Lilley's initials or christian name in the account of it.

However, throughout his long career Lilley remained a warm favourite with cricket supporters—a popularity equipment manu-facturers recognised when they made him one of the first cricketers paid to endorse a brand of leg guards and gauntlets bearing his autograph. Accused of endangering his hands and his Test place by playing soccer each winter, he simply said he played because the pay was good and he could not afford to be idle.

After he left Cadbury's chocolate factory, Lilley went into partnership in a sports wholesale business with the Quaife brothers, two of whom played for Warwickshire. Though he seldom touched alcohol, he later became the proprietor of the Oak Hotel at Selly Oak, near Birmingham. Warwickshire gave him benefit matches in 1891 and 1901.

In 1907 Lilley sought an injunction in Birmingham Assizes restraining the Quaifes from using his name in their business. The Quaifes counter-claimed to restrain Lilley from selling certain sporting goods. The court granted both injunctions and the judge told both sides they were better cricketers than businessmen. That same year Lilley was one of four professionals who refused to go to Australia for a basic £300, plus 30 shillings a week to cover expenses on the voyage to Australia and 40 shillings a week in Australia.

Richard Young, the Cambridge University and Sussex keeper, and one of the few to wear glasses, shared the wicket-keeping duties with Derbyshire's Joe Humphries. Both were disappointing in a shoddy England fielding side. Young was a fanatical cricket theorist who taught mathematics at Eton and once suggested that captains should have the right to pour a hundred gallons of water on any part of the pitch. His career dismissals amounted to 144 (115 caught, 29 stumped). Humphries lacked Young's batting prowess, but his absence from the first Test in which Young made numerous errors helped cost England the rubber.

Lilley was the first to discover Arthur Shrewsbury's curious inability to sleep in any other bed but the one in his home at Nottingham. He found that when Shrewsbury went to Birmingham to coach, he could not sleep at any of the hotels suggested and had to return to Nottingham to sleep. Shrewsbury finally conquered the problem of taking long sea voyages to Australia by going to bed in the same nightcap he wore at home.

Both Shrewsbury and Lilley won the respect of the Lord's hierarchy and helped secure better working conditions for their fellow professionals through a combination of playing skill and good sense. Lilley's lack of animosity towards rivals for his spot in the England team delighted Lord Harris, Lord Hawke and the other MCC stalwarts. When Gloucestershire keeper John Henry Board emerged, Lilley went out of his way to encourage Board, who eventually kept wicket in six Tests in South Africa, two in 1898–99 and four in 1905–06, with Lilley unavailable for both tours.

Lilley was the 13th keeper to appear in Tests for England, but none of those who preceded him did as much to raise public respect for their calling. Down the years all other county keepers benefited from the high standards set by Lilley in 35 Tests—among them Tom Sidwell (Leicestershire), William Farrimond (Lancashire), James Sheffield (Essex), John Hubble (Kent) and Malcolm Lyon (Somerset).

Demand for English professionals to coach provided many keepers with handy incomes from trips overseas. Board coached at Hawkes Bay, New Zealand, for several seasons and had his centuries there, 134 and 195, included in his first-class average of 19.37 from 15,674 runs.

The only pique Lilley ever showed was reserved for his beloved Warwickshire. He had supported the county in the fight for promotion to first-class status, which came in 1894, and seen them survive lean years around the turn of the century, but by 1911 when they won the championship he had been forced to play as a batsman, field while E.J. ('Tiger') Smith kept wicket and play under the captaincy of Frank Foster. Selectors' preference for Smith was particularly galling as Smith had been on the Lord's ground staff for 10 years and

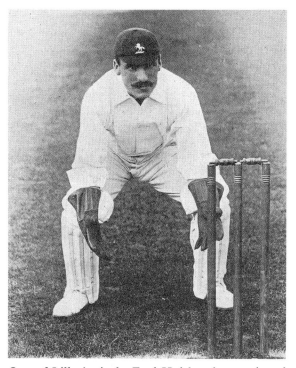

One of Lilley's rivals, Fred Huish, who continued the great tradition for high-class wicket-keeping for the Kent county XI.

Warwickshire had to get permission from Lord's to play him.

Foster was a young tearaway of a bowler who kept splitting the webbing of Lilley's fingers and when it became clear Lilley could not take their main strike bowler, Warwickshire had no alternative but to bring in Smith. Foster generated exceptional pace from a deceptively lazy run-up. Standing up on the legside to Foster, Smith brought off some amazing stumpings and they became a legendary partnership.

'Tiger' Smith said in his autobiography that Lilley angered Foster by moving fieldsmen into deep positions to catch David Denton's lofted cover drive when Denton came in to bat for Yorkshire. 'I'll take your advice if you come to me, Dick, but don't make me look a fool,' Foster told Lilley. In the same match Foster told Smith he was keeping particularly well for a man who had been out till three in the morning.

Asked who told him that, Foster said: 'Dick Lilley'. Smith explained that the truth was he had been up until three adjusting the bandages Lilley had to wear for his varicose veins and had hardly had a drink. Smith added:

'Lilley's differences of opinion with his team-mates and the captain marked a sad end to a great career, and I thought the Warwickshire committee were unfair to him when they left him off the team list when we won the county championship in 1911. He'd done so much for the county he deserved to be acknowledged.'

Lilley settled in Bristol after his enforced retirement from county cricket through lameness and took a keen interest in trying to improve South Africa's standing in international cricket. Percy Sherwell, captain of the first South African team to tour England in 1907, was among his closest friends. Lilley often said that even Blackham could not have surpassed Sherwell's keeping to Johannes ('Kodgee') Kotze. After World War I Dick Lilley served on a special advisory committee to help re-establish cricket in Gloucestershire. He died at Brislington, near Bristol, on 17 November 1929, aged 62.

Before he left Warwickshire Lilley spent many hours coaching 'Tiger' Smith, who had lost the top joints of the third and little fingers of his left hand and the little finger of the left hand in Cadbury's factory. After he left Cadbury's, Smith

'Tiger' Smith succeeded Lilley in the Warwickshire team and was indebted to the county's fast bowler Frank Foster for his selection in England's Test team.

was playing cards when rain stopped Warwickshire's match and a fight began. Smith laid out a big fellow who was accusing team-mates of cheating and Dick Lilley said: 'We'll call him "Tiger" Smith'—a reference to a prominent pugilist of the time. The name stuck, helped by Smith's gruff bark in appealing. Smith took Lilley's place in the Warwickshire first team when Lilley was away on Test duty but he preferred the guaranteed income as a member of Lord's staff.

Smith acknowledged that Frank Foster's bowling lifted him into the Test team because he was the only keeper who could take Foster comfortably. Foster never went to the nets. He would just stroll onto the pitch and from a loping six-pace run let the ball go from high up with a very loose left arm. Batsmen were constantly surprised by the pace Foster's deliveries gathered off the pitch.

Smith stood back to 'sight them' for an over or two and then stood right up on the stumps to Foster—and this made Smith's reputation. The partnership accounted for numerous important Test dismissals from the time Smith toured Australia in the 1911–12 England team captained by Johnny Douglas. Asked by manager 'Plum' Warner how they would get Clem Hill out before the Adelaide Test Smith said, 'Stumped Smith, bowled Foster'. The plan worked and Hill was out for a duck.

Smith took 16 catches and made two stumpings on that Australian tour, his combination with Foster enabling him to displace Herbert Strudwick as keeper after the first Test. They played a major role in England winning the series four–one from an Australian side studded with talent but inhibited by internal strife. This culminated in the infamous 20-minute fist fight between team captain Clem Hill and selector Percy McAlister and in the withdrawal of key players from the 1912 tour of England for the Triangular tournament.

England held exhaustive trials before selecting the side Charles Fry captained in this tournament. In three of his four innings in the trials Phil Mead was out stumped Smith, bowled Foster—a feat that allowed Smith to fend off Strudwick's challenge yet again. 'Foster and I never had any planned signals for stumping,' said Smith. 'His normal line was middle and leg and I'd stand there. Between overs I'd say, "Down the legside when you're ready", and I was ready.'

Foster, the handsome, dashing lady's man, overreached himself gambling on his billiards ability and lost a lot of money on racehorses. His life was an anti-climax after his headlined triumphs in Australia and in 1914 he had a motorbike smash that damaged a foot and prevented him playing again. Smith kept going for 26 years.

Smith played in all England's six matches in the Triangular tournament and toured South Africa in the 1913–14 team led by Johnny Douglas. Without Foster, his keeping lacked its former histrionics and Strudwick was preferred in all five Tests, with Smith playing as a batsman in the second Test.

Strudwick and Smith prevented gifted keepers Tom Oates and James Stone playing for England. Oates had 993 victims (758 caught, 235 stumped) for Nottinghamshire, Stone 524 (394 caught, 130 stumped) for Hampshire and Glamorgan.

Smith made 20 centuries in his 16,997 first-class runs, average 22.39, but his Test average was 8.69.

'Tiger' Smith after he retired and became the Warwickshire county coach enjoyed holding court and telling his fans how he bandaged Lilley's legs at night to keep him in cricket.

In a career that lasted from 1904 to 1930, he dismissed 878 batsmen (722 caught, 156 stumped). He became an umpire on retirement and later the Warwickshire coach. Until he death in 1979, aged 93, he held court in the Edgbaston pavilion, telling cricket yarns and advising youngsters. He won a lasting place in the memory of Australians when he gave Eddie Paynter out lbw to Bill O'Reilly for 99 in the 1938 Lord's Test.

However, Smith always claimed the event he cherished most came at Melbourne in 1911–12. His England captain, Johnny Douglas, liked to open the bowling with Frank Foster but at the beginning of the third over Smith threw the ball to Sidney Barnes who was disgruntled about not being given the new ball. Douglas was too much of a gentleman to take the ball from Barnes as

Hanson Carter took his stance well behind the stumps but had a curious step-forward stumping style shown here.

he paced out his run, and in the next 45 minutes Barnes took four for none as Australia slumped to 4 for 11. This amazing spell enabled England to turn round a series they appeared certain to lose after they lost the first Test by 146 runs.

England clinched the rubber by winning the fourth Test to take an unbeatable three–one lead, scoring a record 589 in the fourth Test in Melbourne after Hobbs and Rhodes had an opening stand of 323. Australian newspapers mercilessly condemned their team and completely ignored Hanson Carter's remarkable feat in allowing only two byes in the 589 runs England scored. Throughout that long innings Carter squatted down before every ball was bowled, maintaining his normal composure from his position a metre behind the stumps, but he never once failed to move in to take the ball over the stumps as it arrived. It was an unorthodox method that puzzled Bert Oldfield as he watched Carter's displays in the series which many said Australia lost in the committee room.

The disputes between players and selectors were so intense Clem Hill did not know the make-up of his team when he went out to toss before the fifth Test. Johnny Douglas refused to toss until Hill named his side, which Hill could not do. Hill had to go off and consult the selectors to learn whom they had picked.

Although it did not impress Oldfield, Carter's move-with-the-batsman technique was copied by Andrew Thomas Ratcliffe, who played 18 matches for New South Wales between 1913–14 and 1929–30 and spent most of those 16 seasons as reserve keeper to Carter and Oldfield. Ratcliffe toured New Zealand with an Australian XI in 1920–21 and a second time with a New South Wales side in 1923–24. He appeared in 43 first-class matches, scoring four centuries and often forced his way into the state side with his left-handed batting. From the same position as Carter, about a metre behind the stumps, Ratcliffe moved his right foot forward when a right-hand batsman played forward to an offside ball. For balls likely to finish on the leg side, he advanced the left foot, and if the batsman played back Ratcliffe found his extra depth gave him a fraction longer to sight the ball. But he preferred not to squat like Carter, arguing that he moved faster if he did not get down low. He rested his weight on his calves.

Ratcliffe's technique was exceptionally successful and provided him with 27 stumpings for the Balmain club in the 1915–16 season when he took the bowling of master spinner Arthur Mailey. He achieved this outsanding tally despite having to share the keeping duties with Hampden Stanley ('Hammy') Love, who became so frustrated by the lack of opportunity in New South Wales with Carter and Oldfield available that he switched to Victoria, where he had five years as state keeper (1922–23 to 1927–28). Love had plenty of success with the bat, but the keeping talents of the Melbourne building contractor Jack Ellis restricted his chances behind the stumps and he returned to Sydney.

6

A Trick with Steak

At Polygon Wood in 1917 in a heavy German bombardment a string of whining shells landed on the 15th Australian Field Ambulance Brigade, killing three men and leaving Corporal William Albert Stanley Oldfield buried and unconscious. Oldfield, who had seen service in Egypt, was dragged from the mess of mud and scorched timber suffering badly from shell shock. He was invalided back to a hospital in Gloucestershire. Germany surrendered before he recovered.

Oldfield was on leave in an unpretentious boarding house not far from the Australian Imperial Forces' cricket team's headquarters in Horseferry Road, London, when the team captain, Herbie Collins, found him. The AIF team had been established as one of a variety of sporting ventures aimed at keeping the troops amused while they waited for ships to take them home. Exhaustive trials were held as cricket practice replaced drill sessions before a team drawn from Australian units through Europe was named.

Some exceptional talent had been unearthed, with players like Jack Gregory, Johnny Taylor, Charles Kelleway, Cyril Docker, 'Nip' Pellew, Allie Lampard, Jack Murray and Collins available, 'Plum' Warner began negotiations from Lord's with the Australian Cricket Board for the AIF XI to play a series of 'Victory Tests' against England. The Board refused to give the matches Test status when Charlie Macartney, Dr Roy Park, Dr Eric Barbour, Dr Claude Tozer and Johnny Moyes announced they were unavailable, depriving the side of outstanding talent and experience.

Further complications beset the AIF team when the GOC of Australian troops in Europe, Field Marshal Birdwood, sacked Kelleway as captain after a series of disagreements with groundsmen in the team's five warm-up matches. Birdwood considered that Captain Kelleway was a quarrelsome character and replaced him with Collins, a lance-corporal with proven skills at two-up and mixing with people. Collins saw that he had a fine team but when 'Hammy' Love withdrew to go home early, he urgently needed a reliable keeper to replace him.

Collins did not even know Oldfield's name when he knocked on his door, only that servicemen cricketers all talked about his skills. Oldfield scoffed at the notion that he was a top-class cricketer and explained that he had no gear. Collins' players supplied him with an array of battered inner gloves and gauntlets, which he wrapped in brown paper, and that night he joined the side on the train to Oxford.

After the first day of the AIF XI's match against Oxford, Ted Long, the reserve wicketkeeper, told Collins they had found a keeper of the highest quality in Oldfield. Long said he would not be needed to play but agreed to stay in case Oldfield was injured.

In the summer that followed Oldfield became a disciple of the Surrey keeper Herbert Strudwick, confirmed by then as the finest gloveman in England. He carefully studied Strudwick's technique and decided there was more value in standing square-on to the stumps, close enough to touch the bails without stretching, weight evenly balanced, forearms resting on his pad tops, body

Bert Oldfield, who was almost buried alive in World War I, recovered to keep wicket for Australia in 54 Test matches. He became a disciple of the great English keeper Herbert Strudwick.

Oldfield stumping England's dashing allrounder Percy Chapman, who has grounded his bat too late to avoid dismissal.

slightly crouched, than in Carter's method of stalking the batsmen.

Ray Robinson, in his detailed assessment of Strudwick's approach, said he had a habit of bringing his hands up towards the bails, his blue eyes watching the batsman's feet. His rather loose gloves lessened the shock of impact. Strudwick attributed his success in taking yorkers and other awkward balls to the practice he had without pads, an intriguing sidelight for those who have watched Australian Ian Healy working out.

Strudwick ignored advice that keepers should always remain at the stumps. He enjoyed chasing balls nicked into vacant legside regions, scooting away with padded legs accelerating as crowds cheered him on. *Wisden* rebuked him for the habit but he said it relieved his concentration as well as delighting spectators.

One of Strudwick's close friends was Harry Murrell, who kept for Kent and Middlesex and played soccer for Arsenal. Murrell had 834 victims between 1899 and 1926 (565 caught, 269 stumped) but joked that if he played Test cricket he would have to switch to left-arm bowling because of Strudwick's superiority behind the stumps.

All Strudwick's fingers were broken, some so badly people wondered how he held a pen when he became Surrey's scorer in 1927. He pointed out that Hanson Carter's fingers were twisted and mutilated 'like pieces of sun-dried vine'. Strudwick's 25 years as a keeper included 28 Tests in which he sent back 72 batsmen.

'In all his years as a keeper Strudwick used to wear brass bars across each hand from the first to third fingers, themselves knotted, as a device to spare the longest finger, which was in no shape for any further hammering,' wrote Ray Robinson. 'Occasionally batsmen heard him moan when the ball hit a tender joint, but he never missed a beat in taking express balls or wristy throws. No cricketer wore his scars with greater honour, a testimony to his unflinching steadfastness on nasty wickets, some so treacherous that he wore a chest pad to protect his ribs from kickers.'

Oldfield and Strudwick were the same height, 5 feet 6 inches (165 cm) but Oldfield was heavier at 10 stone 7 pounds (67 kg) and was known as 'Hercy', short for Hercules by team-mates in the AIF side because of his resilient frame. In the Australian team he was called 'Cracker' because of his habit of cheerfully greeting incoming batsmen with 'Hullo, Crack'.

Oldfield developed quickly under Collins' captaincy. He was in the AIF team during its 34 matches around England, 28 of them first-class, and his keeping to the bowling of Jack Gregory helped clinch many of the team's triumphs. The

Oldfield's hero, Herbert Strudwick, covering a shot in one of his matches in Australia. He toured Australia four times between 1903–04 and 1924–25, reaching 1496 career dismissals.

team played 10 matches in South Africa on its way home, and three matches in Australia when they arrived early in 1920. They defeated Victoria, drew with Queensland and, in the last match before they broke up, had a marvellous 203-run win over the powerful New South Wales side. In all of these matches, Oldfield's keeping of Gregory's fastest deliveries and the left-arm spin of Collins delighted spectators.

Andy Ratcliffe was the incumbent New South Wales wicket-keeper but when the 1920–21 season started selectors dropped him for Oldfield. Carter played for an Australian XI against England that season but Oldfield was preferred for the first three Tests. Oldfield did well, stumping Douglas off Mailey in the first Test, stumping Howell off Armstrong in the second Test, followed by a tenacious half century in the third Test. His cricket was all style and neat efficiency, disciplined to ignore pain in the ribs or fingers from Gregory's wilder balls. He was free of gesticulation or pained grimaces and recovered so quickly even keen eyes missed his rare fumbles.

Shrewd old-timers remained convinced, however, that Carter was superior, and the duel for the Test spot intensified when selectors recalled Carter from his funeral parlours for the fourth and fifth Tests. Carter responded by dismissing six batsmen in the fourth Test, three artistically stumped off Mailey's googly, and followed with five dismissals in the fifth Test.

Jack Ellis (Victoria), Leo O'Connor (Queensland), Albert Ambler (South Australia) and Ratcliffe (New South Wales) performed splendidly but found competition for the Test berth too strong. Every weekend in club matches 'Hammy' Love (Carlton), Allie Lampard (Prahran) and Gordon Inkster (Port Adelaide) excelled without hope of state selection, Ratcliffe producing a ferociously struck left-handed straight drive to thrill fans.

Inkster, born in 1893, started in the B grade XI for Port Adelaide in October 1913 with an innings of 139, but went to work in the Northern Territory as a bookkeeper on a cattle station after one appearance. He joined the AIF in 1918 and

One of Oldfield's most brilliant dismissals was this stumping of Jack Hobbs, who momentarily lifted his back foot in the Fifth Test of the 1924–25 series.

was invited by English cricket authority Howard Lacy to play in preliminary matches which were trials for the First AIF XI. Instead he returned home and joined Port Adelaide for the 1919–20 season. A massive 6 foot 4 inch (190-cm) athlete with a huge reach and superb build who played Australian football for Ports, a football-crazy industrial area that made the semi-finals in all but five seasons between 1897 and 1982, Inkster had a big influence on the cricket club after Percy Rundell's transfer by his bank left the club without a captain. Assisted by players like Gordon Harris, who made 2,053 runs for South Australia and Norman Watkins, who took 116 wickets for the state and 995 for Ports, Inkster's leadership and agile keeping lifted the club to premierships in 1927–28, 1928–29 and 1929–30. His 8 dismissals for South Australia against Queensland in 1926–27 was a record until Gil Langley beat it in the 1950s. Inkster was a diligent businessman who once overstayed his visa in the U.S. to clinch a big deal.

Jack Ellis was the antithesis of Oldfield, shirt-tail loose, pad straps aflap, ready to affront purists by donning brown pads and persistently irritating for batsmen with his blunt prattle. He disclosed that the bowling was rubbish, fieldsmen clumsy, the pitch dead, ignoring the need for concentration. He wore a cap in carefree style, peak behind his ears, ruddy face open to the sun, and if batsmen objected to his commentary he directed it to the slips.

English players said Ellis reminded them of Malcolm Lyon, the Somerset orator, whose loquacity made him the most discussed keeper in county cricket. Lyon was first discovered at Cambridge University and was said to have been excluded from Tests despite 14 forceful first-class centuries because of his foghorn banter. He was later a magistrate in Gambia, chief justice in the Seychelles and a puisne judge in Uganda.

Australians found the 1920 English team had a rival for Ellis in Arthur Dolphin, Strudwick's deputy. Ellis and Dolphin, whose Yorkshire brogue needed a translator, turned the England v. Victoria match of 1920 into a gabfest. Dolphin stood with his body pointing towards mid-off, left foot in advance of his torso, a technique developed keeping to left-handers Roy Kilner and Wilfred Rhodes which gave him extra time to reach the bails. He joined Yorkshire in 1905 and by the time

he toured Australia his fingers were so twisted and mutilated he had trouble holding his beer mug. He never wore a hat and the damage to his pale northern face from the Australian sun gave him the look of a barbecued shrimp.

For all his faults, there was no denying Ellis' skill in taking Victorian fast bowler Ted McDonald in that 1920–21 summer. Australia opened her attack with Gregory and Kelleway in the first two Tests but by the third Test McDonald forced his way into the side, forming a legendary opening partnership with Gregory. Ellis was offered a trip to New Zealand at the end of the season but declined because of a surfeit of building work.

Oldfield sustained a painful injury in the third Test when a McDonald fireball cracked two ribs. He concealed the injury until X-rays confirmed the breaks and kept going for the five days that saw the Ashes go to Australia. Selectors could have relied on any one of seven keepers doing well but they stuck with Oldfield and Carter for the 1921 tour of England.

More contentious was Warwick Armstrong's appointment as captain by a single vote in a Board of Control poll. At Perth when he tossed with Western Australia's keeper–captain Harold Evers, their combined weight was 45 stone (286 kg). At 23 stone (146 kg), Evers was the biggest-ever state keeper.

On the voyage to England Carter schooled Oldfield on English conditions. 'From Carter I learned the trick of applying eucalyptus to the rubber palms of my gloves,' Oldfield said. Carter's hands were battered beyond repair but he disliked fingerstalls inside his gloves as he felt they reduced the speed of his hands. However, the pace of Gregory and McDonald occasionally forced him to borrow Oldfield's fingerstalls on rough pitches.

Oldfield prepared for keeping sessions with meticulous care, taping the first joints of each finger and thumbs before covering them with thimble-shaped leather stalls capped by rubber tips that absorbed shock. The stalls sat snugly inside his gloves, protecting the second joints. Over this he wore two pairs of chamois inner gloves that he always soaked first. The brown leather gloves he pulled on over all this had reinforced palms. He was well aware that his fitness to a fielding side was vital and to be injured

Hanson Carter taking one of the great catches in cricket history, anticipating a genuine leg glance from Jack Hobbs, taking the ball as he falls in the Fourth Test at Melbourne in 1920–21.

could cost them the match; substitutes recruited from fieldsmen specialists seldom performed without vital errors.

Selectors preferred Carter for the first four Tests, but overall Oldfield played in four more matches—23 compared with Carter's 19. Both averaged in the low twenties and made the stumpings and catches that mattered. Aware that at 43 he was on his last tour, Carter suggested Oldfield replace him after Australia took an unbeatable three–nil lead but Armstrong kept Carter in the side.

Rain reduced the fourth Test to a two-day match and as the Australians took the field on the second day for England's first innings, Carter handed his well-thumbed Laws of Cricket to Dr Rowley Pope, the lifelong companion of Australian teams. 'We may need this,' said Carter. At 5.50 p.m. when the Hon. Lionel Tennyson attempted to close the England innings, the English batsmen left the field. The former

England captain Archie MacLaren saw Carter move over to Armstrong with those characteristic bird-like movements and point to the clock. 'Hello, there's Sammy objecting,' said MacLaren. 'I bet an even pound we've made a mistake.'

Accepting Carter's advice that a declaration was illegal, Armstrong told his players to remain while he got Tennyson to consult the two-day laws in the book Pope had in his pocket. Carter was proved right, with the law clearly stating that no declaration was possible unless 100 minutes batting was available to the fielding side on that day. In the confusion caused by the 25-minute delay, players forgot that Armstrong had bowled the last over before the English batsmen went off. Armstrong bowled the first over on resumption to become the only player in Test history to bowl consecutive overs.

Oldfield, a non-smoking teetotaller like Carter, made his initial appearance in a Test in England at The Oval. He dismissed the first English batsman Charles Russell with a clever catch off McDonald, did not allow a bye in England's first innings of 8 declared for 403 and made 28 not out with the bat. When the Australians made their first appearance in South Africa on the way home Carter was preferred in two of the three Tests. Oldfield's place as Australia's number-one keeper was not confirmed until the 1924–25 series in Australia against Arthur Gilligan's English tourists.

In the fourth Test in Melbourne, in February 1925, Oldfield became the first wicket-keeper to dismiss five batsmen in an innings. He began with a remarkable stumping of Hobbs, who momentarily lifted his toe to a ball from Ryder. When spectators cheered Oldfield, Hobbs turned and asked: 'What's up, Bert?' Informed that he had been given out, Hobbs looked down at his crease in disbelief. 'Oh, then, I'd better go', he said, accepting Oldfield's word that the verdict was fair.

Oldfield followed by stumping Frank Woolley off Mailey, and the giant Percy Chapman off Mailey. When he made his fourth stumping to send back William ('Dodge') Whysall off Kelleway's bowling, the crowd went wild with glee. His fifth victim came when he caught Gilligan for a duck off Kelleway. England had made 548, which proved enough to win by an innings and 29 runs, but Oldfield was the crowd's hero. Two weeks later in the fifth Test at Sydney he dismissed Hobbs with a spectacular legside catch. Oldfield's position was never challenged after these feats until the 1936–37 season, when he was nearing 40.

Meanwhile exciting developments in West Indian cricket had seen the emergence of world-class keepers as the teams pushed claims for Test status. West Indian teams had toured England in 1900, 1906 and 1923, while teams labelled as West Indian elevens had played against visiting English teams at home in 1895, 1905, 1911 and 1923. From the start the West Indians recognised keeping as a job for specialists, but their cricket was handicapped by conflict between white and black administrators.

The first keeper recognised as their best by West Indian selectors was Lebrun Samuel Constantine, who kept wicket for the first-ever West Indies XI against Priestley's touring England XI in 1897. His son Learie became Sir Learie and subsequently Lord Constantine, a magnificent all-rounder who represented the West Indies for 16 years from 1923. Lebrun Constantine, an overseer on a sugar estate, toured England with West Indian teams in 1900, when he shared keeping duties with George Learmond—who represented Guyana, Trinidad and Barbados and was Steve Camacho's grandfather—and again in 1906, when Claude Keith Bancroft, of Barbados, sometimes kept wicket.

In 1923, George Alric Dewhurst, a Trinidadian nicknamed 'Fatty', got the job as keeper with Robert Karl Nunes as his deputy. They performed impressively in a superb fielding side. Nunes was the first of a long line of West Indian keepers from Wolmer Boys' School in Jamaica. Nunes, who also went to Dulwich College in England, became a prominent lawyer and was president of the West Indies Board of Control from 1945 to 1952.

C.L.R. James in his famous book, *Beyond a Boundary*, lavishly praised the keeping skills shown in the 1920s by a keeper named Piggott, or 'Piggie' to his team-mates. James was convinced Dewhurst was preferred to Piggott for the 1923 tour of England because Dewhurst was white and Piggott was black. Dewhurst played for the exclusive Queen's Park Club, Piggott for the unknown 'Stingo' club.

Piggott seldom wore a white shirt and usually played in shirts with coloured stripes. He was 6 foot 4 inches (190 cm) tall and kept wicket standing right up on the stumps to the great George John, whom James called the knight errant of pace bowlers.

'Piggott was without the slightest doubt the finest keeper we West Indians had ever seen,' wrote James. 'To this day I have not seen or heard of any West Indian who surpassed him. The sight of him standing up to the fast bowling of George John and George Francis in England in 1923 would have been one of the never-to-be-forgotten sights of modern cricket. Yet, to the astonishment of all Trinidadians, when the 1923 side was selected he was left out and Dewhurst selected instead. Poor Piggott was a nobody and I felt the injustice deeply. . . One day at Queen's Park Oval I saw ordinary people come up to Piggott and tell him that if he had Dewhurst's skin he would be behind the sticks.'

By the time the England team returned to the West Indies in 1926 Cecil Nascimento, a reliable Guianese, had taken over as keeper, and through

Oldfield, crouching behind the stumps as Wally Hammond cover drives, provides a classic shot of Test cricket action in 1928–29.

Oldfield shows his remarkable speed and dexterity as he dismisses Jack Hobbs' famous partner Herbert Sutcliffe off Arthur Mailey's bowling in Sydney.

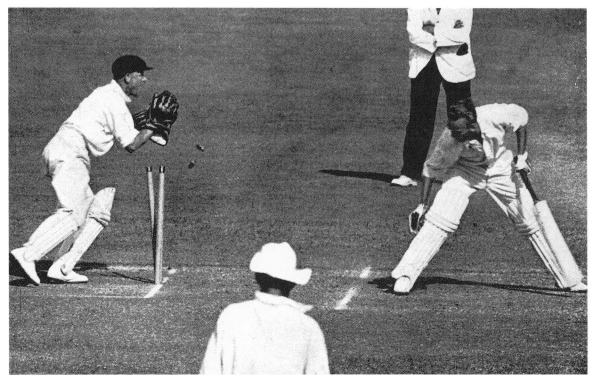

Oldfield breaking the world wicket-keeping record by stumping Hardstaff off Ward in the first Test at Brisbane in 1936. This was Oldfield's 85th Test dismissal in Tests against England.

the brilliance of Learie Constantine, George Challenor and the fast bowling of George Francis and Herman Griffiths, West Indies cricket had taken on a flavour all its own that cried out for international recognition.

When Australia and England met again in 1926, Herbie Collins took over the captaincy. Oldfield had established a deadly understanding with Grimmett, which was to provide Grimmett with 22 Test wickets. The powerful Hampshire keeper George Brown had become an automatic Test selection in matches against South Africa, but with the Ashes at stake again, Strudwick returned for England and a chubby Lancastrian named George Duckworth began pressing for the Test berth he had held for one Test against South Africa in 1924 when Strudwick was unavailable.

With Mailey partnering Grimmett, Arthur Richardson and Charlie Macartney supporting them, Australia relied on spinners in 1926 whereas pace bowling had taken most of the wickets in the two previous rubbers against England. They

failed to get wickets fast enough to win Tests over three days and after four disappointing draws Hobbs and Sutcliffe clinched the series for England with a 172-run stand in the fifth Test. Oldfield's seven dismissals included a superb stumping of Chapman for 49 in The Oval Test that was applauded all round the ground. Collins said at the end of that tour he could not recall Oldfield making a single mistake in any of the 27 matches in which he played.

Immediately after their Ashes triumph England toured South Africa, where Horace Brakendridge ('Jock') Cameron was introduced to Test cricket. Cameron became one of the greatest of all wicket-keeper batsmen, a player whose stumping displays dazzled the eye. One writer said his keeping style was 'the perfection of ease and rapidity without unnecessary show'. Another critic said Cameron stumped his victims 'with the nonchalance of a smoker flicking ash from a cigarette'. He quite overshadowed England's keeper and captain in this series, Lieutenant-Colonel Ronald Stanyforth, the army amateur who later wrote a textbook on the art of keeping. Apart from keeping in spectacular fashion, Cameron's punishing right-handed batting enabled South Africa to share the rubber at two Tests apiece.

Cameron established a strong claim to be ranked the finest of all South African keepers in his 26 Tests, but he had a high percentage of byes, allowing 277 in all, an average of 10.68 per Test. His 11 years in first-class cricket yielded 224 dismissals with 155 catches and 69 stumpings. But he also hit 11 first-class centuries.

Oldfield had a high percentage of stumpings—39.6 per cent or more than one a match—in his career total of 661 dismissals, but he never allowed anywhere near as many byes. A lot of Cameron's byes could be accounted for by the unpredictable pitches South Africans were given during their transition from matting to turf.

The West Indies made a crucial mistake in picking their team for their first official tour of England in 1928—the first tour on which they played Tests—by not including a specialist keeper. They paid dearly for this blunder. Karl Nunes,

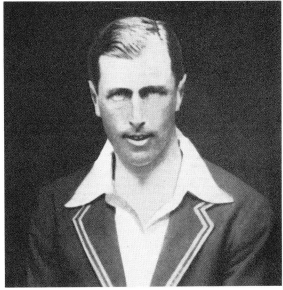

Major Ronald Thomas Stanyforth captained England on their 1927–28 South African tour, a surprising appointment since he had never appeared for a first-class county, only in Army matches. He led England in five Tests, and kept wicket in four of them.

who had made an unbeaten 200 and 108 against Tennyson's English team in Jamaica the previous year, and Claude Vibart Wight, the senior member of a well-known British Guiana cricket family, were expected to share the keeping role but they were primarily batsmen and proved inefficient taking the hostile bowling of Learie Constantine, George Francis, Tommy Scott, 'Snuffie' Brown and Herman Griffith.

English critics said the West Indies had the most alarming pace attack seen in England since Gregory and McDonald opened for Australia in 1921. Chances galore were spilled from their bowling in the Tests. *The Cricketer* commented: 'Nunes kept wicket. He did a horrid job. He does not consider himself or his hands. As captain he should give himself a rest from acting all day long as the target for fast bowling.'

England won all three Tests, with the inimitable George Duckworth behind the stumps in the third Test after Harry Smith (Gloucestershire) and Harry Elliott (Derbyshire) had been tried in the first two Tests. Duckworth proved one of the most talkative and demonstrative keepers in the history of cricket, a shrewd, tough Lancastrian who skidded, bounced and stumbled and sometimes took catches on his knees. One critic said his chest-pad must have been handy as landing gear.

Duckworth could take the bowling of medium-pacer Maurice Tate better than any keeper, picking the swing that hoodwinked batsmen. He wore thin strips of steak inside his gloves facing bowlers of Larwood's pace, with inner gloves keeping the steak in place. Stanyforth's keepers' textbook recommended plasticine or sponge rubber to insulate the hands against fast bowling but George preferred to put up with the smell and flies.

Spectators invariably reacted boisterously to Duckworth diving for balls like a soccer goalie and he never failed to show them an injustice had been done if one of his banshee-like appeals was ignored. On his first visit to Australia in 1928–29 he developed such a close understanding with Tate and Larwood Australian batsmen became wary playing the leg glance. He converted faint nicks off Larwood into catches and those who lifted a boot in playing the shot against Tate often found themselves stumped.

Oldfield was all style; Duckworth would not have a bar of it. Duckworth's pads were wider than Australian models, with additional outer protection, and made him look laboured compared with Oldfield. But he was always in position to collect the ball. Batting in front of him unnerved batsmen not accustomed to his high-pitched and persistent appeals. The words 'Howzat, sir?' tickled the crowd's fancy in virtually every over when George was in full cry.

On his 1928–29 Australian visit Duckworth was clearly superior to his deputy Leslie Ethelbert George Ames, four years Duckworth's junior and not yet 23. This twosome came again in 1932–33 for the notorious Bodyline series and by then Ames had begun to make his bid for a unique place among the keepers of the world.

George Duckworth making one of the stentorian appeals for which he was famous. His 'Howzats' echoed round the cricket world.

7

Cricket Courtier

Kent has a special place among England's counties because of the brand of cricket played there and the contribution of Kentish players to the success of the national team. Les Ames has a special niche in the history of both county and national elevens. He was the first wicket-keeper to score 100 first-class centuries, three times dismissed more than 100 batsmen in a season and formed a deadly wicket-taking partnership with leg-spinner 'Tich' Freeman.

Before Ames came along captains treated whatever runs their keepers contributed as an unexpected bonus. Lilley had a highest Test score of 84 and averaged 20.52 in 35 matches, Carter's best Test innings produced 72 and he averaged 22.97 in 28 Tests. Blackham had a similar record, with a highest score of 74 and a Test average of 15.68. Oldfield's highest Test innings yielded 65 not out and he averaged 22.65. Ames changed all that with 102 first-class centuries, a best Test score of 149 and a Test average of 40.56. At his prime he was good enough to hold a place in the English team as a batsman, and he had a total of 37,248 runs in a first-class career that lasted 15 years (1926 to 1951). After World War II he forsook his place behind the stumps to give Godfrey Evans more opportunities and played for the Kent XI solely as a batsman.

Ames was the outstanding English wicket-keeper of the 1930s, rivalled only at the international level by his close friend, Australia's Bert Oldfield. Together they lifted the standard of Test wicket-keeping to a very high level, bringing polish, skilled glove-work, and sportsmanship to their difficult roles. Ames' career did not yield the string of spectacular dismissals that featured in Oldfield's record, but overall he has strong claims to be rated the finest wicket-keeper batsman of all time. In retrospect, it is clear England's selectors erred badly by not including him in their teams immediately after World War II. Ames scored 9,000-odd of his 37,247 first-class runs in that period.

Ames was born in the farming village of Elham, between Folkestone and Canterbury, and given the middle name of Ethelbert by parents anxious to retain the memory of a Kentish king. He went to Harvey Grammar School, Folkestone, where teachers recorded that he was interested in nothing apart from sport. His father Harold was a well-known local slow left-arm bowler, and his grandfather umpired in Elham for more than 30 years.

He was encouraged to develop his cricket talents by a local squire, Francis Mackinnon, 35th chieftan of the clan Mackinnon, who had played for Cambridge University and Kent and been a member of Lord Harris' team to Australia in 1878–79, and by Jack Hubble, the Kent County XI keeper. Hubble came to Elham for a week each year to stay with his grocer brother Lewis during Canterbury Cricket Week. By the time he enrolled at grammar school, young Ames realised that Kent cricket had a quality all its own, with boys from the lovely farmland villages providing ample talent for school matches, from which the best players developed their aspirations for trials with the county team. Les scored his first century, 104

Cricket's greatest wicket-keeper batsman Leslie Ethelbert George Ames. No other keeper comes near his record of 102 first-class centuries. He also dismissed 1121 batsmen.

not out, for Harvey Grammar against Dover County School at 14 in 1920.

Les was a brilliant outfielder who aimed to emulate his father as a slow bowler until he joined Smeeth, a village club, soon after leaving school. The Smeeth captain was a splendid leg-spinner, but opposing batsmen often survived because catches and stumpings were missed. Les told his captain their wicket-keeper wasted too many opportunities and reluctantly took over himself. Although he did not consider the job would be permanent, he managed to stump three or four village batsmen in every innings for his captain. By 1924 Ames had made such impressive progress he earned a trial against the Kent County Club and Ground XI, captained by Gerry Weigall, the former Cambridge blue and Kent player.

Weigall was impressed by Ames' batting and included him in the Kent side that played Hythe shortly afterwards. Weigall insisted that Ames take over as wicket-keeper, but Les said he was unsuitable for the job and in any case had not brought gloves or pads. Weigall overcame that problem by instructing Arthur Povey, the regular Kent keeper, to lend Ames his gear. Fearful of the ordeal he faced, Ames went out and made three catches and a stumping, helping to dismiss Hythe for 92. This won him a place in the 1925 Kent Second XI.

His wicket-keeping and batting steadily improved and in 1926 he headed the Kent seconds' batting averages and had clearly established himself as a keeper of great promise through a flurry of stumpings and catches. He made his debut for Kent in July 1926, against Warwickshire at Tunbridge Wells. By then his ambition to become a soccer forward had been aired and frustrated in stints with Folkestone and Clapton Orient and he had gone into a sports store business at Gillingham with Jack Hubble. He also played soccer for Gillingham.

The Yorkshire-born journalist Alan Hill, Ames' biographer, continually stressed Ames' early reluctance to keep wicket. Hill gives Fred Huish the honour of establishing the great tradition of Kent wicket-keeping in his 19 years as county keeper, 1895 to 1914. Australians remembered Huish for his quick thinking in Kent's match against the Australians in 1902 at Canterbury. Reg Duff tried to steal a quick single

to give Trumper the strike, with Huish standing back to a fast bowler. Huish did not have time to gather the ball but kicked it on to the stumps at the far end to run Duff out. Huish formed a match-winning combination with the master left-arm spinner Colin Blythe and Ames was to have a similar association with 'Tich' Freeman.

Alfred Percy Freeman remains the only bowler to take more than 300 wickets in an English season, a leg-break and googly bowler of wondrous consistency whose 304 wickets at 18.05 in 1928, when aged 40, is unlikely to be surpassed. Freeman took more than 200 wickets in the seven seasons following that feat and exceeded 100 victims in a season 17 times. But he played in only 12 Tests and in his great years from 1930 to 1935 played in not a single one. He made three tours to Australia, in 1922-23, 1924-25, and 1928-29

The men who founded Kent's great tradition of producing outstanding keepers—Leslie Ames and Godfrey Evans at the back, Jack Hubble and Fred Huish seated in front. –*Kent County Cricket Club*

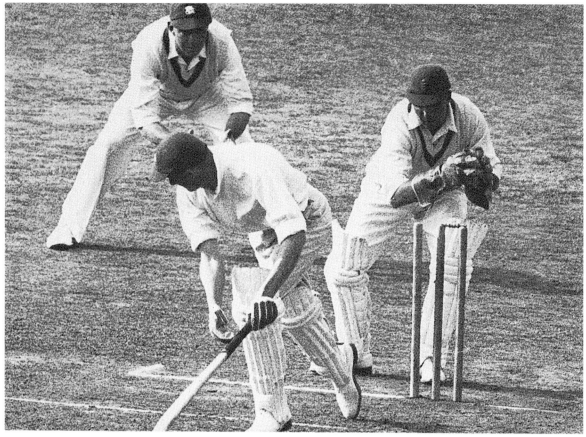

Ames stumping a batsman who has been foolish enough to lift his back foot, as Wally Hammond looks on from the slips. Many of Ames' victims were off Kent team-mate 'Tich' Freeman. –*Kent County Cricket Club*

but on hard, heavily rolled pitches he failed to tempt batsmen into frequent indiscretions as he did in county cricket.

In 1926, Jack Hubble stepped down as Kent's keeper at the age of 45 to make way for Ames, who, thanks to a loan provided by his father, was to remain Hubble's business partner for 40 years. Ames took over for the opening match of the 1927 season against Worcestershire at Folkestone. He immediately justified his selection by scoring 90, adding 155 in 65 minutes with Percy Chapman, who went on to 158. He then took a catch and made three stumpings off Freeman. Frank Woolley had explained how to read Freeman's leg-breaks and googlies at a practice session.

At Southampton against Hampshire, in his sixth county match, Ames hit his initial first-class century. Hampshire at the time had a very useful keeper in Walter Livsey, who went to South Africa with England in 1922–23 but could not play there because of injury. Livsey had a high rate of stumpings (265 or 40.8 per cent) among his 649 career victims, whereas Tom Sidwell, who kept for Leicestershire at that time and was mentioned as a Test candidate, stumped 137 or 19 per cent of his 720 career victims.

Ames' batting lifted him above them and, despite the disadvantage of going in at number eight for Kent, he was picked for Test trials. By the end of the 1927 season he had made more than 1,000 runs at 34.53 and built up a big following among Kent supporters. Then in a hot 1928 English summer he boosted his aggregate to 1,736 runs, with four centuries.

The selectors persisted with the view that specialist keepers should be chosen for Tests and gave both George Duckworth and Derbyshire's Harry Elliott the job in Tests against the West Indies. By the end of the summer Ames' confident batting and his rapid improvement behind the stumps won him selection in Percy Chapman's touring team for Australia as Duckworth's deputy. The selection elated Ames' predecessors behind the stumps for Kent, Jack Hubble and Fred Huish, who forecast that he would become the finest keeper in England. Just as delighted by Ames' inclusion was 'Tich' Freeman.

Duckworth kept wicket in all five Tests in Australia. Ames appeared in only eight of the tour matches, but he had the satisfaction of *Wisden* labelling him one of its Five Cricketers Of The Year and predicting he would become the finest wicket-keeper batsman England had ever had. The duel for the England job intrigued because of the marked contrast in styles of the two aspirants.

The Ames–Duckworth duel for the Test job was closely monitored because of England's need to find a keeper to match Oldfield. The most punctilious of keepers on the field, Oldfield prepared for matches off the field by asking staff in his sports store to throw parcels at him, a risky ploy Carter said, but one which Oldfield claimed sharpened his reflexes. He differed with Carter, too, by sprinting after legside deflections, which Carter said meant deserting your post. Oldfield claimed a brief run improved concentration.

Ames' problem was that he made wicket-keeping look so easy spectators doubted that he had a hard job. He kept wicket without Duckworth's fuss or acrobatics and seldom dirtied his flannels. He was quick with congratulatory comments when opponents reached 50 or 100 and never showed annoyance with umpiring decisions. He looked young and inexperienced long after he had absorbed the hard lessons of life as a cricket professional, whereas Duckworth always managed to convey the demeanour of a master tactician, quick to spot rival players' ethical breaches.

Selectors preferred Duckworth until the fifth Test against South Africa at The Oval in 1929, sadly 'Tich' Freeman's last, and Ames played in all four Tests in the West Indies in 1929–30. He had established an English record in 1928 by dismissing 121 batsmen in the season and in 1929

dismissed 127 (79 caught, 48 stumped). He also scored five centuries in 1929, finishing with a total of 1,795 runs. Ames caught nine Oxford University batsmen in 1928 and a year later caught five and stumped four against Sussex.

However, when Australia toured England in 1930 with a team that included only four players who had been to England before—Oldfield, Grimmett, Ponsford and the captain Bill Woodfull—selectors reverted to the inelegant Duckworth. They reasoned that Duckworth handled the great medium-pacer Maurice Tate better than Ames or any of the county keepers. Australia took the Ashes with a decisive win in the fifth Test due to Bradman and Ponsford (110). Duckworth dropped Bradman off Hammond after he had made 82 but Bradman was given out off Larwood at 232 when the ball did not touch the bat. Asked why he appealed, Duckworth simply said: 'Well, Bradman had made enough.'

Compared to the bustling, untidy Duckworth, Ames kept wicket in a leisurely, unhurried fashion, taking position early as bowlers walked back to their marks, toes and knee flaps well out, elbows inside his knees, showing his teeth through a winning smile in moments of triumph. He got down very low and although he stood up quickly and took the ball sweetly with perfect timing there were doubts about his method and lack of practice in standing back to take fast bowling. Oldfield's sole criticism of Ames' technique was that in standing up on the stumps to medium-pace bowlers he did not cover good-length deliveries outside the leg stump. Instead of stepping across to the leg, he lunged at these legside balls with his left hand. His concentration was unequalled, however, and he missed fewer chances than any keeper of his period.

By 1931 Ames had closed the gap between himself and Duckworth to become England's first-choice keeper for all three Tests against New Zealand. In the four Tests in the West Indies he hit two centuries and in the first Test against New Zealand he made 137, rescuing England, who were on 5 for 129 when he went to the crease. In this innings he helped 'Gubby' Allen put on 246 for the eighth wicket and became the first English keeper to make a Test century. He was to make eight Test centuries in all, including 120 in 1934 at Lord's, the first 100 by a wicket-keeper in England v. Australia Tests.

Ames played in the inaugural Test between India and England in 1932 and then joined Douglas Jardine's team on the infamous Bodyline tour of Australia. He was a professional cricketer, successful sports store proprietor, good-looking, and at the height of his powers at 27. If he had any misgivings about the sportsmanship of the tactics Jardine adopted, he kept them to himself. He came from a village where cricket had been played for more than 200 years between teams who gave their captains unswerving loyalty and he stuck with that concept in his dealings with Jardine. He was ready to criticise England's cricket Establishment for their treatment of Freeman but he remained silent when Jardine's obsession with curbing Bradman's prodigious scoring threatened the future of international cricket.

The fieldsmen and wicket-keeper played important roles in Jardine's Bodyline planning. Ames had to adjust to standing back to the bowling of Voce, Larwood, Allen and Bowes, and covering an incessant legside attack. With only one man on the offside in front of the stumps, and seven men between mid-on and fine leg, batsmen who tried to protect their bodies with the bat could not avoid dismissal. Ames dismissed 10 batsmen in the five Tests standing further from the stumps than he ever did for Kent.

Ames found Australian first-class cricket bristling with wicket-keeping talent. Oldfield remained supreme, but around the states a lengthy list of gifted keepers were ready to take his place if he faltered. The talkative Jack Ellis had been replaced in the Victorian team by Ben Barnett, who had to resist challenges from two highly capable keepers in North Melbourne's Stan Quin and Prahran's Jack Kroger.

Barnett, an effective left-hand batsman who made 131 for Victoria against Tasmania in only his second first-class match in 1929–30, was a cheerful, curly-haired keeper with a flair for amateur acting and conjuring that enlivened the long train trips undertaken by the Sheffield Shield teams. He was the complete antithesis to his predecessor in the Victorian team, extrovert builder Ellis, notorious for smoking big cigars between innings and for seeking to upset batsmen with his chatter. Ellis played for Prahran from

Jack Ellis as Melbourne cricket fans saw him regularly. He was probably the most talkative keeper of them all, continually advising batsmen in front of him on the quality of the bowling.

Jack Ellis, Oldfield's longtime deputy, finally moved over in the Victorian team to make room for Ben Barnett. Reduced to appearances in grade cricket, Jack remained loquacious.

1917 to 1932, headed the club's batting averages in 1919–20 with an average of 68.00, and made three tours with Australian teams.

When Victoria scored the world-record total of 1,107 in 1926–27, Ellis played the pull shot off Tommy Andrews that took Victoria past 1,000. 'Come on, there's three in it,' he hollered. 'Three for me and 1,000 for Victoria.' He remained casual in his dress, and wore his cap with the peak round near his neck, upset purists by wearing brown pads, and there were always laces or straps hanging loose from his calves. But he was one of the wisest men on how wickets would play, and given to encouraging young batsmen suffering from nervousness. Mature players who tried to ignore his commentaries found him bawling into their shoulder blades or turning to say his piece to his slips fieldsmen.

Bill Ponsford and Bill Woodfull opened for Victoria in Ellis' time and together had 22 century partnerships, five over 200. When they went to the crease, Ellis went to inspect one of his building jobs or to visit a bookmaker to lay bets for his team-mates. He was the man who jumped the fence at Adelaide Oval to exchange blows with a spectator whose comments upset him.

Halford Hooker told me how Ellis greeted him when he went out to join Allan Kippax in 1928–29 at the MCG: 'Have a go, Hal, the bowling's rubbish'. Hooker stayed until he and Kippax had enjoyed a world record 10th-wicket stand of 307, a partnership that deprived Ellis and his colleagues of their Christmas Day celebration lunch. Facing Charlie Kelleway's swingers, Ellis played and missed several deliveries and then demanded: 'Why don't you put 'em where I can reach 'em?'

Ellis went to England in 1926 at the age of 36 as Oldfield's deputy, after touring New Zealand with Victoria in 1924–25. At 45, he joined Frank Tarrant's Australian team on the Indian tour funded by the Maharajah of Patialia and captained by Jack Ryder. He took Ryder's medium-pacers two or three paces behind the stumps in a half-and-half position seldom seen since. He was regarded as an outstanding keeper to spinners, and made 294 first-class dismissals (187 caught, 107 stumped), but among Shield players he was more famous as the man who told Bradman to get out because he had had enough batting in scoring a century.

Benjamin Arthur Barnett was as noted for his neatness as Ellis was for his careless appearance. Barnett was born in the Melbourne suburb of Auburn in 1908, and from the time he took over from Ellis at the age of 21, built a reputation for his skill in taking spinners like Fleetwood-Smith and for his conjuring tricks with matches, ribbons, cards and coins.

Charles William Walker, born at Brompton, South Australia, was a year younger than Barnett and won the job as Oldfield's deputy in England on the 1930 tour, partly because of his skill in taking the bowling of guileful leg-spinner Clarrie Grimmett. *The Times* of London found their keeping a revelation. Watching Walker stump three batsmen at Leicester, *The Times* said that with two bowlers of the same calibre as Oldfield and Walker Australia would be formidable.

Walker, who made only 43 runs at an average of 4.77 in England, followed in the comic tradition of Albert Mark Ambler. Ambler, who played for North Adelaide before that club changed its name to Prospect when it moved to Prospect Oval, once ran a two on his own while his partner Dave Pritchard remained stationary at the crease. New

South Wales fieldsmen threw wildly at either wicket and joined spectators in laughter as the umpire signalled to perplexed scorers that the runs did not count. In a club match, commemorating a milestone in South Australian cricket, Ambler took the field in a frockcoat.

The jockey-sized Cyril Norman Parry took over from Ambler in 1925–26. Parry was a fraction over 5 feet (150 cm) tall and weighed only 8 stone 7 pounds (54 kg). He could have ridden in the Melbourne Cup. He left his native Tasmania to further his Test chances in South Australia. Wicket-keeping gloves always looked too big for his slender arms but he was often rated with Oldfield for skill. Clayvell Lindsay ('Jack') Badcock, also a Tasmanian, considered Parry as fast a stumper as Don Tallon.

Respected Australian captain Monty Noble went into the South Australian dressing-room during the 1930 South Australia v. New South Wales match in Sydney and asked: 'How could they play Walker ahead of Parry? He's one of the finest keepers I've seen.'

When Oldfield's skull was cracked in the third Bodyline Test in Adelaide, many critics believed Parry should have replaced him, but the job went to 'Hammy' Love, who made six first-class centuries, top score 192 v. Archie MacLaren's England XI in 1923. Love, a Services XI star in England, had moved from Sydney to Melbourne since Oldfield was blocking his state team selection. With Jack Ellis growing old, Love felt he had more chance of pressing his claim to first-class status in the Victorian side.

Love was a popular, jovial figure who had begun keeping as a pupil at St Andrew's Cathedral School in Sydney, where he captained the First XI in 1911–12. He joined the Balmain club on leaving school and built a reputation as a free-scoring wicket-keeper-batsman. He served as a corporal with the AIF in England in World War I and was one of the keepers picked for the AIF side, but had to return home for family reasons. He played for Carlton and later for St Kilda in Melbourne and in 1922–23 began five seasons as Victoria's keeper. Hampden Stanley Bray ('Hammy') Love had a natural gift for catching; as a schoolboy he caught, without gloves, stones thrown to him by his mates. He trained himself to always receive the ball in his palms, fingers

Popular keeper Hampden Stanley Bray ('Hammy') Love, who left Sydney to try his luck, only to find Jack Ellis blocked his path to State selection as Oldfield had in Sydney. He played in one Test in the Bodyline series when Oldfield was hurt.

down, and finished 30 years of cricket with unmarked hands.

He returned to Sydney in 1927 and was near the end of five years of occasional appearances for New South Wales when he was picked to replace Oldfield for the fourth Test. While Oldfield's head was in bandages, Love made 5 and 3 and took three catches. Oldfield went back into the team for the fifth Test. Three years later, Love, a member of eight first-grade premiership teams in Sydney and Melbourne, toured India with Jack Ryder's Australian team.

Oldfield refused to blame England's bowlers for his narrow escape from serious injury in Adelaide. He said it was all his own fault that a ball deflected from his bat on to his skull, causing a small fracture. Doctors said that if the injury had been an inch or two either side of where Larwood hit him, it could have proved fatal. Oldfield retired after scoring 41 and took no further part in the match, Vic Richardson taking over as Australia's keeper in England's second innings. Considering Oldfield's and Ellis' dominance of the keeping roles in New South

Wales and Victoria, Love did well to reach 102 first-class dismissals (73 caught and 29 stumped).

Love was not alone among the splendid keepers frustrated by Oldfield's presence. Hugh Lavery Davidson (1907–60), whose wide-armed stance collected many victims for the Waverley club, dismissed nine South Australian batsmen in one of his few appearances for New South Wales when Oldfield was away. Frank Alexander Easton (1910–89), who played for Glebe and Balmain clubs, dismissed 44 batsmen in 18 first-class matches, most of them while Oldfield was absent on overseas tours, before an injury to his left thigh in World War II forced him to forsake keeping.

A similar situation prevailed in Victoria, where Stan Quin spent the period from 1930 to 1937 as Barnett's deputy. Quin, who played for North Melbourne, dismissed 59 batsmen in first-class matches, but his fame rested on his partnership of 424 for the fourth wicket with Ian Lee, in the 1933–34 season at Melbourne against Tasmania. Lee made 268, Quin 210, but Tasmania forced a draw. Quin and Lee lifted Victoria's second innings to 560 after they had collapsed for 68 in the first innings. Quin enjoyed playing against the Tasmanian bowling as he also made 114 not out against them in 1931 and 113 in 1933.

Duckworth sustained the reputation of wicket-keepers spotting opponents' weaknesses and is given credit for Jardine's Bodyline tactics. He reported to Jardine that in an over Larwood bowled to Bradman in 1930 at The Oval Bradman clearly flinched when the ball was directed at his body. Larwood confirmed that Bradman had backed away and suggested that Bradman could well have a weakness against fast rising deliveries on the leg stump. Before he died Archie Jackson, who batted with Bradman at The Oval, confirmed that Duckworth had been the first to notice Bradman recoil.

These powers of observation did not help Duckworth in Australia on the Bodyline tour. Ames was preferred in all five Tests, pressing his claims with centuries against Queensland Country at Toowoomba (121 not out) and against Tasmania at Launceston (107). He further distinguished himself with an innings of 103 in the Test against New Zealand at Christchurch.

By the end of the tour all Ames' reluctance to keep wicket had disappeared and he developed into a dignified exponent of a difficult role, dismissing batsmen with a swift flick of the bails. He had dismissed Vic Richardson in the fourth Test at Brisbane with a magnificent legside stumping off Hammond and followed with a fine catch to send back Len Darling, standing back to 'Gubby' Allen.

Despite the intense rivalry of their supporters, Ames and Duckworth were close friends. Ames said: 'I was more friendly with Duckie than any other cricketer in my entire playing career'. They were the first to congratulate each other for outstanding dismissals. 'Ames was the quickest executioner I ever saw', said one-time England captain Bob Wyatt, who favoured Duckworth against fast-medium bowlers like Tate or George Geary, but rated Ames the best ever in taking slow bowling.

Ames, of course, had almost daily practice facing spin bowling. After Freeman retired Doug Wright became Kent's match-winning spinner. Ames' heavy scoring forced selectors to look for keepers who could bat, but it meant he could not easily be replaced in Tests. His Australian contemporaries, Don Bradman, Bill O'Reilly, Leo O'Brien and Bill Brown agreed he was the greatest ever wicket-keeper batsman, an unsurpassed combination of two demanding Test skills, and statistics support that ranking. Among his contemporaries, Ames' supremacy was challenged only by South African Horace Brakendridge ('Jock') Cameron, whose first-class career began on matting pitches in 1924, when he was 19.

Like Ames, Cameron's stumping style was neither noisy nor flamboyant, but was compared to a smoker flicking ash from a cigarette. He took the ball cleanly and easily from all styles of bowling, and team-mates could not recall him fumbling. Like Ames, he was clean-cut and good-looking, an ethical cricketer with rare stamina. He first appeared for South Africa in 1927–28 against England and toured England in Springbok sides in 1929 and 1935. He opened the 1929 tour with a century against Worcestershire and against Somerset at Taunton had seven victims.

Cameron was given the South African captaincy in a Test against England in 1930–31 and did well enough to hold the job for South Africa's 1931–32 tour of Australia. They encountered Bradman and Grimmett at their best.

Horace Brakendridge ('Jock') Cameron, brilliant South African wicket-keeper-batsman, found captaincy burdensome. He died of enteric fever shortly before Australia arrived in South Africa in 1935, in his 30th year.

Bradman averaged 201.50 against the South Africans, scoring 226, 112, 167 and 299 not out in the Tests and 219 and 135 against them for New South Wales. Grimmett took 33 wickets at 16.87 apiece in the Tests, but had little chance to continue his devastation in the fifth Test at Melbourne, where Ironmonger took 5 for 6 and 6 for 18 to have South Africa out for 36 and 45.

Cameron found the captaincy burdensome, though he lost none of his powers as a batsman or wicket-keeper after this drubbing. He returned to England in 1935 under Herb Wade's captaincy. In the Lord's Test he went to the crease after South Africa lost four cheap wickets and hit 90 of the 126 runs scored in the next 105 minutes. This innings paved the way for South Africa's first Test

victory in England, Bruce Mitchell supporting him with 164 in the second innings and Xenophon Constantine ('Bally') Balaskas taking 9 for 103. At Sheffield on that tour Cameron shocked Yorkshire stalwarts by hitting Hedley Verity for 30 in an over.

Cameron had sent back 224 batsmen (155 caught, 69 stumped) when he returned home after that triumph to greet the Australian side led by Vic Richardson. However, he died from enteric fever while the Australians were at sea. At 30 he had scored 5,396 runs at 37.47 with 11 centuries and won a niche among the game's great hitters.

The Australians had what the players agreed was their most enjoyable tour and after the last match played a baseball game for the benefit of Cameron's widow. Bert Oldfield kept wicket in all five Tests, Australia winning four–nil. Oldfield dismissed 12 batsmen in the Tests but unjustified reports reached Australia that he often fumbled taking the spin of Fleetwood-Smith, Grimmett and O'Reilly.

South Africans disagreed with suggestions Oldfield had declined. They had seen faultless displays from the short, dapper little man Ray Robinson said would have made a fine courtier. 'You could picture him in the ballroom at Versailles with powdered wig, gleaming shoe-buckles, and snowy lace at his wrists,' wrote Robinson. 'Never a thing out of place—except a bail flicked from its groove as a dandy might whisk a speck of snuff from his jacket.' But the gossip about his South African performance eventually led to Oldfield's disappearance from the Australian side.

A year after Cameron's death another famous South African keeper died when Tom Ward was electrocuted while working at the West Springs gold mine. Ward, who was often knocked about during his cricket career, appeared in 23 Tests and was noted for his stubborn defence with the bat. He toured England with South African teams in 1912 and 1924 and dismissed 175 batsmen (107 caught and 68 stumped), including three stumpings and two catches against the 1921 Australians when they appeared in South Africa on their way home from England.

8

The Ben and Charlie Show

By the mid-1930s wicket-keeping had become a vital tactical role for winning cricket teams. Improvement in pitches and equipment transformed the job but so did the mastery of Hanson Carter, George Duckworth, Bert Oldfield and Les Ames. Their match-winning dismissals made headlines but they all had to overcome tough opposition for their places in national teams.

Carter overcame challenges from Joe Kelly, Barlow Carkeek and later from Oldfield, who in turn had Gordon Inkster, Ben Barnett, Albert Ambler, Cyril Parry and Charlie Walker bidding for his spot. Duckworth outdid Sussex wizard Walter Latter ('Tich') Cornford and a rival from within his Lancashire club, William Farrimond. Twice in a month Cornford stumped Jack Hobbs down the leg side, and he made regular stumpings off Maurice Tate and Arthur Gilligan. Farrimond toured South Africa with England in 1930–31 and the West Indies in 1934–35, appearing in four Tests. But Duckworth kept him out of the Lancashire XI. Ames, too, had an impressive deputy in the farmer 'Hopper' Levett, who had some inspiring days.

Levett played four times for the Gentlemen against the Players and dismissed 478 batsmen in a 175-match first-class career, including one appearance for England. 'Hopper was the best amateur keeper in England,' said Ames. 'What I particularly liked about him was his loyalty to Kent. He rejected all offers to switch counties.' Levett was a favourite of Kent crowds, renowned for the roar of laughter that carried across the

ground when he took an important catch, and just as noisy in his rage if he dropped a chance.

Ames' batting gave Levett few chances to display his keeping skill and the same talent enabled him to beat off Duckworth's bid for England team selection. Duckworth showed no animosity towards his rival and in the 1931 Test at Old Trafford against New Zealand lent Ames his gear until Ames' equipment was found by railway porters. On the Bodyline tour of Australia when the pace of Larwood, Voce and Allen threatened to bruise Ames' hands, Duckworth introduced Ames to his trick with strips of steak.

Despite his impeccable timing, Ames' hands took such a pummelling he could scarcely take the ball without pain, but even then the steak was converted to pulp by the bowlers. 'Duckie looked after me like a valet,' Ames told biographer Hill. 'He would be the first person to greet me when we returned to the pavilion. He would wash my gloves and cut up fresh slices of meat with scissors before we went out again.'

The steak worked well until Ames threw down his gloves after a hot, tiring day in the field, and in Duckworth's absence, forgot about the steak. Next day was the Sunday rest day and when the Englishmen returned to their dressing-room on Monday morning they found hordes of flies clinging to the rotten steak in Ames' gloves. The stench drove team-mates from the dressing-room and Ames had to find a new pair of gloves.

By then Ames had silenced Duckworth's supporters who accepted the view that Ames' batting prevented England fielding a vulnerable tail. Ames held his place in the England team until 1939, when he gave up keeping because of recurring back problems. He had lost the Test keeping job in the fourth Test against Australia the previous season when he fractured a finger. The Middlesex keeper Wilfred Frederick Frank Price, who had 987 career dismissals, took his place for the Headingley Test, and Yorkshire's Arthur Wood for the final Test at The Oval. Wood went in at 6 for 770 and made 35. 'I'm always at my best in a crisis,' he said. Wood played in three Tests against the West Indies in 1939 and took one astounding catch just inside the long-leg fence. Sprinting hard, he just got his gloves to the ball. 'Just as well I was standing back,' he said.

Wicket-keepers' sense of fun figured strongly in the make-up of Fred Price, too. Price, who often opened the batting for Middlesex, held seven

Arthur Wood, the Yorkshireman who was so delighted to be picked for England he rode in a taxi from Nottingham to London, keeping wicket in a county game to the batting of Surrey's left-hand opener Laurie Fishlock.

catches in Yorkshire's first innings at Lord's in 1937. When the Middlesex team came off a woman spectator said she was so thrilled by Fred's display she almost fell off the balcony. 'If you had, madam, I would have caught you, too,' said Price.

The same good humour was not evident in Australia in the 1930s, where some officials did their best to discredit successors to Oldfield's Test place. Queensland president Jack Hutcheon asked the Board of Control to ban the webbed-thumbed gloves used by Ben Barnett when Barnett won Test selection ahead of Queensland's Bundaberg prodigy, Don Tallon. The move failed.

Barnett replaced Charlie Walker as Oldfield's deputy in England in 1934 and in South Africa in 1935–36, but at a time when slow bowlers dominated Australian cricket both had marvellous days, Barnett in taking the freakish left-arm spinner 'Chuck' Fleetwood-Smith, Walker in adding to Clarrie Grimmett's long list of dismissals.

Oldfield retained a big following because of his expertise in taking Bill O'Reilly and Hughie Chilvers, hostile leg-spinners, but his detractors kept repeating that he had been born in 1894 and could not be expected to be as good as he was in the 1920s. Victorians enjoyed spreading the rumour that Oldfield had been a flop in South Africa in 1935–36 and had performed poorly when Fleetwood-Smith bowled.

O'Reilly called this poppycock and stressed that most keepers had problems when they first encountered Fleetwood-Smith, an unorthodox left-armer who spun the ball prodigiously. 'Oldfield started the South African trip badly but after a month was at his very best—he just needed to get used to "Chuck" and the matting wickets,' O'Reilly said. Oldfield had similar problems with some deliveries from Bill Hunt, the New South Wales left-arm spinner who played one Test against South Africa in Adelaide in 1931–32 before he went off to complete his career in the Lancashire League with Rishton. Oldfield went into the nets with both Hunt and Fleetwood-Smith and rehearsed with them until he could read them with unerring reliability.

Oldfield resisted the challenges from Walker, Barnett and Tallon until the end of the 1937–38 Australian summer. The selectors preferred him for all five Tests against 'Gubby' Allen's 1936–37

Oldfield resisted challenges from Charlie Walker and Ben Barnett until the end of the 1937–38 Australian summer. The threat he posed standing right up on the stumps to spinners Grimmett, O'Reilly, Ward and Fleetwood-Smith is clear in this shot of him behind 'Patsy' Hendren.

English tourists when he had his 40th birthday. By then he had played in seven home series, five of them against England, made five tours of England (including the AIF series), and kept wicket in a record 54 Tests. His 82 matches for New South Wales and appearances for the First AIF team gave him a total of 245 first-class matches during which he caught 399 batsmen and stumped 262. His percentage of stumpings remains a remarkable statistic. He had the benefit of keeping to some great slow-bowlers but to stump 52 batsmen in 54 Tests out of his total Test bag of 130 dismissals has caused many cricket statisticians to check it out in the belief that it might be a misprint. His stumpings were achieved with the stealth of a cat, quietly and efficiently, without dislodging the stumps or deafening the batsmen with his appeals.

Selection of Barnett and Walker for Australia's 1938 tour angered New South Wales fans, who believed that Oldfield was badly misrepresented by the stories of his alleged decline on the South African tour. He was as fit and wiry as ever and

comfortably resisted challenges for his New South Wales spot from a young Western Suburbs keeper named Stan Sismey and the St George club's Ernie Laidler.

Oldfield's big-match days started when he rose from bed. He immediately tested the wind and noted the weather conditions that might affect flighted deliveries. At the ground he made careful inspections of the pitch before batsmen arrived. His thoroughness was such that in 245 first-class matches he allowed only 302 byes, and averaged one bye for every 68.6 runs scored against his teams. He was the first Australian to dismiss five batsmen in a Test innings (four stumped), in 1924–25. This was the series in which he was responsible for Jack Hobbs' first duck in Australia. Hobbs said he glided Jack Gregory down the leg side in the Sydney Test and felt perfectly satisfied with the shot until he saw Oldfield 'going like a hare' towards square leg and pulling in the catch with an outstretched left glove without losing his feet or diving. In the second innings he stumped Hobbs off Grimmett with a speed most batsmen would have disputed. Knowing who had flicked off the bails, Hobbs showed faith in his tormentor's integrity and walked off.

Oldfield, ahead of Ames with the gloves, was reliable but not as prolific as Ames with the bat. He made 1,427 runs at 22.65 in Tests, with a top score of 65 not out, and hit six centuries in all first-class matches, top score 137. When Larwood knocked him down in the fifth Test of the Bodyline series he continued the match with two broken ribs and made 52.

Between 15 and 19 January 1938, on the Sydney Cricket Ground, Charlie Walker broke a finger keeping wicket for South Australia against New South Wales. Bradman, who already had cut his lip in a midfield collision and had a cut finger strapped, looked around his players for a replacement. He remembered his days with the Bowral team, captained by his uncle Dick Whatman, and the advice Whatman gave him on keeping, and took the gloves for the rest of the match.

Cricket commentators said Bradman took an unnecessary risk and damage to his hands could have lessened his run-scoring. Bradman, in fact, enjoyed keeping wicket and answered the critics by stumping Bill O'Reilly off leg-spinner Frank Ward, standing well up on the stumps. In the second innings he stood back to his swing bowlers Merv Waite and Graham Williams and took a catch off each of them to send back Stan McCabe and Bede McCauley, and then caught Vic Jackson off Ward to finish with four dismissals. To show that his batting was not affected by keeping, he made 104 not out in South Australia's second innings, reaching 1,000 runs for the ninth successive season.

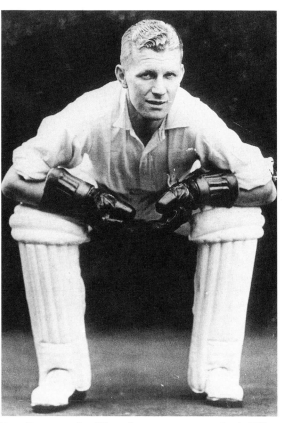

Ben Barnett, the Victorian successor to Jack Ellis, entertained fellow cricketers on tour with his skilful conjuring tricks.

Charlie Walker, the South Australian who made two tours to England without appearing in a Test. Injuries sapped his confidence and he was forced to wear special gloves. He was killed in action in World War II.

Bill O'Reilly, who conducted a feud with Bradman for more than half a century, claimed that the practice of keepers standing back to medium-pacers began when Bradman did so to Waite and Williams. O'Reilly argued that Maurice Tate always preferred Herbert Strudwick to stand up on the stumps to his bowling and later said Alec Bedser was most effective when Godfrey Evans stood right up on the stumps.

In 1988 O'Reilly wrote: 'Bradman swore on his sword hilt that the stand-back position was the safest and best for a keeper keen to get a good eyeful of those snicked legside chances. Schoolboys of 1938 who read Bradman's remark took it to heart and carried it down through the ages to this day. I have been spoiled by the assistance I received from the great Bertie Oldfield and later from Don Tallon. I also received incredible support from Ernie Laidler, whose efforts went unnoticed by short-sighted selectors who attended Sydney grade matches where wizard keepers such as Stan Sismey, Les Fallowfield and Frank Easton plied their brilliant trade in support of spin bowlers, but from my angle the standing back ploy is wrong—dead wrong.'

Most experts believed that when Oldfield retired, Tallon would succeed him, but Queenslanders lacked support among southern-state board members, and when the 1938 team for England was named Ben Barnett and Charlie Walker were preferred. Queenslanders were stunned. For O'Reilly, the omission of Grimmett was a similar selection gaffe.

Bradman admits that he underestimated Tallon's ability in 1938 when he was one of the three selectors who named the team for England. Lindsay Hassett, who followed Bradman as Australian captain, had no reservations. 'I knew Tallon was something out of the box when he caught me twice from authentic leg glances that went exactly where I aimed them.'

Walker broke a finger before the team played the first match in England and missed so many matches team-mates asked who the stranger was when he took the field against Somerset. He had damaged a finger earlier in his career and to support this finger wore a three-fingered glove. He put the first two fingers for half their length into a leather stall packed with sponge rubber and jammed the hand into one enlarged compartment

in his left glove. He could not get enough cricket to seriously bid for the Test spot and Barnett kept in all five Tests.

Australia retained the Ashes by winning the fourth Test at Leeds after three Tests without a result, leaving England chasing lost prestige in the fifth Test at The Oval. The England selectors called up Arthur Wood to keep wicket at short notice. Wood was so elated he hired a taxi to take him to London from Nottingham, where he was playing when he heard of his selection. The meter clicked up £7 15s. 0d., more than two weeks' pay for most people at that time, but Wood laughed it off. Wood was the keeper at Bramall Lane in 1935 when South Africa's Jock Cameron hit Hedley Verity for 30 runs in an over. 'Keep 'em there, Hedley,' said Wood. 'You've got him in two minds—he doesn't know whether to smack you for four or six.'

At The Oval, Barnett had a horror of a Test. Len Hutton had reached 40 when he moved down the pitch to drive and completely missed a ball from Fleetwood-Smith. Barnett dropped the ball with Hutton stranded metres down the pitch, missing a simple stumping. Hutton went on to a world record Test score of 364, 30 more than Bradman's previous record. Author Ray Robinson wrote that conjuror Barnett must have felt like sawing Hutton in half when he stayed for 13 hours 17 minutes.

Watching Barnett's costly lapse, Bill O'Reilly could not help reflecting on the mistake-free record of Oldfield and his St George clubmate Ernie Laidler. O'Reilly said: 'Laidler was one of the finest wicket-keepers I ever encountered, and a great assistance to his bowlers. He was just as fast as Oldfield as a stumper and few people at St George could recall him ever missing a chance. It was a tragedy that he was never chosen for his state.'

Laidler said he and spin bowler Frank Ward were promised places in the Queensland team if they went north. They went to Brisbane, but after weeks of searching could not find jobs and had to return to Sydney. Meanwhile Tallon blossomed as Queensland's keeper, carrying on the tradition of excellence started by William Thomas ('Poley') Evans. Evans dismissed 40 batsmen in 27 appearances between 1898 and 1913. Leo O'Connor and John Farquhar also reached a high standard but

Barnett's lapses on the 1938 English tour brought forecasts of his imminent departure from the Australian team. Here he misses an easy stumping of Walter Robins in the match against The Gentlemen.

were similarly frustrated before Queensland's admission to the Sheffield Shield competition in 1926–27. Farquhar's expertise was acknowledged but he could not bat like O'Connor, who had eight centuries in his 3,311 first-class runs, average 39.89, to go with his 103 dismissals (82 caught, 21 stumped).

Barnett's sporting career began at the Auburn state school. He had a distinguished record as a cricketer and Australian rules footballer at Melbourne's Scotch College, and like Australia's original Test keeper Jack Blackham, was captain of Hawthorn–East Melbourne. He was a natural left-hander, with appealing fair curly hair and a preference for a low, squatting stance between deliveries. His misfortune in missing Hutton was compounded by his splendid form in the four Tests preceding The Oval showdown.

In the first Test at Nottingham, he conceded only one bye in England's massive total of 658. Between matches he often joined pace bowlers Ernie McCormick in practice sessions to try and eliminate McCormick's no-ball problems—McCormick bowled eight no-balls in his first over in England and sent down 46 more in his next 47 overs. At Lord's in the second Test Barnett won accolades from critics for his part in lifting

Australia's out cricket and, after the third Test had been rained off, achieved some spectacular dismissals in the fourth Test at Leeds. He took a fine catch when England's Charlie Barnett flicked at a wideish ball from McCormick, stumped Eddie Paynter and Bill Edrich off Fleetwood-Smith, and caught Barnett for the second time in England's second innings.

Despite Barnett's errors in the fifth Test—he missed a simple stumping against Maurice Leyland when Leyland was 40 on his way to 187, as well as missing Hutton—*Cricketer* magazine said that overall his displays in the Tests were of the highest class. In Australia Bert Oldfield predicted that Barnett would have to be replaced in the Test team within two years.

Sid Barnes, unlucky to fracture a wrist bone in deck games on the voyage to England, was unfit for the first 16 matches, but eased Barnett's work-load by keeping late in the tour in county matches. Walker was still sidelined by his broken finger, one of a long list of hand injuries that sapped his confidence.

The Australians found county keepers divided on the merit of standing back or on the stumps at a time when medium-pace and spin bowling prevailed. New Zealander Kenneth Cecil James, who first went to England in 1927 as second-string keeper to his captain Tom Lowry but quickly won promotion, was building a strong reputation with Northants because of his stumping—37 per cent of his victims or 45 out of the 218 batsmen he sent back in five years with Northants.

James, who visited Australia in 1925–26, kept for New Zealand in their first ever Test at Christchurch in 1929–30 when 'Tich' Cornford kept for England. Cornford was behind the stumps at Auckland in the fourth Test when sundries totalled 51, 37 of them byes, which was the Test record for years. Cornford was still keeping for Sussex in his 47th year, but his longevity did not compare with that of Arthur Newton, who made his debut for Somerset in 1880, toured Australia with Vernon's England team in 1887–88, had 35 seasons with his county, and was still playing club cricket at 81.

Indian keepers had the same devotion to their calling but lacked the opportunities of their Australian and English counterparts. Janardhan Gnanoba Navle kept wicket for Hindus in the Bombay tournament for 36 years and claimed 135 victims (100 caught, 35 stumped) but made only one tour overseas. He opened the batting in the First Test against England at Lord's in 1932 and at Bombay in 1933–34. Jack Hobbs rated Navle in the same class as Oldfield, Ames and Duckworth. Dattaram Dharmaji Hindlekar had a 10-year wait between his English tours in 1936 and 1946. He remained India's first-choice keeper despite blurred vision, chipped fingers and numerous strains and bruises. Like Navle, he opened the batting at Lord's. Hindlekar made 183 dismissals (125 caught, 58 stumped).

West Indian Errol Ashton Clairmore Hunte was another keeper who opened the batting in Tests. A tall, extremely fit man, he had played in only three first-class matches for Trinidad when he was chosen for the West Indies, during England's 1930 tour. He batted at number 10 for Trinidad and at number 11 in his first Test, where he scored 10 not out and 0, but was promoted to open in the next two Tests. He performed creditably, scoring 58 in the first innings at Queen's Park Oval and sharing an opening stand of 144 with Clifford Roach in the first innings of the third Test at Bourda when he made 53.

Costs and travel difficulties forced his omission in the final Test at Sabina Park, where he was replaced by 19-year-old Jamaican Ivan Barrow. The West Indian team included eight Jamaicans. Barrow had a daunting introduction to Test cricket: he was behind the stumps while Andy Sandham scored 325, the first triple century in international matches. England's total reached 849, but he sustained a high standard of keeping and kept the job for the next eight Tests, including five on the West Indies' 1930–31 Australian tour, and three in England in 1933 when he beat George Headley to the honour of scoring the West Indies' first Test century. Opening the batting, Barrow shared a second-wicket stand of 200 in 205 minutes with Headley and was out for 105. Headley went on to 169 not out.

Barrow's reign was interrupted by the emergence of Cyril Marcel Christiani, whose career blossomed when he was picked for British Guiana at the age of 18 for the 1932 inter-island tournament in Barbados when Cecil Nascimento was unavailable. Christiani grabbed his chance and in 1933 went to England as Barrow's deputy. Christiani was considered superior to Barrow as a keeper, so rapid was his improvement, and when England returned for the 1935 Tests he was preferred, with Barrow winning selection as an opening batsman in the fourth Test. Cyril Christiani was unchallenged as the West Indies' number-one keeper when he died of malaria in 1938, aged 24. His place in the British Guiana team went to his brother Robert Julian Christiani, who was inferior to Cyril behind the stumps but appeared in 22 Tests because of his batting.

Cyril Christiani's death shocked the West Indian selectors, who recalled Barrow for the 1939 tour of England. Barrow had not played cricket for years and lived in the United States. He disappointed on tour and had to be replaced by James Edward Derek Sealy, a talented all-round sportsman who had played soccer for Barbados, where he worked as a school teacher. One of his pupils was Frank Worrell.

Back in 1929–30, Sealy had become the youngest ever West Indian Test player when he appeared against England at Bridgetown at the age of 17 years 122 days, scoring 58 and 15. He was an overnight success as a keeper, but his speed of foot was no surprise to those who knew his background as a soccer player. He dismissed 80

The keeper Australians expected to replace Oldfield when he quit, Queenslander Don Tallon, was inexplicably left behind when the team for the 1938 English tour was named.

batsmen, 67 caught and 13 stumped, in his period as a keeper and had a career aggregate of 3,831 runs at 30.40, with eight centuries, the best of which was a dashing 181 in three hours at Lord's in 1939.

Don Tallon vindicated the criticism of his exclusion from the 1938 tour in the season after the team returned. Playing for Queensland against New South Wales he achieved a world record with 12 dismissals—nine caught, three stumped—at the Sydney Cricket Ground. This matched Ted Pooley's performance for Surrey against Sussex at The Oval in 1868.

Tallon joined the army on the outbreak of war in 1939, but was discharged in 1942 with a ruptured ulcer that worried him until he had a large section of his stomach removed. His main rivals for the Australian Test spot, Ben Barnett and Charlie Walker, were not as fortunate. Barnett was appointed Victorian captain on his return from the tour of England following the retirement of Keith Rigg. He set a splendid example when he took over in the absence of a regular opening batsman and put on more than a century in each innings with Ian Lee against Queensland. He made his first Sheffield Shield century, 104 not out, after scoring 92 in the first innings.

Barnett served as an officer in the militia and when war began became a captain in the Eighth Division. He was taken prisoner in Singapore and spent three and a half years on the disease-ridden Bangkok–Moulmein railway. He met Geoff Edrich, brother of English Test player Bill Edrich, in Changi prison camp and together they organised cricket matches between the inmates, stitching together old mats to cover the mud pitch. He joined Nicholas Brothers, the Aspro firm, after his repatriation and represented them in Singapore and London, where he also did invaluable work for the Australian Cricket Board and the Lawn Tennis Association of Australia. He returned to the Victorian team in 1946 and retired at the end of the 1946–47 season, aged 39.

Walker had a recurrence of the injury to his left index finger while playing against Queensland after his return from the 1938 England tour and had to wear a three-fingered glove to support his fragile left forefinger, packing his glove with sponge rubber. He played his last match for South Australia against Victoria in Melbourne in December 1940, before joining the RAAF as a Pilot Officer. He qualified as an air-gunner, and in one of his 15 raids over enemy territory had one engine shot out over Genoa, with the aircraft limping home over the Alps.

In January 1943 Walker's squadron was told that a very important air battle against the Germans was expected that night. One of the Lancasters that would participate lacked a mid-upper gunner. Walker volunteered. The Lancaster took off for a mission over Germany but did not break radio silence on a trip from which it never returned. He was 33, with eyesight so keen he had become noted for his skill in night raids.

Some reports said Walker had been killed in an air battle over the Bay of Biscay but the RAAF said he died in a duel with German fighters over Soltau, Russia. In 109 first-class matches, none of them Tests, Charlie Walker dismissed 320 batsmen (171 caught, 149 stumped), many of them off Clarrie Grimmett. His 1,754 runs were accumulated at the rate of 14.99 an innings, highest score 71.

The war also ended the career of the colourful Western Australian keeper, Ossie Lovelock, who played 21 matches for his state between 1932–33 and 1939–40 in which he figured in 34 dismissals (19 catches, 17 stumpings). Lovelock, who was a member of the East Perth Australian football premiership side in 1929 and represented Western Australia in baseball and football, twice sent back Don Bradman. 'The days I remember most in big cricket were when I got Bradman out,' said Lovelock. 'I thought everyone would be pleased, but they'd all come to see him bat. They did not want to see a smart stumping or a good catch from me.' On 19 March 1938 Lovelock stumped Bradman, playing for an Australian XI, for 102, and on 10 February 1940 he caught the great man for 42 in a Shield match on the same WACA pitch. 'Not many keepers can have dismissed Bradman twice and each time found themselves the villain of the piece,' said Lovelock.

9

The Bundaberg Kid

Bert Oldfield took every opportunity to coach Don Tallon in the techniques of keeping, impressing on him the need to eliminate flamboyance and acrobatics from his tidy, unobtrusive glovework. Oldfield recalled his own modest beginnings as a clerk in the Sydney tramways department and felt prompted to encourage Tallon to overcome a similar background in the country town of Bundaberg, birthplace of pioneer aviator Bert Hinkler. Don's father had been a handy slow bowler for Bundaberg in inter-city matches and his four sons practised all day long on a backyard pitch rolled by their dad. One of Don's earliest memories was helping to push Hinkler's plane down the main street after Hinkler landed at Bundaberg on his return from his record England–Australia flight.

Don's brother Bill was a leg-spinner and Don developed his skills keeping to him. At North Bundaberg state school the boys were coached by former wicket-keeper Tom O'Shea, who gave Don the school captaincy at the age of eleven. He played A-grade cricket at 14 and at 16 kept wicket for Queensland Country against the 1932–33 England side, conceding only five byes in England's innings of 376 and stumping the famous Herbert Sutcliffe. He impressed spectators with the ease with which he took the awesome pace of Aboriginal Eddie Gilbert in Country Week carnivals. In December 1933, aged 17, he made his debut for Queensland against Victoria, who made 542, which included only six byes, but selectors believed he was too young to take on the southern tour, preferring makeshift keeper Roy Levy.

Tallon removed the bails with the precision of a surgeon, following the advice of his mentor Bert Oldfield not to smash down all the stumps. His opposite number Godfrey Evans lacked Tallon's stumping speed but made confident appeals.

Levy was preferred, Eric Bensted taking over when he was unavailable, until Queensland met South Australia in Adelaide in December 1935. Tallon made such a big impression in the Adelaide match he held the state keeping job for the next 20 years. He took two catches and allowed only seven byes in South Australia's innings of 642 (Bradman 233) and scored 88 in Queensland's second innings, hitting 10 fours with firm, crisp driving.

At 19, in February 1936, Tallon made 193, the highest score of his career, against Victoria. This followed some very useful innings, including 88 against South Australia in Adelaide over Christmas. His mistake-free keeping and his heavy scoring with the bat took him to the forefront of candidates for the 1938 tour of England, but to the dismay of Queenslanders the selectors preferred Barnett and Walker. He continued to set records and after his Army service won selection in the Australian team captained by Bill Brown for a short New Zealand tour.

Tallon's glovework made a big impression on Bill O'Reilly on that tour and O'Reilly compared him with Oldfield in his writing for the next 40 years. Tallon developed a notable combination with the Sydney-born leg-spinner Colin McCool, when McCool migrated to Queensland to further his Test chances. Together they won places in the Australian team that opposed Wally Hammond's English tourists in 1946–47 when Tallon broke all Australian records by dismissing 20 batsmen.

He probably was still on trial as the Test keeper when in the space of a few overs in the second Test at Sydney he caught Hutton, spun round to take a dramatic rebound catch off Ian Johnson's chest to dismiss Compton, and then caught Hammond and Yardley. In an hour of sustained brilliance Tallon had virtually won the Ashes for Australia. He stumped Evans and caught Wright in the second innings for a match bag of six, which confirmed a Test position he held for the next seven years. At Melbourne he backed up his spectacular keeping by decimating the English attack with powerful driving that produced a stand of 154 in only 88 minutes with Ray Lindwall. Tallon made 92, Lindwall 100. It was the closest Tallon ever got to a Test century, although he made nine in other first-class matches.

Don Tallon in 1948 after he had been named one of *Wisden*'s five Cricketers of the Year. His brilliance in 1939–40 immediately following his omission from the English tour was spell binding.

He went to England in 1948 ranked the world's best keeper and proceeded to make up for his missed opportunities before the war with a sequence of brilliant displays. He played in four Tests on that tour, missing the Leeds Test because of a finger injury that allowed Ron Saggers to make his Test debut. Tallon completed the tour with honours thick upon him and it was no surprise when he was named one of *Wisden*'s Five Cricketers of the Year.

Wisden recalled how the four Tallon brothers played in their backyard until after dark in Bundaberg and, if their parents went out, cleared away the kitchen furniture and continued their matches. *Wisden* said: 'The unobtrusive way in which Tallon keeps caused much of his skilled work to go unappreciated but critics and those who play with and against him recognise a cricketer worthy of following such renowned Australians as Blackham, Kelly, Carter and Oldfield. Tallon introduces no flourish or

Stan Sismey had to leave the field in Services XI matches when pieces of shrapnel worked their way through his skin and had to be removed. He had been shot down in the Bay of Biscay.

flamboyance into his displays. He folds himself up nearly double as his bowler approaches, and does not move again until he has seen all he needs to know from the flight, length and spin of the ball. For over after over his wicket-keeping is unnoticed. Then along comes the chance of a stumping and the bails are off in a flash; or the batsman snicks a ball down the leg side and Tallon dives for a catch that has the crowd rising to its feet. His dismissal of Hutton was rated the catch of the season, but such acrobatics are reserved for special occasions. He has the virtue of inspiring bowlers, who meet with unexpected success brought about by wicket-keeping brilliance. His hands bear so little evidence of long years as a keeper they could be mistaken for those of a violinist.'

Tallon's dominance prevented Stanley George Sismey, the Services XI's stylish keeper, Victorian Ian Lee, from South Melbourne club, West Australian Gwilym ('Glyn') Kessey and Victorian Bert Wright, from Footscray, pushing their Test claims and delayed the Test appearances of South Australian Gil Langley, Ron Saggers, from the Marrickville club in Sydney who toured as Tallon's deputy, and Wally Grout, his substitute in the Queensland side.

Sismey was particularly unfortunate. He played for the Western Suburbs club in Sydney for 25 years and in 20 matches for New South Wales between 1938–39 and 1950–51. He was elegant and reliable in all his work, one of the few who stood up on the stumps through most of each innings. Born in the New South Wales Riverina town of Junee in 1916, he was the same age as Tallon. His 20 catches and seven stumpings for Western Suburbs in 1938–39 earned him a place in the state side after Oldfield retired, but after two seasons he joined the RAAF and left for Europe. He had a distinguished war record and appeared frequently at Lord's and other major venues as the captain of air force teams. In 1942, as a squadron leader, he was shot down in the Mediterranean while piloting a Catalina in a mission off Algiers. Eight hours later a Royal Navy destroyer fished him out of the water, unconscious, his back full of shrapnel. He joked that he had so much shrapnel in his back it affected compass readings when he resumed flying.

Sismey became the keeper for the Services team captained by Lindsay Hassett that toured England, India and Ceylon immediately after the war, often leaving the field to have pieces of shrapnel removed when the heat and his exertions forced splinters through the skin surface. In India when Keith Carmody substituted for him, Carmody conceded 42 byes. Sismey resumed as New South Wales' keeper in 1946–47 and went to New Zealand in Bill Brown's Australian team in 1949–50. His craftsmanship delighted Services team-mates and spectators alike, and he won respect for the gentlemanly approach he brought to his role.

Sismey played for Scotland in 1952, and in a career that spanned 12 seasons made 88 catches and 18 stumpings. After he retired he gave New South Wales outstanding service as state selector. He was a reliable right-hand tail-end batsman whose 725 first-class runs came at an average of 17.68.

Saggers was a smart, polished keeper with exceptional stumping speed who practised hard through the war years and was able to throw out a strong challenge to Tallon when peace arrived. They were both tall, lean men who seldom conceded a bye and they had an equal number of dismissals on the 1948 tour of England, 43. Tallon caught 29 and stumped 14; Saggers caught 23 and stumped 20. Australia lost nothing by playing Saggers when Tallon was injured in the Leeds Test, but Saggers was below Tallon's class as a batsman, though Saggers remains one of the few batsmen to score more than 1,000 runs in a Sydney grade season. At Southend in 1948 on the day Australia scored 721 in a six-hour day, Saggers was one of four century-makers, adding 166 in 65 minutes with Sam Loxton on his way to 104 not out, his career top score.

Saggers took over as Australian keeper on the 1949–50 tour of South Africa when Tallon was unavailable, playing in all five Tests. He enjoyed

Ron Saggers, Tallon's deputy in England in 1948, got his chance when Tallon was unavailable for the 1949–50 Australian tour of South Africa. He acquitted himself splendidly in all five Tests.

spectacular success in the second Test at Cape Town when he stumped Colin McCool's first three victims on his way to a match-winning 5 for 41. The long hours of patience in the Marrickville club's nets paid off in the speed and sureness with which he despatched batsmen who momentarily erred.

Saggers retired after that tour to concentrate on his work in insurance, with 221 first-class dismissals to his credit (147 catches, 74 stumpings), 24 of them in Tests (16 catches, eight stumpings). He had shown flair and the all-important reliability in supporting Australian attacks that included a happy blend of pace (Lindwall, Miller, Bill Johnston), medium-pace (Loxton), and spin (McCool, Doug Ring, Ian Johnson), and contributed 1,888 first-class runs at 23.89.

His retirement opened the way in the New South Wales team for Geoff Trueman and for Gilbert Roche Andrews Langley to move closer to Test selection. Langley was a ruddy, often untidy figure with an ample midriff whose shirt-tail usually fluttered loose. He lacked Tallon's stumping speed and the neat appearance of Ames or Oldfield, and at first glance looked like the keepers sighted in park cricket who cannot get down to the low catches because of their girth. He appeared capable of accepting whatever chances came his way but unlikely to create chances. But when you talked to the bowlers he worked with they were all ecstatic about the threat he added to their bowling and the manner in which he converted half-chances into dismissals.

Langley took to wicket-keeping at school in Adelaide at the age of 12 with no family history in cricket except for a grandfather who once umpired a match between Fiji and South Australia. He was self-taught, eager to accept any advice that came his way at Colonel Light Gardens school or from his Sturt club captain Vic Richardson, who recommended him for the Colt XI, the side that enabled the most promising youngsters to gain experience in first-grade competition. Sturt's coach Alfred Hodder found him a remarkably dexterous lad who needed to work on his right-hand batting. In 1947–48 Langley succeeded Roley Vaughton as the South Australian keeper. Every winter Langley played top-class Australian rules as a rover.

When Tallon withdrew from the South African

tour in 1949–50, Langley got the job as Saggers' deputy. He sustained a broken finger when a ball from Allan Walker bounced awkwardly but he had 22 dismissals in six matches on that tour. Most critics regarded him as a stopgap keeper when he was chosen for the first Test against the West Indies in 1951 at Brisbane, but he laid strong claims for a permanent spot by figuring in seven dismissals, a record for a Test newcomer. He retained his place for all five Tests and at the end of the series had 21 victims, a bag only Herbert Strudwick had previously matched—in England's 1913–14 series against South Africa. Apart from absences through injury and Tallon's reappearance for a Test at Nottingham in 1953, Langley remained Australia's keeper until he retired in 1956.

Tallon had the misfortune of going deaf when he was ranked the world's finest keeper and towards the end of his career was known to team-mates as 'Deafy'. He accepted this damning fate for a wicket-keeper with good humour, but Queenslanders blamed the shortness of his career (21 Tests) on the selectors who had not discovered his unsurpassed talents until he was in his 31st year.

Lindsay Hassett was among the first to discover Tallon's hearing defect when he sent out a message in a Test against England in 1950–51 for Tallon 'to go for the light', which meant he wanted Tallon to appeal against the fading light. Tallon misheard the instruction and thought it was that he should 'go for the lash'. He proceeded to hit out at almost every ball and only discovered his mistake when he got back to the pavilion.

Langley's appeals lacked the stridency of a Tallon roar but were usually favourably received. Behind the stumps he watched the bowler's arm carefully, his gloves in front of his knees but not touching the turf as many modern keepers prefer. He waited with the right foot flat and the left heel raised. An English critic watched him at Lord's and wrote that he looked like an apple orchardist who had strayed on to the hallowed pitch. He appeared to lack mobility but was adept at going down on the point of one shoulder to reach low catches.

Tallon fitted the English conception of an Australian keeper more precisely—sun-dried and sparely built like a jackaroo. Ray Robinson said

Tallon's appeals were bad for batsmen's nerves; they burst from him, demanding satisfaction, and he often held the ball aloft as he awaited confirmation of a catch. Refusal of an appeal was a wounding injustice. Robinson said that omission from the 1938 tour of England had left Tallon in a ferment of bewilderment and frustration, and hurt him like a kick in the face. Robinson wrote:

'Some writers professed to know that each of the three selectors included Tallon on their original team list—Bradman (South Australia), Walker and Tallon; E.A. Dwyer (New South Wales), Oldfield and Tallon; W.J. Johnson (Victoria), Barnett and Tallon. I doubt that he was on all three lists, but believe he would have been chosen had he been the keeper for one of the older cricketing states. After that experience Tallon gritted his teeth and set out to show how wrong his omission had been. Between then and his disappearance into the army I believe he reached the highest standard ever attained by a keeper. In

Gil Langley in his Speaker's wig and the Sturt Australian Rules club's jersey after his departure from big cricket. He represented South Australia 15 times at football and played 26 cricket Tests.

Shirt-tail hanging out, stomach bulging, Langley still seldom missed a catch. He took many superb grabs like this one in the Lord's Test in 1956 which sent back Johnny Wardle.

Langley and his West Indian counterpart Clyde Walcott produced keeping of a very high standard in the 1951–52 series in Australia. Here Walcott stumps Washbrook off Ramadhin at Lord's in 1950.

the 1938–39 season he evicted 34 batsmen in Queensland's six matches—figures no other keeper has attained in an Australian season. Four times in 10 innings at least six batsmen fell to his deft glovework.'

Tallon's omission remains one of the most amazing blunders in the history of Australian cricket team selection. He made it appear even more unjustified with every brilliant Test display, but the frustration he suffered pursued him all his cricket career. He had sleepless nights before Test sides were announced and even reassurances from team-mates never completely banished his fear of being denied his rightful place in Australian teams.

He dominated Queensland's immediate postwar matches, establishing a formidable combination with leg-spinner McCool and, in the Sydney Test in December 1946, described earlier, simply took charge of the match against England, menacing the batsmen constantly from behind the bails, darting and prancing to dismiss six batsmen. The following summer the Indian captain Lala Amarnath, who had played international cricket since 1933, agreed with the Australian assessment that Tallon was the greatest keeper who ever lived.

Watching Tallon in England in 1948 George Duckworth said: 'He gets smoothly to balls that would have had me scrambling. In fielding the ball with gloves on he is the cleanest I have ever seen.' Ray Robinson replied that England had not seen Tallon at his peak. The 1948 summer in England was too cold for Tallon, who damaged fingers taking balls that came to him out of cool, almost misty air and found that with Bradman preferring pace bowling to spin he spent most of each innings standing back.

Tallon knew that the peak he reached in 1939–40 had gone forever and, although he tried hard to regain his former brilliance, his increasing deafness and a tendency to fumble brought an end to his Test career after the first Test in England in 1953. Gil Langley, who had proved such an able replacement against the West Indies in Australia in 1951–52 and against South Africa in 1952–53, took over.

Langley built an unprecedented safety record, accepting virtually every chance that came his way. *Wisden* called him the greatest ally Australian bowlers ever had. Langley dismissed five batsmen in an innings three times and his record of nine victims in a Test has not been matched by an Australian.

Langley and his opposite number Clyde Leopold Walcott provided keeping of a very high calibre in the 1951–52 summer, though both were bulky, even cumbersome in appearance. Walcott weighed 21 stone 6 pounds (136 kg), stood 6 feet 3 inches (188 cm) and was part of the famous 'W Formation' that did so much for West Indian cricket immediately after World War II. The other players in the formation were Frank Worrell and Everton Weekes.

Walcott made his Test debut against England at Bridgetown in 1947–48 after he and his schoolmate Frank Worrell had created a West Indian record by scoring an undefeated 574 for Barbados against Trinidad at Port-of-Spain in 1945–46. Walcott was just 20 years of age and his 314 not out remained the highest score of his career. He proved a wonderfully entertaining international cricketer whose driving bruised the hands of many fieldsmen. He had to crouch because of his height but he was very sound in defence and could cut with striking force and deft placement. When he was at full flow fieldsmen felt themselves under constant bombardment.

Walcott held his place behind the stumps for 15 successive Tests during which his reading of the spinners Sonny Ramadhin and Alf Valentine was invaluable to his side. He had reached a total of 64 Test dismissals (53 caught, 11 stumped) when a doctor found that he had a slipped disc and advised him to give up keeping. After the second Test of that 1951–52 series against Australia, Walcott moved to first slip and Simpson Clement Guillen took his place behind the stumps. Walcott became a very useful fast–medium change bowler and retained his Test place because of his batting prowess in the West Indies against England in 1953–54 and against Australia in 1954–55 when Ian Johnson took the first Australian team to the West Indies.

Guillen, son of a Test umpire and brother of a Trinidad player, seemed assured of a long Test career in the West Indies after standing in the last three Tests against Australia and in the two that followed in New Zealand, but he was enchanted by New Zealand and later migrated there to become the only West Indian to have represented two countries in Tests. Walcott never kept wicket again after he left Australia but continued his Test career until he reached 44 Tests, in which he scored 3,798 runs at 56.68 with 15 centuries. In all first-class matches he made 11,820 runs at 56.55 with 40 centuries.

Guillen appeared in three Tests for New Zealand against the West Indies in New Zealand in 1956 and played a big part in New Zealand's first win in any Test. He top scored with 41 in New Zealand's second innings and stumped the last West Indian batsman Alf Valentine to give New Zealand victory by 190 runs. He had not been resident in New Zealand for the stipulated four years at the time, but the West Indies raised no objection to his selection. The following season Guillen also appeared for a New Zealand XI in three matches against Ian Craig's Australian team.

With Walcott unable to keep and Guillen absent in New Zealand, West Indian selectors tried several candidates in an effort to find a permanent Test keeper. When India visited the Caribbean in 1953 for the first time, Alfred Phillip Binns was tried for the first Test but then dropped for Ralph Archibald Legall, a Barbadian resident in Trinidad. Neither did enough to hold the job permanently and when the West Indian team to tour England in 1953 was named selectors opted for Clifford Aubrey McWatt, who had played for British Guiana since the early 1940s and had been Walcott's deputy in India in 1948–49. He appeared in all five Tests in England but lacked consistency.

The West Indies tested three keepers for the first three Tests against Ian Johnson's Australians in 1955, Binns for the first, McWatt for the second and the Barbadian Clairemonte Depeiza for the third before settling on Depeiza for the rest of the series. Binns and Depeiza went to New Zealand in 1956 but it was not until 1957 that the problem was solved with the emergence of·Franz Copeland Murray ('Gerry') Alexander, who made the job his own. Alexander, a Cambridge blue in 1952 and 1953, playd in 25 consecutive Tests.

He made his initial appearance in a first-class match in the West Indies in March 1957, for Jamaica against the Duke of Norfolk's XI. The West Indian selectors held special trials soon afterwards at Port-of-Spain and most critics believed that a Dominican named Alex Reid had done enough to tour as Alexander's deputy, but the selectors chose the dashing young Guianese batsman Rohan Kanhai, a part-time keeper. Then they left Alexander out of the first three Tests in England, allowing Kanhai to make his Test debut as a keeper.

After England had taken a one–nil lead Kanhai was relieved of his unfair burden and Alexander came into the side. *Wisden* said Kanhai, later revealed as a brilliant fieldsman, had been 'little more than a stopper' behind the stumps. Kanhai went on to play 79 Tests and was established as one of the finest batsmen of all time when he took the gloves to substitute briefly for Deryck Murray in his final Test.

Alexander, a specialist for a specialist's job, was an outstanding sportsman who represented both Jamaica and England as an amateur soccer halfback. Captain of the West Indies in 18 of his 25 Tests, he proved a popular and astute leader. Against England in 1959–60 he dismissed 23 batsmen to equal the world record, though his team lost the rubber. In Australia in 1960–61 he scored at least 50 in every Test, with 108 in Sydney being the best effort of his Test career, and he headed the West Indies' tour batting averages with 484 runs at 60.50.

Alexander was a fine physical specimen with wide shoulders and a powerful chest, handy attributes when taking bowlers like Wes Hall for long periods. He took some astounding catches off Hall. Team-mates admired the manner in which he accepted his replacement as captain by Frank Worrell, and Alexander's value to Worrell as vice-captain was enormous. He appeared at the peak of his powers when he retired after the 1960–61 Australian tour to concentrate on his work as a veterinary surgeon.

Alexander's deputy on two tours to India, Sri Lanka and Pakistan, and in Australia, Jackie Hendriks went into the West Indian team for the first Test against India in 1962, but he broke a finger in his debut. Although he could not keep for the rest of the series he scored 64 in the West Indies' first innings. Hendriks went to work in the United States when his finger mended and did not return to the West Indies' team until 1964–65.

During Hendriks' three-year absence in America Ivor Leon Mendonça and David Walter Allan were tried. Mendonça had splendid results with the bat and in his first Test at Kingston added

127 for the fourth wicket with Gary Sobers, scoring 78, but was unavailable for the 1963 tour of England. The selectors turned to the Trinidad keeper Deryck Murray, at 19 just out of Queen's Royal College and an unknown quantity. Allan arrived in England as the first-choice keeper but illness put him out of contention for the first Test and Murray took his place, taking an attack that comprised Hall, Charlie Griffith, Sobers and Lance Gibbs. He was so dependable that he held his place for the entire series, and with 24 dismissals created a West Indian tour record.

Murray had no ambitions at the time to pursue a career in Test cricket and he dropped out of the West Indian team after that series to go to Cambridge University. He won blues in 1965 and 1966, when he was captain, and later played for Nottinghamshire and Warwickshire. This gave Hendriks the chance to return to the West Indian team. Despite a setback in the fourth Test at Bridgetown against Australia in the 1964–65 series, when he was hit by a ball from Graham McKenzie and required brain surgery, Hendriks toured England in 1966 and 1969, India in 1966–67 and Australia in 1968–69, playing in a further 15 Tests before he retired and Deryck Murray replaced him. Clive Lloyd rated Hendriks the best West Indian keeper of his time, a gloveman who never seemed to have a bad day.

The standard all these keepers tried to match as big cricket opened up for nations apart from England and Australia was that achieved by the 'Bundaberg Kid', Don Tallon. As international tours multiplied through the second half of the century, Tallon's reputation spread world-wide. Nobody could stump with his lightning precision, and few have ever matched the catching he made look easy. Selectors may have restricted his Test career to seven years, but they could not stamp out his genius. In the end he was philosophical about it all and mindful of old Queensland team-mates like Ron Oxenham, who never had the trip to England his talents deserved, and Frank Sides, the gifted left-hander killed in action at Salamaua in north-east New Guinea at the age of 30. Sides was a talkative cricketer like Don's brother Les, a humourist who enjoyed chatting up opponents and sometimes took the gloves for Queensland. Tallon remembered Sides' style and claimed Les Ames' successor in the Kent and England team, Thomas Godfrey Evans, had the same showy qualities. Evans was irrepressible, an extrovert whose sound performance could always be relied on when it mattered.

Deryck Murray, regarded by many critics as the best of all West Indian keepers, falls in taking a fine catch for Warwickshire to dismiss Derbyshire's Alan Hill. Murray played 62 Tests and accounted for 849 first-class batsmen. He also appeared for Cambridge University and Nottinghamshire.

10

Godfrey the Showman

Godfrey Evans made nonsense of the concept that wicket-keepers should be reliable but not flamboyant. He relished the big audiences common in Australia, and regularly combined his flair for sinewy showmanship with glovework that lifted the performance of his team and delighted spectators. His energy was boundless and his enthusiasm infectious as he dived to convert half chances into dismissals. 'There has been nobody like him for lifting tired fieldsmen late on a hot day,' said great Australian allrounder Keith Miller. 'His value to England was incalculable.'

Australians had their first glimpse of Evans in the summer of 1946–47. He arrived as a virtually unknown 26-year-old ex-boxer with a battered nose, a Test against India and three summers for Kent behind him, the second-choice keeper in Wally Hammond's 24th England team to Paul Gibb. They were a beguiling pair. Gibb, a Yorkshireman who had won his blue at Cambridge, captained a Yorkshire XI on a prewar Jamaica tour, and survived a rugged war in Coastal Command. Evans lacked the old-school-tie background and had come through the war as an army sergeant.

Gibb began his first-class career as a specialist batsman and was recruited into the Cambridge XI as a freshman when S.C. ('Billy') Griffith was injured. He was the first amateur to score a century on debut for Yorkshire, 157 against Nottinghamshire at Bramall Lane in 1935. He was seven years older than Evans and had made an equally dramatic Test debut by scoring 93 and 106 in his first Test at Johannesburg in 1938–39. Gibb

was bald and bespectacled and kept with the wide brim of his white hat turned up in front. Every bit as extroverted as Evans, he was philosophical about the risk of keeping in glasses. An amateur who turned professional, Gibb played 36 games for Yorkshire and 145 for Essex.

Evans quickly proved Gibb's superior behind the stumps. His popularity grew when he was preferred for the second Test at Sydney, his Ashes debut. He demonstrated a magnificent flair for lifting the flagging spirits of England's bowlers, communicating his confidence and enthusiasm to them and his fieldsmen. He did not allow a single bye while Australia scored 1,024 runs, 659 in Sydney and 365 in Melbourne, and he added immeasurably to the threat of Alec Bedser's bowling by standing right up on the stumps to his medium-pacers.

At Adelaide Evans showed renewed confidence in his batting in a memorable partnership with Denis Compton that saved England from defeat. He batted 95 minutes before scoring, a Test record, and reached 10 not out after 133 minutes. This allowed Compton to add 103 not out to his first innings 147 and match Arthur Morris, who also made a century in each innings. The Evans-Compton stand yielded 85 runs and left Australia to score 314 runs in 195 minutes, a challenge they could not meet.

Evans impressed with his handling of the bowling of Kent team-mate, Doug Wright, who gave his leg-breaks a lively pace that confused Gibb. The tour ended with four matches in New Zealand and Evans claimed 33 dismissals (28

Godfrey Evans, one-time prizefighter, was quick on his feet and for 91 Tests, through eight overseas tours, kept England's fieldsmen alert with his special brand of extrovert keeping.

caught and 5 stumped) from the entire 39 matches involved. The New Zealand trip included a drawn Test at Wellington in which Eric Tindall, who had been a first-class wicket-keeper since 1933 and had shown versatility by playing Rugby for the All Blacks, failed to add to his total of 126 dismissals (93 caught, 33 stumped).

Evans returned home after that triumphant tour firmly convinced that keepers should stand up on the stumps whenever possible. Unlike his idol Les Ames, who had to be persuaded to take up keeping by Kent stalwart Gerry Weigall ('In modern cricket, it pays to have a skill to add to your batting'), Evans had taken naturally to keeping from early schooldays and revelled in the exposure the task provided. 'By standing back the keeper misses plenty of catches that do not carry to him and accepting these compensates for the more difficult ones he may drop by standing up,' Evans said. 'Not to mention the lack of chances for stumpings.'

Evans supported this view with some of the fastest footwork seen in big cricket, taking several catches in front of the stumps which no other keeper could have reached. He retained a boyish sprightliness for almost 30 years and even in the grimmest of Test matches he looked along the pitch with merriment in his blue-grey eyes. His brilliance on the blind side in stumping Victorian Ken Meuleman off a fastish ball from Reg Pollard was a hallmark of his good days.

His work depended heavily on confidence and on his bad days—all keepers have them—over-confidence began the slump by causing him to arrive too late for catches he normally accepted. He missed four catches at Melbourne in 1946–47, including Morris off the first ball of an innings and Bradman later on. In 1947 South African batsmen snicked five deliveries from Bedser without penalty. At Leeds in 1948, Evans fumbled chances to stump Hassett, Morris and Bradman off Bedser and Laker, escapes that allowed Australia to go on to an extraordinary victory and compelled Ray Robinson to write that cricket's 'Jack-in-the-box' had been struck by the lid. 'It was the only time I ever saw him dispirited,' added Robinson.

Matched against this were Evans' brilliant days. In the Nottingham Test of that 1948 rubber Sid Barnes chopped a Laker off-break on to Evans'

Evans catching Australia's Colin McDonald off the bowling of Fred Trueman in the third Test at Leeds in 1956.

right leg. The ball bounded up behind the keeper's right shoulder. Evans sensed the location of the ball and dived backwards, clutching in the catch with a backhand action three metres from the stumps. Denzil Batchelor likened Evans' dive to that of a zoo seal at feeding time.

Evan's presence up on the stumps encouraged Alec Bedser to bowl a fuller length, which caused the ball to swing a lot. Bedser could rely on Evans preventing byes. His exuberance caused Evans to chase after balls deflected down the leg side in a match race with team-mates, sprinting hard as they approached the boundary fence. At Hobart on the 1946–47 tour he pounced on the ball centimetres ahead of Bill Edrich and celebrated with a throw that went for overthrows at the bowler's end. In Sydney he was in such a hurry to gather a ball Morris played to short leg he climbed up Morris' back, arousing ribald comments from characters on the Hill.

Evans taking Bedser carried old-timers back to the years when Duckworth took similar swinging deliveries from Maurice Tate and when Oldfield had to take Jack Ryder, Hans Ebeling

and Alan Fairfax in Tests or Halford Hooker in matches for New South Wales.

A broad-shouldered figure, 5 feet 9 inches (173 cm) tall, Evans approached even desperate positions with characteristic merriment. He went to the crease at Old Trafford in 1950 against the West Indies with England 5 for 88 and with a smart mix of precise cuts and well-timed front-foot drives produced his first Test century, 104 in 140 minutes with 17 fours. This lifted England's total to 312 and enabled them to win the match by 202 runs after Evans made three stumpings and took a catch.

Evans favoured a turf-touching technique in which he pressed his knuckles into the ground outside the off stump, and as bowlers ran up to bowl, they could see the lurid red palms of his gloves. Experts gave Ames the credit of introducing this style, generally adopted by English county keepers who were forced to lift their heels off the ground by leaning forward. It was a style that went against the advice of Jack Hubble, an earlier Kent keeper who in 1923, at the age of 42, had 10 victims in a match. Ray Robinson found Hubble's technique described in verse in an old issue of *The Cricketer*:

> Keep both feet flat upon the ground,
> 'Twill save you endless trouble,
> Don't put your weight upon your toes—
> Sage words from J.C. Hubble.

Hubble believed the leaners swayed back and ground their heels into the turf as they rose to take the ball, whereas followers of the traditional flat-foot style like Tallon came up to take the ball from a level stance. Robinson, on tour with Bradman's team in 1948, had the chance to assess how many county keepers followed the hands-on-turf stance. He found that tall, thin men like Leslie Compton (Middlesex), George Dawkes (Derbyshire), Jack Andrews (Hampshire), Alan Wilson (Lancashire) and former schoolmaster 'Billy' Griffith (Sussex) used the hands down between the knees stance, whereas Percy Corrall (Leicestershire), Tom Wade (Essex), Richard Spooner (Warwickshire) and Harold Stephenson (Somerset) held their hands high and balanced on the balls of their feet.

Stewart Cathie Griffith, like a lot of talented cricketers, lost his best years to World War II, but in the final 'Victory Test' in 1945 he caught seven

One of the quality keepers whom Evans prevented winning Test team spots was the late Billy Griffiths. He celebrated his Test debut with a century in the Port-of-Spain Test in 1947–48.

of the Australian Services XI. But he was 31 and selectors preferred the younger—by six years—Evans, although they brought Griffith in as an emergency opening bat for the Port-of-Spain Test in 1947–48. Griffith celebrated by scoring his initial first-class century. A year later England preferred Griffith to Evans for the last two Tests in South Africa. Griffith took five catches. There was a lot of the pluck that had won him a DFC with the Airborne Division at Arnhem in Holland in Griffith's cricket. Griffiths served as MCC secretary, 1962–74, and president, 1979–80 and was widely mourned when he died in 1993, aged 79, after a long fight against cancer.

Another keeper who lost his best years to the war was Henry Yarnold, who made his debut for Worcestershire in 1938. Yarnold dismissed 110 batsmen in the 1949 season, and in 1951 stumped six batsmen in an innings, for Worcestershire against Scotland. He stumped 231 of his 694 victims, near enough to one out of three.

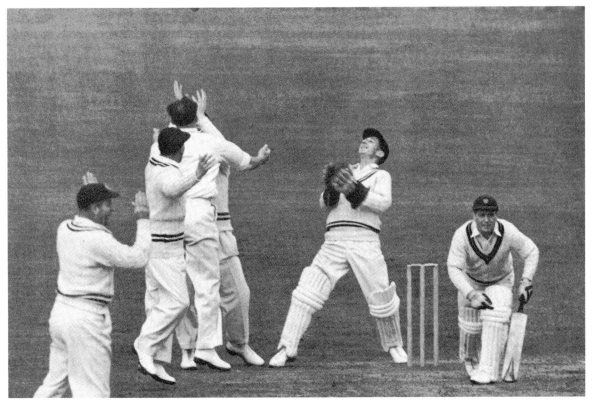

Another talented keeper who missed higher honours during war service was Worcestershire's Hugo Yarnold, seen here caught behind by Dick Spooner off Eric Hollies.

In Australia, where Tallon, Langley and Saggers dominated the role in postwar years, Victoria boasted a zealous keeper in Dr Ian McDonald. In 39 matches for his state, some with his brother Colin, Dr McDonald had 129 victims, many in support of spinners Ian Johnson and Doug Ring. West Australian John Munro backed his state's bid for a place in the Sheffield Shield competition with 58 dismissals (55 caught, three stumped). New South Wales found a highly capable substitute for injured keepers in Sid Barnes, who filled the role when he first joined Petersham.

In India, Hindlekar's run as his country's leading keeper ended after 13 years. Evans' first Test at The Oval in 1946 was Hindlekar's last, and when the West Indies toured India in 1948–49 nimble-footed Bengali Probir Sen took over. Australians saw Sen the previous summer when he allowed only four byes in the Melbourne Test in Australia's sole innings of 8 for 575 declared. Sen's anticipation accounted for many of the catches and stumpings he made, which swung the balance of big matches. He captained Bengal province, for whom he once achieved a bowling hat-trick, and on tour in Australia in 1947–48 looked a safe, reliable keeper who remained tidy when Australian batsmen ran up big scores. Sen had a career total of 143 dismissals (107 caught, 36 stumped) and died of a heart attack playing cricket in Calcutta, aged 44.

Sen represented India immediately after Partition when the new nation, Pakistan, played their first Test at Delhi in 1952–53. All the Pakistan team except A.H. Kardar and Amir Elahi had previously played for India, including Pakistan's keeper in that match, Hanif Mohammad, one of the most gifted members of a famous family. Three of Hanif's brothers, Sadiq, Mushtaq and Wazir, also played for Pakistan in Tests. Their feat of three brothers appearing in the same Test has only been emulated by the Graces and the Hearnes. Hanif is one of the few to score more than 300 in a Test innings, and his 499 for Karachi against Bahawalpur in 1958–59 on the mat at Karachi remains the highest score in all first-class cricket—he was run out trying for his 500th run.

Hanif captained Pakistan in 11 Tests, a small, compact right-hand batsman of infinite patience who often seemed impregnable. He took up residence rather than briefly visiting the crease, and from the time he made his Test debut in 1951–52 at 17 years 300 days gave few chances and took no risks. He made 287 runs at 35.87 in the five Tests against India in 1952–53, and in 1954 in Pakistan's first official Test in England he took 340 minutes to score 59 runs (20 and 39).

Selectors preferred to rest Hanif for his long innings by playing Imtiaz Ahmed as the Pakistan keeper, with Hanif only going behind the stumps if Imtiaz Ahmed was injured. As Pakistan's number-one keeper in their first five years of Test cricket, Imtiaz Ahmed made 93 dismissals (87 caught, 16 stumped) in 41 Tests. Abdul Kadir took over from him for four Tests in 1964–65. Abdul Kadir was the unfortunate batsman run out for 95 in his Test debut against Australia in 1964–65. Altogether, he made 59 dismissals for Pakistan (46 caught, 13 stumped) before Naushad Ali took over for six Tests in 1964–65, when Wasim Bari was preferred.

Despite the policy of resting him for batting by allowing others to keep wicket Hanif, in a first-class career that lasted from 1951 to 1976, made 190 dismissals, comprising 178 catches and 12 stumpings. Pakistan made only limited use of him as a keeper, apparently fearing he might damage a finger or sustain an injury that would upset his run-getting. He was a cricketer of amazing patience who in only his third Test innings demonstrated his powers of concentration by batting for six hours at cavernous Brabourne Stadium for 96.

Hanif, known in Pakistan as the 'Little Master', played in all his country's first 24 Tests, before a knee injury forced him out of the 1958–59 series against the West Indies after he scored 103 in the first innings of the First Test. Hanif shared a stand of 178 for the second wicket with Saeed Ahmed, a record against the West Indies. Hanif showed his versatility by taking 53 first-class wickets with his right-arm off-breaks.

Despite his obvious gifts Hanif was little more than a backstop behind the stumps and one of the most tedious batsmen of all times. Like the legendary Australian stonewallers Alick Bannerman and Charles Kelleway, he was a consistent 'weariness of the flesh' to spectators. Lord's members had a sample of his patience on his first English tour in 1954 when he batted for

314 minutes to score 59. In the West Indies in 1957–58 he batted for 16 hours and 10 minutes to make 337 in Pakistan's total of 657. At home against England in 1981–82 he drove bowlers to distraction by batting for 14 hours and 43 minutes to score 111 and 104 in the second Test at Dacca.

Australians had a good look at him in Pakistan's first Test in Australia in 1964–65. From 4 to 8 December, he was seldom off the field, top scoring in both innings with 104 and 93, and keeping wicket in place of the injured Abdul Kadir. His 197 runs helped him become the first Pakistani to score 3,000 runs in Tests. In 1967, spectators at Lord's suffered another dose of his slow batting when he made 187 not out off 556 balls in 542 minutes.

Imtiaz Ahmed, who relieved Hanif of the wicket-keeping duties in Tests, was the direct opposite in his approach, a stroke-maker whose aggressive qualities excited crowds. He missed only one of Pakistan's first 42 Tests and has been rightfully called one of the founders of Pakistan's high reputation. He was prepared to sweep and hook from the time he appeared for Northern India at 16 in the Ranji Trophy competition. He visited India twice, in 1952–53 and 1960–61, and proved a safe, reliable keeper.

On his first tour of England in 1954, he dismissed 80 batsmen while keeping wicket and another six while a fieldsman, a record for any touring team. At The Oval, in the final match of that tour, he caught seven batsmen behind the stumps—all off Fazal Mahmood. At home he made 209 in the Lahore Test against New Zealand, then the highest score by a wicket-keeper in a Test. His ability to stand right up on the stumps to Fazal Mahmood made them a deadly combination, comparable with the Bedser–Evans duo for England.

Imtiaz Ahmed had 30 years in first-class cricket, 1944–74, during which he accounted for 391 batsmen behind the stumps, 314 of them caught and 77 stumped. With the bat, he made 10,323 runs at 37.26, with 22 centuries. His top score, 300 not out for the Prime Minister's XI against the Commonwealth XI at Bombay in 1950–51, entitles him to a very high rating among wicket-keeper batsmen. Three of his centuries and 93 of his dismissals (77 caught, 16 stumped) came in his 41 Tests.

Imtiaz Ahmed, like Godfrey Evans, was an observant cricketer who improved with every tour. He thrived on the big occasion, as he demonstrated when Australia first met Pakistan in October 1956, at Karachi. He took three vital catches in Australia's first innings of 80, all off Fazal, who had 6 for 34, and in the second innings caught Richie Benaud off Khan Mohammad for 37 when Benaud appeared likely to rescue Australia.

Another keeper who always rose to the big occasion was the South African John Waite, who appeared in 50 Tests between 1951 and 1965. A quietly-spoken, modest player, Waite was a tall man for keeping. Blessed with intense powers of concentration, he relished the challenge of Test cricket. He played for both Eastern Province and Transvaal but never seemed as effective for them as he was in Tests. The English commentator Christopher Martin-Jenkins rated Waite the best wicket-keeper batsman of his time.

He had a very short backlift and extremely

John Waite who dismissed 137 batsmen in 50 Tests, took 29 catches on South Africa's 1952–53 Australian tour, some of them amazing efforts.

South Africa keeper John Waite, rated by critics the best wicket-keeper-batsman of his time, watches as team-mate Eric Rowan catches Australian Keith Dollery off the bowling of his brother Athol in the match with Warwickshire, in England, 1951.

sound defence which made him equally dangerous opening the innings or in the middle order. Waite went to England for the first of his three tours there in 1951 as the reserve keeper but was preferred for the first Test, contributing 76 runs towards a match-winning total of 483. His 76-run stand with Jackie McGlew for the second wicket subdued England's pace attack and allowed Dudley Nourse to come in and score 208. Nourse batted in pain for much of the 550 minutes he was at the crease. Waite took four catches in the two England innings, his all-round contribution on debut helping to clinch South Africa's first win over England for 16 years.

Waite was unfit for the fifth Test and his replacement, William Russell Endean, was involved in a rare dismissal when a ball from Athol Rowan ballooned up from Hutton's bat. Hutton tried to fend the ball away from his stumps and obstructed Endean's lunge for the catch. Hutton was given out 'obstructed the field'—the first and only time this has occurred in Tests and

only the fifth time in first-class cricket. Five years later in the second Test at Cape Town, Endean was the victim in a similar incident when he tried to fend a ball from Laker away from his stumps and was given out 'handled the ball'.

Waite's superiority as a keeper compelled Endean to concentrate on fielding and he became one of the most spectacular fieldsmen Australians have seen. He took 29 catches on South Africa's 1952–53 Australian tour in a variety of positions, some of them miraculous efforts that made him the star of a marvellous fielding side captained by Jack Cheetham.

South Africa appeared to have so little chance against a powerful Australian line-up that the Australian Cricket Board doubted there would be enough spectators to make the tour pay. The South African Board of Control had to provide a £10,000 bond against losses for something they envisaged as an educational trip for their promising youngsters. The Springboks shocked the cricket world by sharing the five-Test rubber, which produced two wins apiece, and the tour made a £3,000 profit. Both Lindwall and Miller, mainstays of Australia's attack, were unfit for the decisive fifth Test, which South Africa won by six wickets after Australia scored 520 in their first innings and appeared safe from defeat.

Waite's keeping had a major influence on South Africa's surprise success. His glovework reached a very high level, inspiring his fieldsmen, and lifting their efforts in catching, throwing and ground fielding. Even Neil Harvey's feat in scoring his eighth century in 10 innings against South Africa failed to dishearten the Springboks. Tayfield countered by dismissing 30 Australians in the Tests and taking 84 wickets on the complete Australasian tour, with South Africans scoring 11 first-class centuries. Freed of keeping responsibilities, Endean scored 1,496 runs on the tour, including three centuries, at an average of 55.40.

South Africa's performance enhanced the view that Australian cricket was in decline and at the end of the season Lindsay Hassett took a patched-up team to England. Langley, who had kept wicket in all five Tests against South Africa, was one of the few newcomers to England to succeed. Jack Hill, Graeme Hole, Ian Craig and Colin McDonald never really settled down to English conditions and Richie Benaud gave no hint of the class he was later to reach. Tallon had a few days of brilliance, but in a wet summer the Australians were thankful that Langley matched Evans for reliability and cheerfulness. Langley appeared incapable of missing a catch, and of his 47 victims on the tour 35 were caught and 12 stumped.

Evans, who had scored centuries against the West Indies in 1950 and India in 1952, found the pace of Lindwall, Miller and Davidson beyond him in the Tests, but he was as brilliant as ever behind the stumps. He supported spinners Laker, Wardle and Lock splendidly and four of his 11 Test victims came from stumpings. His stumping of Arthur Morris for 30 in the Lord's Test ended a threatening Australian opening stand at 65, had Morris shaking his head in disbelief and helped Bedser reach a tally of 200 Test wickets in the match.

Evans made four tours of Australasia (1947–47, 1950–51, 1954–55, 1958–59), two to the West Indies (1947–48, 1953–54) and two to South Africa (1948–49, 1956–57). Even when he approached 40 and played in his 91st and last Test he could not resist the showy touches and pep talks to team-mates that characterised his career. The wonder of it was that his contortions never detracted from his displays. He quit first-class cricket in 1959 after his omission from England's team, but returned to tour South Africa with a Commonwealth XI in 1959–60, India in 1963–64 with the Prime Minister's XI, and Jamaica and the West Indies with the Cavaliers in 1963–64 and 1964–65 respectively. He had a career bag of 1,006 dismissals, 816 caught and 250 stumped, 219 of them in Tests (173 caught, 46 stumped).

Paul Antony Gibb, whom Evans deposed from the England side, retired when he returned from the 1946–47 tour, but made a comeback in 1951 to play for Essex, the first University blue ever to become a professional. He toured England in a caravan when he became an umpire and worked in Guildford as a bus driver until he died in 1977. Gibb wore a wig and contact lenses in his mature years and had to be introduced to former Test team-mates. None of the passengers in his bus knew of his 19 first-class centuries or 548 dismissals (425 caught, 123 stumped).

Evans drifted in and out of jobs. His jewellery business failed, his speculation in green belt land disappointed, and after collapsed marriages he left his job laying the odds at Ladbrokes cricket-ground betting tents ('Godders from Ladders') in 1992. His ebullience remains, as does his unflagging love of cricket.

In the Victorian goldmining town of Ballarat, locals recall one of their batting hopefuls going to the crease against England on one of Evans' tours. He watched patiently as the dandified batsman, superbly attired in freshly pressed pants and new shirt, took guard, adjusted his box, fastened his batting gloves, tugged at his pad flaps, carefully studied the field placings, re-marked his guard and was bowled first ball. Evans surveyed the wreckage and said: 'Pity—just when you were settling in.'

Londoner Arthur McIntyre twice deputised in Tests for Evans when he was injured and once was included for his batting prowess. McIntyre was a leg-break bowler when he first tried out for Surrey at The Oval, but he was persuaded to take on wicket-keeping in an emergency and did so well at it he dismissed 95 batsmen in his first full season. He was a small, nimble man with fast hands and exceptional powers of anticipation who stood right up on the stumps for the spin of Laker and Lock and the late swing of Alec Bedser. Bedser rated him the equal of Evans in executing stumpings from his bowling.

McIntyre scored more than 1,000 runs three times in an English season and had a career bag of 795 dismissals from 639 catches and 156 stumpings. He was appointed Surrey's coach in 1959 but continued playing until 1963. He toured Australia in 1950–51.

Roy Swetman was the same height as McIntyre (5 feet 6 inches; 165 cm) and compensated for his lack of height with an excess of confidence. He was a sensational schoolboy cricketer and made his first-class debut for Combined Services in 1953, while doing his National Service. He played for Surrey from 1954 to 1961, during which time he played in 11 Tests. He toured Pakistan with England in 1955–56 and came to Australia in 1958–59, playing in the third Test at Sydney when Evans fractured a finger. Evans returned for the fourth Test at Adelaide but again broke his finger and had to be replaced at the end of the first day by Graveney. Swetman regained the job for the fifth Test at Melbourne and for the two Tests that

followed in New Zealand. Swetman went on to play for Notts (1966–67) and Gloucestershire (1972–74).

Swetman's efficiency underlined the fact that Evans was past his best—as were Tyson, Bailey and, to a lesser extent, Statham. England lost nothing with Swetman behind the stumps, but in an acrimonious series in which Slater, Burke and Meckiff were accused of chucking, Australia triumphed four–nil. Seven Australian batsmen averaged more than 25 in the Tests, but only three Englishmen did so.

Evans returned for the first two Tests of the 1959 series in England against India, but after India had been easily beaten in each the selectors announced they had omitted him for Swetman 'in the interests of team-building'. Evans realised the hunt for his successor was serious and quit at the end of that summer. But in 1967 he returned at the age of 47, when Allan Knott and Derek Underwood were absent on Test duty, for Kent's vital match against Yorkshire at Canterbury. He was badly overweight, with unruly side-burns down his cheeks, but he was as exuberant as ever. Spectators loved his chirpy vitality and he rewarded them with a virtuoso performance, brilliantly catching Ken Taylor and Ray Illingworth.

11

The Griz

Wally Grout collapsed several times at the Woolloongabba nets while practising with the Queensland cricket team in the 1940s and 1950s. Team-mates like Ken Archer admired the way he quickly bounced up and returned to his batting or keeping drills. Grout shrugged off his temporary indisposition, wisecracked about heavy nights and the heat, apologised for any inconvenience he caused team-mates and completed the sessions before sharing a few beers with them in the Queensland Cricketers' Club.

The Queenslanders came to regard him as one of the toughest of cricketers, a laconic, lantern-jawed figure who loved a bet and whose uncompromising attitude to Sheffield Shield success was urgently needed by Queensland. He spoke of how Queensland had been denied a place in the Shield competition until 1926–27 and of the injustices perpetrated against the state by southern-state umpires and administrators. Over the years his approach mellowed but he never discarded his gritty, inflexible resolve to become a great keeper.

He was a handsome man, immaculate in a dark blue suit, a chain-smoker with leathery, sunburnt skin whose adult geniality replaced his youthful swagger. Eye specialists said he had the keenest sight of anybody they ever tested. Barry Jarman, who was to be Grout's understudy and successor in the Australian XI, said: 'Wally was one of the game's greatest characters. I never begrudged playing second fiddle to him.'

Grout was a brash youngster from Mackay in north Queensland when he first came to Brisbane.

He received valuable grounding as a schoolboy in a combined secondary schools team that played in the Brisbane C-grade competition while he was at Brisbane High School. His ambition was to follow his idol Don Tallon into the Queensland side after a schoolmaster gave him the keeping job because 'you can't run fast enough to field anywhere else'. At age 10 he played for a Brisbane Schoolboys XI against Ipswich as an opening batsman.

Leyland Sanders, a promising right-hand batsman who later played for Queensland, held the keeping spot Grout coveted in that team and they continued their friendly rivalry until the state team needed a substitute for the absent Tallon. The selectors left it to the former Sheffield Shield keeper Jack Farquhar to pick between them, and Farquhar chose Sanders.

'Jack preferred Ley because he had the good keeping habit of moving the ball over the top of the stumps immediately it came into his gloves, whereas I held the ball back behind my body,' said Grout. ' "Move the ball over the sticks, son," said Jack, "and if the batsman lifts his toe you've got him." '

At 14 Wally joined the South Brisbane club after being thrown out of the Valley club because he did not live in their district. His mother bought him his first pair of long trousers when he was chosen to keep for Souths' firsts and he was so proud of these creams he wore them to bed. He was born Arthur Theodore Wallace Grout in 1927 and when he turned 18 interrupted his cricket career to join the army. He scored his first century

Wally Grout, one of Australian cricket's great characters. He had to wait years in the wings while Don Tallon and Gil Langley reigned as Australia's Test keepers, but enjoyed his chance when it came.

as an opening bat while training at Canungra Jungle Warfare school. The army realised immediately that Private Grout had more value for them as a cricketer than as an infantryman and instead of going north as a reinforcement for a fighting unit in the New Guinea jungle he found himself on the Canungra canteen staff, playing midweek cricket for the army and Saturday matches for Souths while on weekend leave.

'A more cocksure pipsqueak would have been hard to find,' Grout wrote in his autobiography. 'A swift kick in the pants would have been good medicine for me.' He was fond of a bet and yelled the odds against team-mates dropping catches. Behind the stumps he regularly goaded batsmen, urging them to get down the pitch and have a go at the bowling. Souths captain Jack ('Smacker') McCarthy, the former Sheffield player, often had to reprimand him for upsetting opponents' concentration.

Keeping on rough wartime pitches to a big variety of servicemen sneaking a bowl before they went north to the war brought early maturity to his cricket. He took a job in a Brisbane sports store after he was discharged and worked there stringing tennis rackets as selectors picked the first Queensland team after the war to go south. Tallon was required for Test duty against India, but Toombul's Doug Siggs, a future Australian hockey captain, was named as Tallon's replacement. A selector told Grout his chatter to batsmen influenced the choice, and the fact that Siggs was a better bat. Grout resolved to improve his batting and did so successfully that in some of his early matches for Queensland he played as an opening bat, fielding at cover.

In 1946 Grout went to Adelaide as Tallon's replacement, after Tallon injured a finger against Hammond's English tourists. He had to wait seven years for Tallon to retire, however, but when he finally did so Wally wondered why he had had the temerity to think he could replace the man most Australians regarded as the greatest keeper cricket had known. He despaired of ever replacing him but when the chance came he felt faint-hearted about it.

Don Bradman said that, up to the end of Tallon's career, he was inclined to hand the laurel for the finest keeper to Tallon, but Grout had not then emerged. 'When he did, the resemblance in style and method was remarkable,' wrote Bradman. 'I don't know whether Tallon was an inspiration to Grout or a model he copied but without doubt their glovework was very similar. They had the same basic timing, the same footwork, the same "swoop" on a snick, the same inevitability on holding a chance, and even the same air of intent.'

Grout developed into cricket's earthy Australian, a man of sardonic humour whose tongue could be as biting as the 'ocker' Paul Hogan's, but an ethical, sportsmanlike keeper whose conduct was never as tough as his tongue. He believed the Australian Test team should always include the best men for the job, even when that meant Tallon kept Grout waiting in the wings.

Grout had one match as Queensland's keeper in 1949 when Tallon asked to be considered as a spin bowler. Keepers often fancy themselves as bowlers, probably because of their years of

Grout running out an opponent on one of his two trips to England. Bradman said his style had an uncanny resemblance to that of Grout's longtime idol, Don Tallon.

reading bowlers' deliveries, but Tallon quickly realised his spin-bowling aspirations were fruitless and returned to wicket-keeping. Grout decided then to emulate Imtiaz Ahmed and John Waite and play his way into the state side as an opening bat. He sought instruction from his South Brisbane club captain, Test opener Bill Brown, and when illness forced Brown out of the state team Grout replaced him as an opener, playing alongside his idol, Tallon, and opening Queensland's innings with Ken Archer.

Studying Tallon close-up, Grout fully appreciated his artistry: 'I felt I could match his work on the off side but never had I believed such legside work was possible. He never snatched the ball, but let it ride gently into his gloves, and I began to adopt his habit of taking the ball on the leg in my right glove so that the left was free for a thick edge. This wasn't easy and it was years before I mastered it.'

Apart from his deafness, Tallon began to complain of a feeling of claustrophobia on the field. 'When I squatted down to take the first ball I felt there were people breathing down my neck,' Tallon said. 'I looked round and there was first slip practically in my pocket and leg slip parked beside my left ear.' Tallon shunted them wider, but his crowded-in feeling opened the way for his successor Gil Langley.

Queenslanders probably would have accepted Grout as Tallon's successor, but when Langley was preferred for the first Test against South Africa at the Gabba in 1952–53 they gave him a torrid reception. On the Saturday when a ball from Ian Johnson sneaked under Jack Cheetham's bat, thumped Langley in the chest and felled him, the crowd on the hill, fortified by their customary half dozen beers, gave Langley a blast and then switched their abuse to selector Jack Ryder, sitting in the Members' Stand. In the stand Grout was irate over the demonstration, for he knew that the off-spinner's yorker was the hardest ball of all for a keeper to take, a delivery the keeper does not see until it passes the stumps.

Tallon went to England as Langley's deputy in 1953 but retired soon after his return because of his claustrophobia and a recurring finger injury. This gave Grout his chance as Queensland's regular keeper. However, when Langley was hurt Jack Ryder was among the selectors who picked Len Maddocks to replace him for the final Tests against England. Wiry and dependable, Maddocks got into the Victorian team two years before his brother Richard, and in the 1970s saw his son Ian play for Victoria.

At the time of his Test selection Len Maddocks had an injured finger, but he top scored in the third Test against England in Melbourne and against the bowling of Statham and Tyson gave Australia an unexpected first-innings lead. He also top scored in the fourth Test at Adelaide, where

Victorian Len Maddocks, whose batting success earned him trips to England, the West Indies, India and New Zealand. Selector Jack Ryder tested his injured finger with a firm handshake.

his 92-run stand in 95 minutes with Ian Johnson again rescued Australia.

All this time Ryder was very suspicious about the condition of Maddocks' finger and whenever they met in lifts or hotel lobbies he tested Maddocks by shaking hands firmly. Maddocks responded with a strong, if painful, grip but Ryder kept hounding him. Maddocks survived but played in the Tests with his fingers wrapped in a wire cage that fitted inside his gloves.

Maddocks went to the West Indies in 1955 as Langley's deputy and again beat Grout for the spot on the 1956 tour of England. Grout was disheartened but the selection of his Queensland team-mate 'Slasher' Mackay after 10 years of Shield cricket gave him hope for inclusion on the upcoming 1957–58 tour of South Africa. When 'Slasher' returned from England Grout demanded to know the reason for his omission from touring sides.

'You're unfit,' came the reply. 'Before tea you're the best keeper in the world, but in the last session you're the worst. That's because tiredness breaks your concentration.'

Grout went on a special fitness course of skipping, calisthenics, squash and tennis, cut down on cigarette smoking and lapped the oval after net practice, seeking to 'put a spring into my steps that would last until stumps'. When Langley retired and began a career in politics that would take him to the Speaker's chair in the South Australian parliament, Grout felt confident selectors would send him and Maddocks to South Africa in 1957–58. He reckoned without the rising young South Australian Barrington Noel ('Barry') Jarman.

Australia sent Jarman on a short tour of New Zealand in 1957, with Peter Burge filling in as his deputy, and when the team for South Africa was announced Jarman was named the number-one keeper, with Grout his deputy. Grout's wife Joyce doubled the servings of carrots for every meal until Wally's departure, following the old belief that carrots improved the eyesight.

Few Australian teams have had such a messy start to a tour as that 1957–58 side. Just before their departure, the appointed manager Jack Jantke fell ill and withdrew, leaving Neil Harvey to take charge on the long flight across the Indian Ocean, via the Cocos Islands and Mauritius. Team captain Ian Craig, a surprise appointment, flew in from London while Jantke's replacement, Jack Norton, was recruited in Sydney. Without Jantke's notes on practice arrangements and hotel bookings, Craig had to improvise and when the Australians reached Johannesburg, South African newspapers described them as a 'leaderless legion'. Australian papers labelled them the worst side to have left Australia.

Grout formed a wicket-taking partnership with Alan Davidson, the left-arm bowler from Lisarow on the New South Wales Central Coast who had started life as a fast bowler but been forced to lower his pace by a broken leg. At a brisk fast-medium Davidson found he could swing the ball either way, enough to find the bat edges which provided Grout with 49 of his first 100 Test dismissals. Grout's experience in taking the gifted spinners in the Queensland side, Brian Flynn and Mick ('Possum') Raymer, also allowed him to take the spin of Lindsay Kline and Richie Benaud with style and certainty.

Neil ('Ninna') Harvey gave Grout the nickname 'The Griz' early on the tour and it stuck for the rest of his career. Harvey, unerring with his throwing from the covers, thought Grout grizzled too much when a fieldsman's throw did not arrive over the bails and forced him to scamper about to prevent overthrows.

Grout broke a thumb against Eastern Province at Port Elizabeth when a ball from Ian Meckiff kicked unexpectedly from a rough patch. Although an X-ray and a specialist confirmed the break, he concealed the injury from the tour selectors and found himself picked for the first Test at Johannesburg ahead of Jarman. Only room-mate 'Slasher' Mackay knew of his broken thumb when he turned in a miserable display in South Africa's first innings. He did not miss any chances but he had a bad attack of the fumbles and allowed eight byes in a Springbok total of 9 for 470 declared. Davidson rescued him with a superb exhibition of swing bowling, providing Grout with four catches. He took one each off Jimmy Burke and Ian Meckiff to find himself with six dismissals in the innings, a world record, one more than Oldfield and Gil Langley's old record. Davidson had 6 for 34 from 17.4 overs and Australia escaped with a draw.

This success launched Grout on a brilliant Test career. Australia took a series lead by winning the second Test at Cape Town by an innings and 141 runs following an opening stand of 190 by Jimmy Burke (189) and Colin McDonald (99) and a hat-trick by Linsday Kline. Grout did not dismiss a batsman but allowed only six byes in two innings. His fine form continued in the third Test when, finger mended, he took four catches and made a stumping. The match ended in a draw amid controversy when it was alleged that Neil Adcock had made excessive use of sunburn cream to retain shine on the ball.

Australia clinched the rubber in winning the fourth Test at Johannesburg by 10 wickets, Benaud contributing a century and nine wickets, Grout dismissing six more batsmen, four caught and two stumped off Kline. He got a further two in the fifth Test at Port Elizabeth, where Australia won by eight wickets to give Australian cricket the boost that was needed with a three–nil series triumph. By the end of the tour most Australians felt that Grout in the Test side was a lucky omen.

Benaud was given the captaincy everyone expected to go to Harvey when Craig fell ill with hepatitis just before the 1958–59 series against England. In front of his home crowd at the Gabba, Grout caught Tom Graveney off Davidson after 90 minutes, the first of his 20 dismissals in the rubber. This was the first Test in Australia to be televised and it firmly established Grout as a viewers' favourite as he held four catches and brilliantly stumped Trevor Bailey off Benaud. It was a particularly satisfying dismissal as Bailey consistently belittled leg-break bowling in his books and commentaries. He only lifted his toe momentarily, but Grout had the bails off and the umpire's finger was up before he touched down. Bailey responded by batting for 458 minutes for 68 runs in England's second innings, but he failed to save England.

Grout's support for Davidson's swing and the spin of Benaud continued throughout the summer, Australia winning four–nil, but Grout's 20 dismissals were forgotten by an English press who excused their team's failure with the claim that they were opposed to a team of chuckers. Their barbs were mainly aimed at Ian Meckiff, and they ignored Grout and the simple truth that bowlers with copybook actions, Davidson and Benaud, took most wickets for Australia, and that

Bowler Alan Davidson leaps for joy as Grout dives wide to his right to take a brilliant catch and dismiss Lance Gibbs in the 1960–61 series against the West Indies.

Australia's batsmen had overcome the threat of Laker and England's arch chucker, Tony Lock.

The cohesive teamwork that had shown itself in Australia's cricket against South Africa and England continued on a difficult tour of Pakistan in 1959–60. Australia won the first two Tests in the three-Test rubber to become the first country to defeat Pakistan in Pakistan. Australian fans were surprised by the bowling of 'Slasher' Mackay, but Grout assured team-mates Mackay's bowling was just what was required on the mat, and Mackay underscored this by taking 6 for 42 to set up victory in the first Test at Dacca. Then Kline turned in a match-winning 7 for 75 in Lahore to clinch the second Test. President Eisenhower watched the fourth day of the drawn third Test in which Pakistan made 5 for 105, the second slowest day in Test history, but nine more than the same team had managed in one day on the same Karachi pitch three years earlier.

Practising for the first match on the Indian part of the tour, Davidson kayoed a spectator whose face pressed against the nets. The man went down with blood spurting from his head but before Grout or Davidson could get to him he was passed over the crowd's heads and his place taken by another fan.

Grout helped Australia rout India in the first Test at Delhi by taking four catches in their first innings of 135. Australia responded with 468 and won the match by an innings and 127 runs. When last man Desai skied a catch to Meckiff, spectators who had been pelting bottles on to the field jumped the fence. Grout grabbed a stump, the only available weapon, flourishing it at advancing rioters as he raced for the dressing-room with team-mates. Alone on the field, Meckiff held the catch. Nobody cared that, technically, Desai was not out as the wicket had been broken. Deprived of a day's play, the crowd compensated for it by continuing to throw bottles and fruit on to the field well after dark.

Jarman made his debut in the second Test, although Grout was fit and eager to play. The tour selectors simply wanted to give Jarman, who had only two minor matches, some cricket and overruled Grout when he said the number-one keeper should always play in a Test. They promised Jarman the second and fourth Tests but failed to honour this when the fourth Test came round.

Grout then found himself arguing for Jarman's inclusion because he said it was unfair to tell a player he was to play and disappoint him. India tried three keepers before Australia won the series two–one, with two draws. They played Padmanabh Joshi, a very sound keeper who had toured the West Indies in 1952–53 and England in 1959, in the first Test; Narendra Tamhane, who also toured England in 1959, in the second Test; and Budhisagar Kunderan, an impassive, efficient keeper, developed in India's mass-coaching scheme, in the last three Tests.

Kunderan was to reach a career total of 260 dismissals, despite the whims of selectors. The following season, 1961–62, he achieved a record for an Indian keeper by dismissing five of the eight English batsmen sent back in the first Test but found himself replaced by Farokh Engineer for the rest of the series.

The Australians completed the tour of Pakistan and India with four wins in eight Tests and only one defeat. Grout kept in seven Tests and was one of Australia's 10 first-class century-makers, reaching 101 against Combined Indian Univer-

Barrington Noel Jarman, who made his Test debut as Australia's keeper in 1959–60 when Grout was injured. Jarman became one of the few keepers to captain Australia in a Test match.

sities at Bangalore. Grout proved his value to a touring team which had Gavin Stevens in hospital and Lindsay Kline and Gordon Rorke sent back to Australia with hepatitis that reduced them to skeletons, by opening the innings for the final Test with Les Favell. They put on 76, Grout scoring 50. Back home Grout and Ray Lindwall had just sweated out the incubation period for hepatitis when they were included in the Queensland side to play Western Australia in Brisbane.

Weary from incessant travelling and frequent attacks of 'Asian tummy' that had to be constantly treated by team doctor, Ian McDonald, Grout was not game to bend down in his normal pose before the bowler arrived, but he set a world record by dismissing eight batsmen, all caught.

The following season in Australia, 1960–61, Grout sent back 23 batsmen in the wonderful series against the West Indies. This equalled the world record at the time but was eclipsed by both West Indian Deryck Murray, who claimed 24 Englishmen in 1963, and by South African Johnny Waite, who dismissed 26 New Zealanders in 1961–62.

Grout's fiercely competitive personality was a feature of the series with the West Indies. He dropped Gary Sobers before Sobers went on to 132 in the first Test, was dropped himself when Kanhai and Hall collided, and in the dramatic fifth Test attracted boos from 65,000 spectators, which persisted for the rest of the day, when he appealed against Joe Solomon, whose cap had dislodged the bail. The umpires had no doubt Solomon was out but the crowd considered his dismissal unethical. One man mixed his hoots with the cry: 'Get out of the game, Grout—you're too old'. Grout was too experienced at 34 to let it bother him. (He showed he had a chivalrous streak three years later when he refused to remove the bails when Fred Titmus was stranded in mid-pitch after colliding with Neil Hawke in a Test against England at Nottingham.)

Ironically, Grout survived when a bail fell off as he played a ball through rival keeper Gerry Alexander's legs. Alexander insisted he had not brushed the stumps, but the stump supporting the bail had tilted forwards, not backwards, as it would have done had the ball hit it. The umpires conferred and gave Grout not out. His six catches helped seal Australia's win.

Grout reached 100 Test dismissals in his 24th Test at Lord's in 1962. This was eight Tests faster than Allan Knott (32 Tests), nine Tests faster than Ian Healy (33), 12 Tests faster than John Waite (36), 16 Tests faster than Jim Parks (40), 17 faster than Bert Oldfield (41) and 18 faster than Godfrey Evans (42). His triumphant run was broken after 27 Tests in which he shrugged off many injuries. A broken jaw forced him out of the first three Tests against Ted Dexter's English tourists in 1962–63. Jarman replaced him but as soon as Grout recovered selectors rushed him back for the fourth and fifth Tests. He immediately regained centre stage with five dismissals, including a catch to send back the Rev. David Sheppard that started

The contentious Joe Solomon dismissal, with Grout and Benaud appealing after Joe's cap dislodged a bail. Umpires had not doubt that he was out but spectators thought it unsportsmanlike.

in Benaud's hands at second slip, popped out as Simpson lunged for it at first slip, bounced over Simpson's shoulder and finished in Grout's glove as he dived full-length.

From the time he turned 30 in March 1957, Grout became accustomed to speculation that he was finished, but at the age of 36 he was still in fine form. He went south with the Queensland team in 1964–65 amid expert forecasts that Victorian Ray ('Slug') Jordan would join Jarman in the Australian team on the West Indian tour at the end of that summer. He answered these predictions by taking seven catches for Queensland against South Australia, and that night over dinner found himself matching wits at the Adelaide home of legendary Test selector Don Bradman. Seeking a tip on his tour chances, Grout said he planned to include chapters on the West Indies tour in a book for which Bradman had agreed to write the Foreword.

'Which tour?' said Bradman.

'The approaching one.'

'That's too bad, Wal, the manager's job has been filled and we won't be sending a baggage man.'

At this point Bradman's daughter, Shirley, came to Grout's aid. 'Dad, did you see Wally's wonderful catch that dismissed Brian Hurn?'

'No, I didn't, Shirley. I was in the dressing-room talking to Barry Jarman,' Bradman said, and turning to Grout, twisted the knife by adding: 'I believe you took another great catch but I didn't see that one either.'

Grout believed he only went on that 1965 West Indian trip because of a dazzling legside catch he took to dismiss Doug Walters later in Sydney in front of another tour selector, Dudley Seddon. He played in all five Tests in the West Indies, and in his book *My Country's Keeper* left no doubt over how much he enjoyed dour, tough Test cricket. In the second Test, when he was given out for 35 caught behind by Jackie Hendriks, Gary Sobers told him as he went off: 'I know you weren't out, but this is a Test match'. Grout did not worry about it; he was more concerned that umpires were not no-balling Charlie Griffith, whom all the Australians called 'The Ghoul' and rated a blatant chucker.

Grout dismissed 18 batsmen in the five West Indies Tests and 12 more in the 1965–66 series in Australia against Mike Smith's England team. He dismissed three successive English batsmen with catches off Walters in the fifth Test and later caught Barry Knight off Neil Hawke. This took him to 187 dismissals in 51 Tests, the record for an Australian at that time.

When Grout died of a heart attack at 41, two years after his retirement in 1965–66, there were widespread reports that he had been warned by doctors of heart problems, and had defied their advice to quit to accompany Australia to the West Indies in 1964–65. These reports have been strenuously denied by his widow, Joyce Grout, who on Wally's death was left to bring up a 13-year-old Daughter, Nelma, and an eight-year-old son,

Brian Hedley Taber, who became Australian keeper when Jarman, Maddocks and Grout retired, appeared in 129 first-class matches, 16 of them Tests, dismissing 395 batsmen.

Ian Chappell, one of an impressive list of specialist batsmen that includes Sid Barnes, Arthur Allsopp, Keith Carmondy, Jack Fingleton, Vic Richardson and Don Bradman, who have taken over when their team's keeper was injured, appealing for a catch in a South Australia v. New South Wales match.

Darryl. Grout's old captain, Richie Benaud, does not believe the warning was ever given.

Grout played 94 matches for Queensland, for whom he dismissed 293 batsmen (229 caught and 64 stumped). He had 183 first-class matches in all, scoring four centuries and dismissing 587 batsmen (473 caught and 114 stumped).

They are a tough mob, the Grouts. Wally recalled riding in a tram with his grandfather, a sun-dried old bullock-driver who had been reduced to breaking in brumbies for a living. The old man found the air in Brisbane offensive after years in the Outback and reached over and squashed out the cigar an American serviceman was smoking. The American was too surprised to respond.

Barry Jarman, restricted to 19 Tests by Grout's presence, took over as Australia's top keeper for the 1968 tour of England when he was vice-captain. He had been Grout's understudy for 27 Tests in six series, except for his first Test at Kanpur in 1959, and had distinguished himself with a magnificent diving catch in 1962 against England when he skidded on his right buttock to hold a Geoff Pullar leg glance. He had been unavailable for the South African tour in 1966–67, when Brian Taber was blooded, but at the age of 31 had enjoyed his first full series against India in Australia. In naming him ahead of Taber for the England tour, selectors opted for his greater experience and his aggressive batting style. At Scarborough in 1961 in the festival match against Tom Pearce's XI, Jarman had hit 26 (6, 6, 4, 4, 4, 2) off one over from David Allen, a burly figure of 14 stone (89 kg) who had played first-class cricket at 19.

After sitting in dressing-rooms for years, Jarman found his enthusiasm tested when he broke a finger in three places at the nets during the second Test at Lord's. He pluckily went in to bat but a ball from David Brown further damaged the finger and he had to retire. The finger injury put him out of the third Test, with Taber replacing him, but he took over as captain when he reappeared for the fourth Test following an injury to Bill Lawry (also a broken finger). He was the first keeper to captain Australia since Blackham in 1894, and told cameramen not to miss a very special tossing ceremony. Australians looking for Jarman to chase victory in place of Lawry's boring lack of initiative were disappointed when he allowed the match to dawdle to a tame draw.

Jarman's chance for an illustrious triumph disappeared when he persisted with medium-pacers and denied spinner Gleeson, with England set to make 325 in 300 minutes. Jarman retired at the end of the 1968–69 Australian season after Taber had replaced him for the fifth Test against the West Indies. At that time Jarman was one of three Australian keepers to have dismissed more than 500 batsmen. In 191 first-class matches he sent back 500 batsmen (431 caught, 129 stumped), a total exceeded only by Oldfield (661) and Grout (587). Only 54 of his dismissals came in Tests (50 catches, four stumpings). He scored 5,615 runs at 22.73, with five centuries, top score 196 for South Australia against New South Wales at Adelaide in 1965–66.

12

Wollongong's Finest

When the West Indies prepared in Perth for their exhilarating 1960–61 tour, Arthur Mailey surprisingly championed an unknown keeper named Gordon Becker. Bruce Buggins had been the West Australian keeper since 1954–55, but Mailey, a shrewd judge of cricketers, was impressed with what he saw in the practice nets of Becker, who had not been able to displace Buggins.

Buggins and Becker played important roles in West Australian teams just after the state was admitted to full membership of the Sheffield Shield competition. Eastern-state critics were sceptical about the standard of keeping in the west from the time Sydney-born Keith Carmody took the gloves in 1947–48, but Carmody was merely celebrating his versatility like other top-order batsmen Jack Fingleton, Don Bradman, Vic Richardson, Grahame Thomas, Arthur Allsopp and Warren Saunders, who all had a turn as keepers.

Since Francis Bennett and Horace Wilson, keepers for the first West Australian side to visit eastern states in 1893, proficient keepers played a big part in lifting their state's cricket prestige. They were followed by practised specialists William ('Frosty') Moore (1898), Harold Evers (1905–20), Robert Hewson (1924–31), Ossie Lovelock (1932–39), 'Glyn' Kessey (1945–49), John Munro (1948–54) and other short-term keepers. Moore, born in West Maitland, had played for New South Wales before becoming the first professional coach in Fremantle. Evers had captained New South Wales.

Buggins dismissed 162 batsmen (142 caught, 20 stumped), turning in some eye-catching displays in his 62 matches before he handed over to Becker in 1963–64. By then Western Australia had made big advances under English coach Tony Lock, and there was widespread interest in Becker's performance in Sydney among those who recalled Mailey's forecast. Becker played despite an attack of chickenpox and there was a memorable shot in Sydney newspapers of him eating alone in the SCG dressing-room. He made 52 not out.

Becker fulfilled Mailey's prediction by touring South Africa as second-string keeper to Brian Taber in 1966–67, but he played in only five of the 17 first-class matches on the tour and never appeared in a Test. This was despite 140 first-class dismissals (118 caught, 22 stumped), three first-class centuries including 195 against India in 1967–68 in Perth, and splendid displays for the state's winning Sheffield Shield team that summer.

Hedley Brian Taber, the keeper who frustrated Becker's Test ambitions, was a small, dapper cricketer who had 10 seasons in the first-class arena before becoming an important figure in Board of Control coaching programs. Taber was a polished, unobtrusive keeper who avoided showmanship and extravagant mannerisms or exaggerated appeals. He took some brilliant catches standing back to pace bowling and stumped erring batsmen smartly off spin. His batting was sound and dogged but at the highest level did not produce the big scores forecast when he first appeared in the New South Wales team

Long-serving Western Australian keepers John Munro (*right*) and Bruce Buggins. Munro had 60 dismissals in 26 matches for the state, Buggins 162 dismissals in 62 appearances.

in 1964–65, when he took five catches in his debut against Western Australia. He dismissed 33 batsmen in his initial first-class season and 33 in the following summer. By then it had become clear that he was a very promising batsman, an ideal replacement for Wally Grout or Barry Jarman.

Taber was born in Wagga Wagga in 1940, but spent his teenage years in Wollongong, the steel and coal city on the New South Wales South Coast. He learned cricket on Wollongong paddocks with his brother Ross. The paddock beside the Taber's home at Fairy Meadow was known as 'Tabers' Pitch'.

The Taber boys built an impressive record in matches for Country schoolboy teams in annual matches against Sydney A.W. Green Shield sides. They were invited to join the Gordon club in the Sydney competition and every Saturday travelled 120 miles to appear in club matches. Ross Taber was a good first-grader but did not advance to the state side. Brian became Gordon's first XI keeper at 16, suceeding Sheffield Shield hopeful Ross Englefield.

Douglas Allan Ford had not long vacated the New South Wales keeping job, after 63 appear-

Brian Taber, who learned his cricket in Wollongong, sent back 35 batsmen in his initial first-class season, five of them in his debut for New South Wales against Western Australia.

ances between 1957–58 and 1963–64, during which he accounted for 177 batsmen (120 caught, 57 stumped). The selectors were looking for a player who could give the role similar stability and help build teamwork. Ford had taken the job by accident when the incumbent Ossie Lambert, the Newcastle stumper, dropped out. Selectors named Balmain keeper Keith Herron as Lambert's replacement but had to fall back on Ford when officials could not find Herron, who was holidaying with his family at a South Coast caravan park. Ford did such a fine job Herron did not get a second invitation.

Ford was an agile, athletic keeper with splendid powers of anticipation, reliable in catching and a swift, sure stumper. Many of the internationals who played with him in the state team argued that he was deserving of higher honours. He had to be content with a trip to New Zealand in Ron Roberts' international side in 1961–62, with Grout and Jarman preferred for Test teams.

Taber had a record-making Test debut, dismissing eight South African batsmen at Johannesburg for Bob Simpson's Australian team in 1966–67. This remains the best bag by an Australian keeper against the Springboks. Reporters were amazed to find after this feat that Taber had never before attended a Test.

Burly Barry Jarman, unavailable for the South African tour, replaced Taber for the Indian tour in 1967–68 when Taber scored his sole first-class century, 109 for New South Wales against South Australia in Adelaide. He went to England as Jarman's deputy in 1968, during which tour he sent back 39 batsmen in 14 appearances and scored 365 runs at 26.07, top score 81, compared with Jarman's 27 dismissals in 13 matches and 184 runs at 10.22, top score 41.

The Australians found that there was keen competition for the role of England keeper between Allan Knott and the Derbyshire perfectionist, Bob Taylor. Knott was preferred for the Tests but the Australians were full of admiration for Taylor, who often was condemned to touring as Knott's understudy but still managed to appear in 51 Tests and set some important records.

Taylor took only 15 Tests to reach 50 dismissals, 30 to reach 100, and in his 47th Test reached 150 dismissals and 1,000 runs. He got his chance to play Test cricket when Knott joined Packer's rebels

in 1977–78. He celebrated becoming the first England keeper to catch five Australians in an innings, and in this innings his seven victims equalled Wasim Bari's world record. Taylor dismissed seven batsmen in an innings three times, once for England and twice for Derbyshire. He had a remarkable career record of 1,649 dismissals, exceeding John Murray's world record of 1,527 first-class dismissals. Taylor was a model of good positioning and seldom needed to dive for catches. His slips fieldsmen could hear deliveries from pace bowlers smacking cleanly into his gloves, but his timing was so precise he rarely damaged his hands. Taylor had some great fast bowlers to keep to at Derbyshire, amongst them Harold Rhodes, Brian Jackson, Alan Ward and Mike Hendrick. He was known to team-mates as 'Chat' because of his willingness to socialise at tour functions and on 11 overseas tours never tired of listening to his host. As a right-hand tail-end batsman he was good enough to score 11,521 runs at 16.84, with a top score of 100 and an innings of 97 in Tests.

James Graham Binks was unfortunate to play in only two Tests, for he followed a long line of outstanding Yorkshire keepers with elegance and calm, undemonstrative technique of a high order. Like Don Brennan before him, he was disappointed in his Test aspirations. Godfrey Evans restricted Brennan to two Tests and John Murray and later Allan Knott rationed Binks to the same number. Brennan, who made a big impression on the 1948 Australians, dismissed 434 batsmen in his 14 seasons with Yorkshire which included an England tour of India in 1951–52, and Binks had 1,071 dismissals between 1955 and 1969, including 107 dismissals in 1960 (96 caught, 11 stumped). Binks went to India as a replacement for John Murray in 1961–62. He generally batted in the late order but was used as a makeshift opener. He migrated to America in the 1980s.

Back in Australia after the English tour with Bill Lawry's team, Taber equalled the world record of 12 dismissals in a match (nine caught, three stumped) playing for New South Wales against South Australia in 1968–69. The feat had only previously been performed by Edward Pooley, of Surrey, and by Don Tallon.

Taber played in his only Test of the 1968–69 summer, the fifth against the West Indies, scoring

Bob Taylor brilliantly stumping Derek Chadwick in England's match in Perth against Western Australia in 1970–71. Taylor appeared in 57 Tests for England.

48 in an Australian innings of 619 batting at number nine, and holding six catches. His display completely overshadowed that of Jackie Hendriks, who contributed to a sloppy West Indian fielding and dropped Walters, who made 242, when he was on 75. Taber captained New South Wales in five matches that summer, Walters in three.

Towards the end of the season Taber contracted a lung infection but he went on the tour of India and South Africa while still under treatment, a ruddy-faced figure. He again outshone the rival keeper, Farokh Engineer, who missed easy stumping chances off his spinners Prasanna and Bedi, and his 16 dismissals in the five Tests added to the effectiveness of Mallett and Gleeson in a rubber decided by spinners. Mallett proved the bowler of the series with 28 wickets. Taber was very good, too, taking McKenzie and Connolly.

By the time the Australians arrived in South Africa for the second part of their tour, morale had slumped alarmingly after a riot in Bombay, a crowd invasion of the pitch in Calcutta and stone-throwing in Bangalore. Some members of the team were unhappy with the behaviour of captain Bill Lawry. Victorians in the side found themselves defending Lawry and at odds with players from other states. Taber and Ian Chappell did their best to socialise with South African rivals, with Lawry conspicuously absent once play ended.

Australia sustained a four–nil defeat at the hands of a classy South African XI, with the Pollock brothers, Barry Richards, Eddie Barlow, Mike Proctor, Trevor Goddard and John Lindsay in fine form and splendidly led by Dr Ali Bacher. Dennis Gamsy, who had dismissed nine batsmen

Taber leaps high in elation after another dismissal during the 1968-69 season when he equalled the world record, dismissing 12 batsmen in a match for New South Wales v. Western Australia.

in a Currie Cup match at the age of 19, playing for Natal against Transvaal, kept wicket in the first two Tests, but was replaced by Lindsay for the last two.

Queenslander John Maclean toured New Zealand as keeper for an Australian B team while the Test side was in India and South Africa and at 24 appeared the most likely candidate for Taber's job. Maclean, a civil engineer, had given the Queensland team excellent service, and in New Zealand impressed with his handling of the bowling of Dennis Lillee, Dave Renneberg, Alan ('Froggy') Thomson and Terry Jenner.

Maclean was a powerfully built right-hand batsman of unexpected agility for a player who looked like a Rugby front-row forward. He was a forceful late-order batsman who could cut well and produce fruitful lofted drives, a graduate of Queensland University with an imposing record for South Brisbane club. Queenslanders spoke of him as another Gil Langley, very reliable, but lacking the polish of a Tallon or a Grout.

Taber returned from the arduous tour of Sri Lanka, India and South Africa popping pills to keep his lung infection in check, but because of his florid complexion he became the victim of unfounded rumours about his behaviour. Looking for scapegoats following the disastrous drubbing by South Africa, the Australian selectors brought in Rodney Marsh to keep wicket against England and later in the series created another major shock by sacking Bill Lawry as captain, leaving Ian Chappell to lead the side without a successful opening batsman.

Opposing the inexperienced Marsh, the England captain Ray Illingworth had two outstanding keepers, Knott and Taylor, men of wide experience accustomed to their captain's fondness for legside field placings.

Knott had succeeded Jim Parks as England's number-one keeper on tour in the West Indies in 1967-68. Parks was a dashing right-hand batsman, noted for his footwork against slow bowlers, who had played for Sussex since 1949 and donned keeping gloves for the first time when Sussex's keeper was injured. He scored 2,300 runs in the 1955 and 1959 seasons and the England selectors believed that choosing him vastly improved the side's run-getting potential. He played for England originally as a batsman in

Big, powerful Queenslander John Maclean leaps to take a catch. He appeared Taber's likely successor after taking Dennis Lillee and Dave Renneber well on a New Zealand tour, but Marsh got the job.

1954 and 10 years later was named the top keeper. His keeping improved every summer and he built up a remarkable list of victims, standing back to pace bowling and becoming increasingly at ease with spin, while also scoring valuable runs throughout this educational period.

In his first full season as a keeper, Parks sent back 93 batsmen in 1959, delighting his father James Horace Parks, who had played 434 matches for Sussex between 1924 and 1939 and toured Australia with England in 1935–36. Jim Parks' uncle, Henry William, also played for Sussex, and his son Robert James appeared for Hampshire.

Jim Parks was flown to the West Indies as a replacement batsman when Peter May became ill in 1959–60, and made a match-saving 101 not out in the Test at Port-of-Spain. He was 5 feet 10½ inches (177 cm) tall, with a very open stance, but impressed as a free-flowing strokemaker prepared to hit over the inner ring of fieldsmen. His place as a wicket-keeper batsman appeared secure but illness and indifferent form kept him out of the Test team for several seasons and when he did return to the England XI he shared the keeping duties with John Murray.

Parks scored more than 1,000 runs in an English season 20 times and three times exceeded 2,000 runs. He made 205 not out for Sussex against Somerset in 1955 at Hove. His talent as a leg-spin bowler was untapped because of his keeping triumphs, but he reached 50 dismissals in his 24th Test and 100 dismissals in his 41st Test, going on to 114 dismissals in 46 Tests (103 caught, 11 stumped). He proved one of the world's best limited-over batsmen.

Parks captained Sussex in 1967 and resigned midway through the 1968 season because the job affected his health and his run-scoring. In 1972, following a dispute, he moved to Somerset, but he returned to Sussex after 27 matches as Sussex's marketing manager. His career statistics were highly impressive, reflecting the skill of the man: he made 36,673 runs at 34.76, with 51 centuries, and had 1,181 victims (1,088 caught and 93 stumped).

Jim Parks probably excelled his father in longevity, but he never matched his dad's performance in 1937 when he scored 11 centuries on his way to 3,003 runs at 50.89, took 101 wickets and held 21 catches. James Parks, snr, scored 22 and 7 in his sole Test and trapped three New Zealand batsmen lbw for 36 runs. He appeared in 13 matches on England's 1935–36 tour of Sri Lanka, Australia and New Zealand, averaging 40.40 with two centuries for the side led by Errol Holmes. In 1937, he added 297 for the fifth wicket with his brother Henry at Portsmouth against Hampshire, which remains the Sussex record. Henry hit 1,000 runs in a season 14 times and had a top score of 200 not out against Essex at Chelmsford.

John Thomas Murray, born in North Kensington, London, in 1935, played 508 matches for Middlesex between 1952 and 1975, and became the first Middlesex keeper to score 1,000 runs and dismiss 100 batsmen in a season. In an age when fast bowling accounted for most dismissals and spinners were no longer considered strike bowlers, Parks' form with the bat deteriorated and while he held some splendid catches standing back, selectors began to look for a substitute keeper who would allow Parks to regain his brilliance as a batsman. They settled on Murray, who had been a member of the Lord's ground staff since he was 14.

Murray became a keeper by accident when he

John Murray, batting for Middlesex against Surrey at Lord's in 1962, watches Tony Lock bowling. Murray's batting gave him an advantage when selectors picked England Test teams.

played in the final of the Rugby Boys' club competition and offered his services when the keeper broke a finger. He took naturally to the role and was given a trial at Lord's, but had to wait a year to join the staff when the school leaving age was lifted. He played for the Middlesex senior team within two years, with Andy Wilson and Bert Strudwick his coaches. He hesitated momentarily to consider a career as a soccer professional—he was an amateur inside forward on Arsenal's books—but decided to concentrate on a full-time career in cricket, partly because the longtime Middlesex keeper Leslie Compton was nearing the end of his reign.

He became a regular selection for Middlesex in 1956 after doing his National Service with the RAF, playing occasionally with Gloucestershire in second-class matches by arrangement with Middlesex, because he was stationed there. From the start his association with off-spinner Fred Titmus flourished and within a season of his RAF discharge he became only the second keeper to achieve the double with 1,025 runs and 104 dismissals from 82 catches and 22 stumpings. He repeated the feat in 1960 by catching 95 and stumping seven. This won him selection for the first Test in 1961 against Australia at Edgbaston, following a New Zealand tour with the England A team led by Dennis Silk.

With Grout playing for Australia and Murray for England, television fans saw keeping of a very high standard in 1961. At Old Trafford in the fourth Test, Murray, all style and graceful movement, took seven catches to equal Evans' record for England v. Australia. His total of 18 dismissals for the series was a new England record but Grout surpassed it with 21 dismissals. Murray furthered his claims to a permanent place in the England XI with some valuable innings and went to India in 1961–62. He had a bad attack of the fumbles and conceded 33 byes in India's first innings of the first Test and after the third Test was flown home suffering from varicose vein problems. The team's second-string keeper Geoff Millman, of Nottinghamshire, took over for the remaining Tests and Jimmy Binks flew in as a replacement. Millman also appeared in Tests in England against Pakistan in 1962, but retired when it became clear Murray and Parks were preferred for big matches.

Millman was a splendid keeper who played his way into the Notts county side from Bedfordshire. His limitations with the bat gave Murray and Parks a clear edge over him when Test sides were picked. Millman dismissed 652 batsmen for Notts between 1956 and 1965 (556 caught, 96 stumped). Despite his lack of strokes his stubbornness brought him three first-class centuries and he twice passed 1,000 runs in a season. He equalled the Notts record by accounting for six batsmen against Northants in 1959 and five years later dismissed nine Warwickshire batsmen at Trent Bridge. Millman had the distinction of holding the first catch in limited-over cricket in England in 1962.

The famous Kent keeper 'Hopper' Levett came to Murray's aid, at a time when his career was in the doldrums, by highly praising Murray's keeping during the 1962–63 England tour of Australia. 'Internationally, there is nobody in Murray's class,' said Levett. 'He is streets ahead of anyone else and he would be a more successful keeper if he had someone really pushing him.'

Levett's assessment came at a time when Murray, Northants' Keith Andrew and Warwickshire's Alan Smith, all talented keepers, were in disfavour with England captain Ted Dexter. There was nothing personal about Dexter's attitude, but he believed specialist keepers were a burden in Tests if they displaced potential century-makers. Dexter admitted he was 'not very good at wicket-keepers'.

Smith had a higher run-scoring potential than Murray in Dexter's view and played in 13 matches in Australia, compared with seven by Murray. Smith was an unusually versatile cricketer, nudging 6 feet (182 cm) in height, who developed his keeping at King Edward's School in Edgbaston and won his blue in each of his three years at Oxford University. He kept Murray out of six Tests, four of them on the 1962–63 Australian tour, batting in the middle of the order at first but not delivering the heavy scoring hoped for by selectors. He was not a stylish keeper but he was safe and agile, as befitted a soccer blue. He proved an innovative captain of Warwickshire later in his career, removing his pads to bowl right-arm medium-pacers that swung appreciably. He took a hat-trick at Clacton against Essex in 1965.

Serving as a director of Aston Villa soccer club and as secretary of Warwickshire, Smith also had a term as an England selector and returned to Australia in 1974–75 as assistant manager. He impressed with his handling of problems in the West Indies in 1980–81 when his work as manager earned praise from the Test and County Cricket Board. He became the TCCB's first chief executive in 1987. Twenty of Smith's 776 dismissals (715 caught, 61 stumped) came in his six Tests, the rest in county cricket and on England tours. There were five centuries in his 11,027 first-class runs (average 20.92).

Murray's chances of replacing Smith permanently in Tests on the 1962–63 Australian tour were hampered when he was hurt brilliantly catching Bill Lawry in his sole Test. Murray thrilled the Sydney crowd by diving full-length to catch a Lawry leg glance centimetres from the turf, but he landed on the point of his shoulder and was not fit to resume his place until the first Test in New Zealand. When the Englishmen got home, the selectors dropped both Smith and Murray and brought in Keith Andrew for the first Test against the West Indies.

Andrew was rated the most talented keeper of his generation by some English critics but he played for an unfashionable county, until Freddie Brown and Frank Tyson gave it some glamour. He also suffered from the selectors' preference for inferior keepers who could bat rather than specialists. He dismissed 904 batsmen (723 caught, 181 stumped) between 1952 and 1966, toured Australia and New Zealand in 1954–55 and the West Indies in 1959–60, but was restricted to only

John Ducker (*left*), who dismissed 60 batsmen (48 caught, 12 stumped) for South Australia in his 20 matches from 1952–53 to 1962–63 and Ray ('Slug') Jordon (*right*), whose 79 matches for Victoria produced 260 victims (226 caught, 34 stumped) between 1959 and 1970.

two Tests. His batting average—13.38 in scoring 4,230 runs—probably did not help his Test prospects.

Andrew's tour round Australia found Ross Edwards firmly established as Western Australia's keeper, with John Ducker in South Australia, Ray Jordan in Victoria, Geoff Trueman in New South Wales and Wally Grout in Queensland virtually unchallenged for their jobs, but in Tasmania Rex Davidson was struggling to hold his spot. Later, Jarman came in for Ducker, Richie Robinson for Jordon, Lambert and Taber for Trueman and Maclean for Grout, but the most dramatic change of all in the modern history of wicket-keeping in Australia came in Western Australia, when a chubby little man with billiard-table legs named Rodney William Marsh took over as that state's gloveman.

13

Old Iron Gloves

When Rodney William Marsh went out to bat for Australia against the Rest of the World in January 1972, Sydney Cricket Ground spectators booed him all the way to the crease. Spectators who considered Wollongong's Brian Taber shabbily treated by selectors guffawed at the sight of the overweight, heavy-legged figure from the back-blocks of Western Australia, their prejudices against cricketers from the west and their suspicions that the selectors had lost their marbles confirmed. How could this podgy, gum-chewing oddity with an unbuttoned shirt that showed his hairy chest achieve the athleticism demanded of an Australian keeper? Compared with the trim, quick-stepping Oldfield or the lean, spruce Tallon, he looked completely wrong.

Old-timers in the Gabba Members' Stand had forecast, when he made his Test debut the previous summer against England, that Marsh would disappear after one appearance. Marsh was amazed at his selection but the boos of those first two seasons in a prized job angered him. He immediately raised doubts about the sanity of selectors by dropping Edrich, Fletcher and D'Oliveira. Australia escaped with a draw, thanks to 207 from Stackpole whom cameras showed was favoured by a run-out decision at 18, but unhappy Gabba fans hollered 'We want Maclean' with each Marsh error. When Marsh dropped Boycott off McKenzie in front of his home crowd in Perth in the second Test, even a hard-hitting 44 did not end pleas for his omission. The boos may have abated in Perth's first-ever Test, but across Australia newspapers called for his immediate removal.

Marsh's fumbling compared unfavourably with Alan Knott's virtually unblemished displays. At Sydney in the fourth Test the mob on the Hill hooted Marsh and howled for Taber's rein-statement even when Marsh gloved the ball well. 'I felt like jumping the fence and taking some positive action in defence of my honour,' said Marsh in his biography, *You'll Keep*. 'I learned to live with the abuse but what I did not realise was that worse was yet to come.'

The New South Wales Cricket Association president Alan Davidson dealt Marsh a cruel body blow when he argued for Taber, now restored to fitness, to be included ahead of Marsh for the 1971–72 series against the Rest of the World. Davidson said keeping was a specialist job and Marsh should not be preferred to Taber because he was rated a slightly superior batsman: 'No one can honestly say Marsh played well against England, and Taber is by far the best keeper in Australia'.

Davidson later apologised to Marsh for his comments, but Marsh felt wounded and hurt by critics who refused him a fair go. Originally selected as a top-order batsman by Western Australia, Marsh remained confident his luck and all the years of hard practice would prevail if he could shake off the 'Old Iron Gloves' stigma dished out by eastern critics.

Marsh was born at Armadale, 20 miles south-east of Perth, on 11 November 1947, the son of Ken Marsh, a one-time bush cricketer from Geraldton, 300 miles north of Perth. Ken and his wife Barbara took Rodney and his brother Graham to watch his Saturday matches in the

Armadale district. The boys were not satisfied with just watching and to the annoyance of their mother, a keen gardener, built a pitch in the backyard. They played in the Armadale competition and for their school team, with their father occasionally joining in their backyard matches. Rodney was restricted to sweeps, later the despair of his fans, to protect his mother's prize plants.

Rodney played for Armadale C grade with Frank Pyke, who became a doctor and nursed Dennis Lillee back to fitness when back injuries threatened the bowler's career. A schoolmaster named Geoff Sinclair suggested he take on keeping when he was 10 and his parents gave him a pair of gloves for his 11th birthday. Photographs of him at that age show a well-fed infant with chubby legs and billowing cheeks. Like Bradman, he practiced against a brick fence for hours at a time, counting the catches he made before he dropped one. He was always delighted to reach a thousand without fumbling.

Rodney Marsh when he first came into the Western Australian team in 1968 at the age of 21 and earned the nickname 'Iron Gloves' for his clumsy keeping.

Graham Marsh, three years Rod's senior, beat him to state selection when he won a place in the 1958 West Australian Schoolboys side. Rod tried to emulate his brother, who scored 73 not out in the Adelaide carnival, and felt wounded when he missed selection in 1959. Graham broke his arm high-jumping in the backyard and doctors suggested golf to strengthen the arm. Aged 14 and ready to work on his right-hand swing at the local Gosnells course, Graham was soon lost to cricket as he reduced his handicap. Golf was more difficult for Rodney as left-handed clubs were unavailable, but he found diversion in Australian football.

At the age of 12 Rod played for West Perth Under 16s on Saturday mornings and for West Perth's fourth grade side in the afternoons. After two seasons he was promoted to the seconds. Gordon Becker, the state keeper, kept for the firsts and when he was absent in the eastern states Geoff Hicks took the gloves. This did not suit Rod, who trained with another club with the intention of moving until West Perth promoted him to the firsts as a batsman who could fill in if Becker was unavailable.

Left-handed batting at the top of the order was Rod's strength when he went to Sydney in 1960 with the West Australian Schoolboys XI, with Terry Gale the vice-captain before he, too, became a famous golfer. The Sydney Cricket Ground aroused awe in Rod that returns every time he sights it. In the match against Queensland, captained by John Maclean, he scored 50. That schoolboys' team included Bob Massie and David Goddard among its bowlers. The South Australian team at that carnival included Greg Chappell. On their return to Perth Goddard persuaded Rod to join the West Perth club.

He went on to Kent Street High School, close to Perth, after primary school, and got into trouble with WACA officials when he joined four West Perth youngsters in reinforcing the Ongerup side that arrived for Country Week five men short. Rod made a smart stumping for Ongerup and in the second innings opened the bowling. Association officials recognised the five ring-ins during the third match and hauled them in for an explanation. Ongerup were banished from the competition and the five West Perth men were each fined one guinea.

Marsh hitting one of the big sixes that helped make his critics become his fans. He originally played first-class cricket as a top-order batsman or opener in Shield matches.

Marsh shows the acrobatic agility that characterised his keeping, leaping high to field a wild fieldsman's return.

The next season Rod entered the University of Western Australia, a move that got him away from the West Perth club where Becker barred his progress, and steered him towards a career as a teacher. When lectures clashed with cricket, he always gave cricket preference. In third term he failed his exams and abandoned his teaching aspirations, with tutors warning that he would never make a living from cricket.

The University of Western Australia welcomed his presence in their team, however, and he found himself playing alongside Jock Irvine and John Inverarity, who both played later for Australia. The team included another future Test player, leg-spinner Tony Mann, son of a vigneron from the Swan Valley, who gave Marsh regular practice in taking a bowler who really turned the ball. The team won two premierships as Marsh developed his batting and keeping and in the 1967–68 season he won selection in the state Colts. He thought about moving to another state but when he studied the South Australian side he found Barry Jarman firmly established, Ray Jordon in Victoria, Brian Taber in New South Wales and Lew Cooper in Queensland, none of them likely to relinquish their roles easily.

All he could do to win state selection was improve his value as a batsman and score so many runs he would force selectors to pick him for the Sheffield Shield XI. By then he worked part-time at the WACA as a cleaner and this gave him the opportunity to study Lew Cooper's technique when Queensland played in Perth.

At the start of the 1968–69 season Perth cricket writers listed Marsh as a candidate for a state batting spot, ignoring his keeping skills. When Gary Sobers, Peter and Graeme Pollock, Freddie Trueman, Wes Hall and Colin Milburn arrived in Perth, Marsh was among the WACA ground staff who fielded for them as they prepared for a world double-wicket event. Later that summer he made his debut for Western Australia as a batsman, going in at number four against the West Indies at the WACA. Charlie Griffith bowled him for a duck in his initial first-class innings and he fielded in the covers when the West Indies batted, while Becker kept wicket. He knew as he took guard in the second innings that his future in first-class cricket was at stake, with a place in the Combined XI alongside Doug Walters, Ian Chappell and Paul Sheahan possible if he could perform.

With Western Australia on 2 for 12, Marsh attempted to tickle a ball from Wes Hall down to fine leg, but only managed a faint edge and the ball flew to leg slip. 'My heart sank, and then bounced right back to normal when Richard Edwards dropped the catch,' said Marsh. 'Had the catch been accepted it could easily have been the end of my first-class career, at least for a while. As my score moved into the twenties, the jitters took hold and the crawl up to 100 seemed to last an eternity. Finally it came through a push into the covers off Joey Carew, bowling off-spinners. I had had two chances missed, but I was mighty proud at that moment. I thought to myself, "This is much better than I expected", and when I was bowled for 104 soon afterwards I floated off the WACA. I read that only one other player, N.S.W.'s Arthur Allsopp in 1929–30 v. England, had begun with a century against a touring international team.'

Selectors may have taken a gamble on Marsh batting against the World XI in Sydney, but this did not excuse the spectators who shouted for Taber to be given his spot. He hung on grimly until the tea interval and regained his composure when Taber encouraged him in the dressing-room. The defiance that characterised Marsh's career emerged as he began to bat confidently. He put on 69 with John Benaud, and when Benaud was out, remained while 80 more were added, 50-odd off his bat. Spectators were won over as he swatted Intikhab Alam over the fence twice on the bounce. Around the ground disappointment greeted his departure for 77, although Australia reached 312. He never again lacked crowd support.

Magically, the jibes about 'Iron Gloves', or 'Fat Rodney' and newspaper reports about the 'slips fieldsman in pads and gloves' were replaced by accolades for Marsh's aggression. He dieted and worked hard on a fitness routine, and the dives for apparently impossible catches and big hits out of the park became a crowd-pleasing part of big cricket in the 1970s. Marsh became a phenomenon who gave everything for his team and for the remainder of his 244 first-class matches was the most popular cricketer in Australia in an era that included Lillee, Thomson and the Chappell brothers.

Marsh dives wide to his right to make one of the catches for which he became famous, going on to a world record of 355 Test dismissals and a career total of 870 victims.

Lillee and Marsh both overcame serious physical problems to sustain their wicket-taking. Lillee had to undergo painful exercises to mend a spinal condition; Marsh often had to ignore an arthritic knee that swelled like a balloon. Warren Lees, New Zealand keeper and keen student of world cricket, summed up: 'You can't take it away from Marsh—he's a bloody marvel'.

Now, after Marsh has completed the most successful career of any Australian keeper, selectors can laugh. Despite early criticism, they stuck with Marsh because the demands of keeping in Tests had changed from the days when keepers generally moved up on the stumps, waiting for stumpings. Only 7.4 per cent of Marsh's victims were stumped, compared with 40 per cent by Blackham, 39.6 per cent by Oldfield and 46.5 per cent by Charlie Walker. Blackham and Oldfield always had at least one stumping per match but Marsh went weeks at a time without one and averaged a stumping every fourth match.

Marsh made only 65 stumpings in a first-class

career stretching from 1968 to 1984, in a massive total of 869 dismissals. He fulfilled his ambition of 'giving these young blokes something to catch' by achieving a world record of 355 Test dismissals in 97 matches, but only 12 of his Test victims were stumped. The other 343 were caught. He did not miss a Test in five tours of England and completed 14 years in big cricket with 92 more dismissals than England's most successful keeper, Alan Knott. Both were highly successful in their two seasons with Packer's World Series Cricket, but their dismissals in that period do not count in their career statistics.

A major reason for Marsh's small percentage of stumpings was that he did not encounter many top-class spinners, but kept mainly to a fiery pace attack that included Dennis Lillee and Jeff Thomson. His success revived the old controversy about whether keepers are more effective standing up on the stumps to medium-pace bowlers or standing back. Godfrey Evans was adamant that keepers should move right up on the stumps whenever possible, but Marsh advocated standing back where you could get a good sight of nicks and deflections.

Marsh's special talent was that he could reach firmly struck glances and cuts with acrobatics no other keeper has matched. Paul Sheahan, Marsh's team-mate on overseas tours and now headmaster of Geelong College, assessed Marsh this way for the 1985 *Wisden*: 'The archetypal Australian: strong, disrespectful of authority, yet fiercely loyal to those he admired'.

Bradman and his fellow selectors were strongly aware of the changes in the laws that produced more frequent new balls and gave pace bowling a dominant role. Long spells by slow bowlers were no longer a feature of Test innings, with captains able to call for new balls after 75 overs. Marsh's stumping skill was difficult to assess because he stood up so infrequently, but his reflexes were lightning fast as he dived for wide catches. There is no evidence that he could not have been a fast stumper. He took Johnnie Gleeson, Tony Mann, Ray Bright, Kerry O'Keefe and Tony Lock with enthusiastic efficiency standing up on the bails. His detractors point to the fact that when he equalled the world record by dismissing 26 batsmen in the 1975-76 series against the West Indies all his victims were caught, but keepers can only accept the chances that come along and neither Jenner nor Mallett provided them.

Marsh first played against England in 1970-71 under Bill Lawry and in only his fifth Test (one of which was rained out) appeared within reach of the initial Test century by an Australian keeper when Lawry declared. Marsh remained on 92 not out, but he accepted his captain's declaration as an unlucky break that was necessary, considering the state of the match. Lawry was sacked and Ian Chappell took over as captain two Tests later. Lillee also made his debut against England in that series and when Marsh caught John Hampshire off Lillee in the seventh Test it began a famous partnership.

Marsh went close to a Test century again on his first tour of England in 1972 by scoring 91 in the first Test at Old Trafford. He hit four sixes and nine fours from 111 balls in adding 104 with John Gleeson, an Australian record for the ninth wicket in all overseas Tests. He further boosted his popularity with English crowds by dismissing

23 batsmen in his bulk-defying diving, lurching style.

Although a Test century still eluded him, he ran up his highest first-class score, 236, for Western Australia v. Pakistan at Perth in 1972-73. He carried that form into the Tests and in the first Test at Adelaide hammered all the Pakistan bowlers to become the first Australian wicket-keeper to hit a Test century by scoring 118. He scored further Test centuries against New Zealand (132) in 1973-74 at Adelaide and in the 1977 Centenary Test at Melbourne his 110 not out swung a wonderful match. His stand with Rick McCosker, whose broken jaw was heavily strapped, yielded 54 runs. Australia won by 45 runs.

Marsh's friendship with Lillee, begun in 1966 when they were ambitious youths in Perth club cricket, developed into a marvellous asset for Australia. They often ran their laps together to achieve fitness and they developed a signal system fruitful to Lillee, particularly against left-handed batsmen. Amazingly, Marsh was behind the stumps for every ball Lillee bowled in his 70 Tests, except for the inaugural Test against Sri Lanka in April 1983, at Kandy, when Roger Woolley held five catches, one off Lillee.

Lillee delivered 18,471 balls in Tests, 18,337 with Marsh keeping, and Marsh accounted for 95 of his 355 Test victims. In all first-class matches, Marsh accounted for 219 of Lillee's 845 victims. This was by far the finest wicket-keeper/bowler partnership in the history of cricket, with Roger Taylor's 53 Test victims for Ian Botham, Wally Grout's 45 for Alan Davidson, and Bert Oldfield's 37 for Clarrie Grimmett overshadowed. The Nottinghamshire wicket-keeper, Bruce French, dismissed 115 batsmen for Richard Hadlee. Considering the Marsh/Lillee combination had another 20 victims in 15 World Series Super Tests, it's a record that is likely to remain unsurpassed. No wonder Australians rushed to the grounds or to their TV sets to watch them operating together.

Marsh did not miss a Test on five tours (1972, 1975, 1977, 1980 and 1981) of England. By the second tour a trimmer, fitter Marsh was of immense help to Ian Chappell, and by the third he was acknowledged for his tactical skills. Critics spoke of him as a prospective Australian captain but Australia's state and national selectors have

Marsh behind the stumps for Australia, with Gary Gilmour at silly mid-on, as rival keeper Alan Knott hits a boundary in the 1975 Australia v. England Test at Edgbaston.

always been reluctant to appoint keepers captain. The theory is that they have enough to worry about without the responsibility of leadership. Marsh clearly had the qualifications for captaincy, but remained loyal to the Chappells.

Traditionalists dubbed Marsh a traitor along with his colleagues who joined World Series Cricket, a laughable jibe when applied to Marsh. He agreed with the frustrations Australia's top players felt about their poor rewards. There was a big chance Packer would not succeed but Marsh felt he owed it to his wife and two sons to try to improve his cash returns from cricket. His support for WSC brought unforeseen pressure on his family, whose friends chided them about his disloyalty. Marsh not only toughed it out, but he gave some of the most inspired displays of his career. From the moment Packer turned on the lights at Sydney Cricket Ground on 28 November

1978, for the 50,000 people who had surged through the gates, the make-up of international cricket changed. Within a few months the Australian Cricket Board's losses were so alarming they were glad to negotiate a truce.

In Marsh's absence, Kevin John Wright, born in North Fremantle, had his big chance. An alert, fast-footed redhead, he filled in for Marsh in the West Australian XI from his debut in 1974–75, but moved to South Australia to improve his Test prospects.

Marsh had been through an unhappy tour of England in 1977 when the rebels played alongside establishment loyalists, and on his return saw the Australian Board appoint Steve Rixon to the Test team against India. Rixon appeared in all five Tests as the Board struggled to resist Packer's challenge, establishing himself as the best over-the-stumps keeper of his generation.

Steve Rixon toured the West Indies in 1977–78 and dismissed 13 batsmen in the Tests. He later joined rebels in South Africa, and after he retired coached New South Wales successfully.

Rixon, born in the border town of Albury in 1954, played for Waverley when he first moved to Sydney and later with Western Suburbs and Sutherland. He was regarded as Marsh's deputy after Taber retired in the seasons leading up to the WSC revolt and it was no surprise when he was picked to play in the Australian teams captained by Bob Simpson in Marsh's absence with WSC. Rixon's batting proved a bonus. He made 50 in the second Test against India and, when Australia needed 341 to win in the second innings, helped clinch victory with a timely 23.

The 22 dismissals Rixon executed in that series won him a tour of the West Indies in 1977-78 and he had 13 victims in the series. His 54 and 39 not out in the Georgetown Test was a major contribution to Australia's win. But on the Australians' return home the establishment selectors dropped Rixon and brought in John

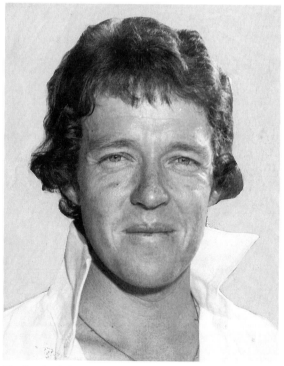

Kevin Wright, who held Marsh's place in the Australian team during the two seasons of the Packer revolt, appeared in 10 successive Tests. Wright was born in Western Australia, but played for South Australia.

Maclean, whom they named vice-captain to Graham Yallop, a punishing left-hand batsman. Burly, ruddy-faced Maclean proved a bonny fighter in the Marsh mould but at 32 appeared past his best. Selectors made him the scapegoat for Australia's disappointing displays and replaced him and Geoff Dymock for the last two Tests against Mike Brearley's England team.

Kevin Wright took over as Australia's keeper for the fifth and sixth Tests against England and retained the job for 10 successive Tests, a sequence which included two matches against Pakistan in 1978-79 and six against India in India in 1979-80. Wright had fashioned a splendid record for South Australia and handled Test cricket with impressive composure. He took six catches in his initial Test and stumped Gooch with a thrilling alertness in the following Test. His two Tests against Pakistan yielded 14 more catches.

In India, Wright batted high in the order for a keeper and in the fourth Test at Delhi made 55 not out. His 14 dismissals in the six Tests did not save him, however, when the Australians returned home to find the Packer rebellion settled. Hilditch, Wood, Yardley and Wright all lost their places in the Australian team and despite some splendid batting for South Australia Wright could not regain his Australian team spot. In 1981, when Australia toured England with the Packer recruits all available, Rixon went as Marsh's deputy.

Marsh accepted 54 catches and scored a century, 103 not out, in WSC's 'Super Tests', and kept wicket for Australia in all 16 of these matches. He did not make a stumping in tense cricket (in which pace bowlers ripped into opposing batsmen's protective equipment) that attracted crowds after a miserable first year. None of his runs or dismissals for WSC count in his first-class averages, an injustice cricket administrators should correct.

Spectators found Marsh just as fearless in his headlong dives for catches, but his batting appeared to have slipped in his time with WSC. He could cut as savagely as he had always done, and bang drives back over the bowler's head just as dramatically, but he was more prone to edging balls outside his off-stump. But as the New Zealanders found at the WACA in 1980-81 when Marsh hit 91 in the second Test, he could still make bowlers work hard for his wicket.

Marsh's instinctive loyalty to his mates helped bring his retirement in January 1984, at the age of 36. Greg Chappell retired during the fifth Test against Pakistan in Sydney after passing Bradman's 6,996 mark to become Australia's highest run-getter in Tests. Lillee followed him the same night, and after Australia had won Marsh joined them, rather than hold on, with the Australian captaincy beckoning.

The three had begun their Test careers together after Australia sustained her worst defeat in losing four–nil to South Africa. Each had set records that transformed their country's fortunes, Rodney Marsh with a unique mix of combativeness and ebullience that overcame a physique unsuited to cricket. He was uplifting to watch as he hammered his way to 11,607 first-class runs, but it will be as a keeper of unsurpassed endeavour that he will be remembered. He was the greatest catcher the wicket-keeping dodge has known.

Marsh shows his mauled hands after keeping to the fearsome pace bowling of Lillee and Thomson. He often played with broken or badly damaged fingers.

14

The Health Advocate

On the field Alan Philip Eric Knott was nimble-footed, quick-witted, with lightning-fast reactions to support his flair for improvisation. Spectators were bemused by his calisthenics behind the stumps, unaware that his quest for supple limbs, cool fingers and fast reflexes began just after daybreak in his hotel room with the English physiotherapist. Every item Knott wore was carefully chosen from the padding inside his gloves to the flannel and vest inside his shirt that absorbed sweat, to the boots he had specially made by a Northants craftsman, with studs of just the right length.

Knott changed his clothing and showered at every interval, existed on a diet of fruit and milk, and was careful about how he disposed of spent chewing-gum, usually in an old stump hole. He was almost paranoid about stiff muscles and fingers and in his half-hour daily warm-up put his hands under hot water or sat with them between his knees. His pads had to have four straps instead of three, his trousers had to have tight seats, his shirt cuffs were taped with plaster if the buttons were too tight. Around the England team's hotels he was permanently suspicious of draughts and wind changes. Originally, he sported a cap, but changed to a more comfortable floppy hat after injuring his neck in a crash at Brands Hatch racing track.

Following these guidelines Knott seldom missed a Test and fashioned a record of 269 dismissals in 95 Tests, figures that have only been bettered by Rod Marsh. In all first-class matches he executed 1,344 dismissals. With the bat, he scored 18,105 first-class runs with 17 centuries and 97 fifties at the handy average of 29.63. In Tests he made 4,389 runs with five hundreds and 30 fifties at an average of 32.75.

Impressive though these statistics are, they could have been vastly improved if Knott, the dedicated family man, had not twice opted to take an increase in pay. He had two seasons with Kerry Packer's World Series Cricket and later joined the rebel tour of South Africa, which virtually ended his career because of the three-year ban on him playing Test cricket that resulted. None of his achievements in these two ventures is included in his first-class figures.

Knott may have been considered eccentric, but among wicket-keepers that is not unusual, and for two decades he gave pleasure to millions of cricket fans around the world. He was a tremendous crowd-pleaser in Australia, despite the regularity with which he frustrated Australia's Test efforts. The sight of him diving and swivelling to bring off remarkable catches or stumpings disclosed a man of astounding dexterity. His surprising virtue, however, was his sometimes unorthodox expertise with the bat. His 106 not out at Adelaide in January 1975, against Lillee and Thomson at their best, remains one of the finest knocks by a keeper in the game's history. In this match Knott joined Les Ames as only the second England keeper to score a Test century against Australia and Godfrey Evans as the second England keeper to pass 200 Test dismissals. Australia won the match by 163 runs but Knott took the honours.

An Alan Knott special—he dives to his right to bring off a spectacular catch to dismiss Dilip Sardesai in the 1971 England v. India Test at Lord's.

Of the 66 players who joined World Series Cricket, Marsh, Knott, Deryck Murray, Richie Robinson, Dennis Yagmich and Ross Edwards all had wicket-keeping experience, although Edwards had forsaken the job for a spot in the covers. Yagmich had dismissed 86 batsmen (73 caught, 13 stumped) in three seasons with South Australia. Kerry Packer's failure to get the Australian Cricket Board to include their performances in the WSC Super Tests, when the 1977–78 dispute was settled, meant dismissals and runs gathered in tense, high-quality matches were not included in their career statistics. Similarly, Knott's feats on the rebel tour of South Africa in 1982 were excluded from his figures. It's an absurd situation, considering that

figures for Oxford and Cambridge University matches, which are about the standard of Melbourne and Sydney third-grade matches, are included in players' averages.

Knott was born at Belvedere, Kent, on 9 April 1946 and grew up in the family home at nearby Erith. His father was the keeper for Belvedere and Alan watched their matches from the age of four. He was forced to make a keen study of the game when Belvedere appointed him their scorer and this encouraged his dad to practise with him and his brother Francis in their back garden. Alan went to Northumberland Heath Secondary Modern School but was too small to play in the first XI. He was desperately keen on a future in cricket but his teachers warned him of the dangers of forsaking his studies in the belief he could make a living playing cricket.

At the indoor nets in Eltham he met Claude Lewis, the Kent county coach, who advised him to bowl spinners. Lewis showed him the grips and promised him sixpence every time Alan bowled him. When Knott presented himself at the Kent selection trials they signed him on as an outstanding batting prospect and off-spin bowler.

His first chance to appear for Kent came in a match for the Club and Ground against Aylesford when selectors surprised him by asking him to keep. He dropped the only chance that came his way, off a bowler named Derek Underwood, but they were both chosen shortly afterwards against an army team at Chatham and Knott made three stumpings. In his debut for the Kent XI Godfrey Evans' deputy Derek Ufton kept wicket and captained the team.

The chance of Knott becoming Kent's keeper looked forlorn with Ufton secure in the role once Evans retired and Tony Catt established as Ufton's substitute. Bowling off-spinners seemed Knott's future. Then at the start of the 1964 season Ufton decided to concentrate on a career in soccer and Catt migrated to South Africa.

Kent gave Knott his chance behind the stumps against Cambridge University at Folkestone. The South African Stuart Leary, who in 10 seasons with Charlton scored 153 goals, drove him to the match in his Jaguar. Knott made the winning hit in the last over of an exciting match. He kept wicket all that season, using a signal pre-arranged with leg-spin and googly bowler Ted Fillary, who went back to his mark and turned anti-clockwise for his leg-break and clockwise for his googly.

He survived the first summer despite a rough pitch against Northants where he conceded a lot of byes, three successive ducks, including one against Yorkshire, and a match against Australia at Canterbury. Northants' Keith Andrew, Yorkshire's Jimmy Binks and Australian Wally Grout gave him models to contemplate.

Andrew pointed out that he had conceded more byes than Knott and added: 'It's wickets that count—not byes'. Supported by a brilliant cordon of close-in fieldsmen, Phil Sharpe, Brian Close, John Hampshire and Fred Trueman, Binks showed why Yorkshiremen ranked him the best keeper in England. Quick to spot batsmen's lapses, Binks was on his way to a remarkable 412 successive county matches, a keeper who debunked the notion that Englishmen play too much cricket. As Yorkshire loyalists argue, if you call down any pit shaft for a skilled bowler or batsmen, one will come up in the next cage. Binks, Don Brennan, Roy Booth (Worcestershire), Terry Gunn (Sussex) and Paul Gibb (Essex), all Yorkshire-born, proved the surplus applied to keepers.

After 10 matches in his initial first-class summer, Knott realised his opportunities were thrilling. He had come into big cricket as the old interchange of international tours by teams that spent weeks at sea had passed. Airlines took tourists to places where national teams that could challenge England and Australia were eager for visitors.

At the end of that first summer Knott went to the Caribbean with the Cavaliers, the team his Kent predecessor Godfrey Evans helped organise, with help from stage stars Ernie Wise and Harry Secombe. Evans repaid careful study. His immense strength made Knott feel puny, and even in his mature years Evans was still flinging himself at apparently hopeless chances after hours in the tropical sun.

On that trip Knott kept wicket to Trevor Bailey and Freddie Trueman on faster pitches than he had ever experienced and faced the subtle repertoire of Jim Laker, veteran of 46 Tests and seven successive county championships with Surrey. He listened to advice from team-mates and opponents alike and returned to Kent knowing he had to become physically stronger and how important were even the smallest details in equipment and technique.

The multiplying challenges of international cricket took him to Pakistan in 1966–67 with an England Under 25 team managed by his county idol Les Ames. This was his first official tour. He was 20 years old. On pitches like billiard tables they played seven first-class matches in 34 days, carefully watching every item of food and unable to drink water. He soon learned that fieldsmen who had to go off to primitive, improvised toilets were easier to replace than keepers, who were forced to endure discomfort to avoid the shedding of pads, box and gloves.

At Peshawar he opened the batting with the team captain Mike Brearley against Northern Zone following an injury to Neal Abberley. He surprised even admirers of his sound strokeplay by scoring his initial first-class century, 101 out of an opening stand of 208. Brearley continued to score 312 in a day's play and England's total of 4 for 514 was the highest ever in Pakistan. Brearley hit 41 fours and three sixes, which completely overshadowed Knott's display.

This splendid performance for England's Under 25 side set Knott on his way to Test selection. The tour gave him a chance to study the keeping of Pakistan's brilliant young keeper Wasim Bari, a wiry, loose-limbed cricketer who retained his zest through the hottest days. Again he was impressed by the physical strength of an opponent, and the observation made him more determined than ever to match the fitness of players like Wasim by applying himself to a rigorous daily calisthenics program.

The following English summer Wasim made his Test debut at Edgbaston in the three-Test rubber against England. Knott's Test debut came in the next Test at Trent Bridge. Wasim made a big impression at his baptism, dismissing three batsmen in a rain-interrupted draw. Knott had a victim in his first hour, catching Billy Ibadulla off Ken Higgs. He dropped Asif Iqbal off Basil D'Oliviera but was relieved when this proved inexpensive. Three catches in all in his first innings of Test keeping, plus four catches in the second innings, helped Knott hold his place and give England a win. Another six victims in the third Test at The Oval and 28 runs with the bat enabled him to resist challenges from proficient county keepers like John Murray and Bob Taylor.

Knott's special acumen handling county colleague Derek Underwood's brisk left-arm spinners was rewarded by selectors, who took Knott to the West Indies early in 1968, but they preferred Jim Parks in the first three Tests because of his batting potential. Knott returned for the last two Tests and immediately proved the selectors

A splendid Patrick Eagar shot of the brilliant Pakistani keeper Wasim Bari. Bari fails in a bid to run out Dennis Ammiss in 1974 against England at The Oval.

Another Patrick Eagar shot of Wasim Bari, this time as he dives full length to catch Basil d'Oliviera, one of his world record of eight catches against England at Leeds in 1971.

were wrong for viewing his batting suspiciously with a fine 69 not out, England pulling off a surprise win by seven wickets. That was enough to win the series despite brilliant batting by Garfield Sobers and Clive Lloyd.

Knott retained his place in all five Tests for the 1968 series in England against Australia, enhancing his growing reputation with 13 victims. His understanding with Underwood continued as a bonus to England's attack in a drawn series. His major coup came off Ray Illingworth, however, in the fourth Test at Headingley when he stumped Cowper, Sheahan and Jarman.

He was cheated of his first Test century in March 1969, at Karachi, when a mob stampeded on to the field just before lunch on the third day.

He was on 96 not out, but the rioters bearing banners could not be dispersed and play had to be abandoned. England were on 7 for 502 at that stage and Wasim had not missed a chance for Pakistan. By averaging 68.25 in his seven matches on a tour marred by frequent demonstrations, Knott earned promotion in the batting order.

When the West Indies toured England in 1969, Knott batted in the middle of the order in all three Tests. At the end of the season *Wisden* voted him one of the Five Cricketers of the Year. By then he had become a tremendous crowd favourite, always active, whether behind the stumps or batting, and training regularly with Charlton Athletic soccer club. Spectators had grown familiar with his trademarks, the buttoned shirt

New Zealand's outstanding keeper Ken Wadsworth behind the stumps as he watches Alvin Kallicharan miss with an attempted sweep in a Test against the West Indies.

collar to protect his neck from the sun, the sleeves rolled down to prevent him skinning his elbows as he dived for catches. His first three seasons of Test cricket had brought 58 dismissals and 666 runs.

Kenneth John Wadsworth kept wicket for New Zealand in the three Tests that immediately followed the series against the West Indies. Wadsworth remained New Zealand's regular keeper for 33 Tests and when he died of cancer at the age of 29 he probably had not reached his potential. In his six Tests in England he dismissed 17 batsmen, and in a first-class career involving all the cricket nations he sent back 291 batsmen (265 caught, 26 stumped). A tall, blond man of very powerful build, Wadsworth was a pugnacious

right-hand batsman who scored 3,664 runs at 25.62 with two centuries. He preferred to stand back when keeping.

Australia first saw Knott in 1970–71 when England won an acrimonious series extended to seven Tests after a washout in Melbourne. Knott's keeping to Illingworth's off-spin and the left-arm spin of Underwood worried the Australians as much as John Snow's barrage of bouncers. Knott also contributed valuable runs, averaging 31.71 in the Tests and 44.91 on the full tour.

He met Bert Oldfield in Sydney. Bert gave him a pair of gloves from his sports store and advised him to persevere with his exercises. Their conversation got down to fingerstalls and the avoidance of injuries, vital to all keepers. At 73, Oldfield was in the midst of negotiations with Haile Selassie, Emperor of Ethiopia, for a team of Australian schoolboys to play in Addas Abbaba, a most unlikely cricket venue, with the Lion Of Judah holding court to teenagers.

Knott had to resist a strong challenge from Bob Taylor for his Test spot in this memorable series. Australian experts believed England had never been represented by two such distinguished keepers. Knott supported his fast bowlers with remarkable agility standing back and held 21 catches in the 10 Australian innings in the rubber, as well as stumping two batsmen. He also had the satisfaction of stumping Ian Chappell, an acknowledged master of good footwork, three times on the tour. Taylor looked the more polished of England's keepers standing up and was rewarded with a Test in New Zealand.

Knott made his first Test century at Auckland thanks to three dropped catches. He batted 180 minutes for 101 and hit 11 fours and one six. He reached 1,000 Test runs in this knock, his 37th in 25 Tests, and went on to 2,000 runs in his 43rd Test after 66 innings, and 3,000 runs in his 66th Test after 102 innings. He later became the first keeper to score more than 4,000 Test runs and secure 200 dismissals, finishing with 4,389 runs in 95 Tests (149 innings).

By comparison his arch rival in the Australian team, Rod Marsh, reached 1,000 runs in his 33rd innings after 23 Tests, 2,000 runs in his 64th Test innings after 43 Tests, and 3,000 runs in his 118th innings in his 75th Test. Marsh's 100th Test dismissal came in his 29th Test, his 200th in his 54th Test, and 300th in his 84th Test.

Knott scored more than 1,000 runs twice in an English season, and dismissed six batsmen in an innings seven times, six of them playing for Kent. At Maidstone in 1977 he sent back nine batsmen in the match against Leicestershire. His many successes with the bat included 127 not out and 118 not out for Kent against Surrey at Maidstone in 1972, and his courageous century against Australia.

Knott breaks the stumps as Australia's Ashley Mallett scrambles home in the Leeds Test in 1977.

Victorian Richie Robinson, Rod Marsh's deputy on the 1977 tour of England, has a ball cut from his gloves, and (*overleaf*) Wayne Phillips suffers a similar fate in England in 1985.

These statistics, impressive as they are, convey little of the high appeal of Knott the man, a cricketer who waved happily to the spectator on the SCG Hill who, after watching his loosening up routine yelled: 'I'll buy a pogo stick, Knott'. He made six overseas tours in all with England and four others on coaching ventures or with the Cavaliers. For some of these trips he and Derek Underwood were inseparable.

On his second big Australian tour in 1974-75 (he played twice for Tasmania on a 1969-70 coaching trip), Knott remained defiant as Lillee and Thomson battered Mike Denness' batsmen. He made 51 in the second Test, 52 in the third, 82 in the fourth and his captivating undefeated century in the fifth Test, notable feats in a team beaten four-nil. By then he had devised an array of defensive strokes and scoring dabs to combat head-high deliveries, often leaping high with the bat up around his collarbone but under control.

His technique defied coaching creeds, but was enormously effective. When he joined Packer's WSC he had plenty of chances to improve it facing Lillee, Thomson, Joel Garner, Colin Croft, Michael Holding, Garth Le Roux, Wayne Daniel, Mike Proctor and Imran Khan. He regained his place in the England team after the Packer settlement, batting like a contortionist. He faced pace without backing away, using his bat like a wand, but the edges opponents expected did not come and he stayed batting with bold improvisation right to the end.

In Knott's time at the top, international cricket's expansion brought forth some fine keepers from unexpected sources. Farokh Meneksha Engineer, a dashing Parsee, emerged as one of the world's best keepers, a man who revelled in flicking off the bails, diving sideways, and quickly disposing of the ball. From his debut for Combined Indian Universities in 1958 until he hung up his gloves after 18 years in first-class cricket that took him from Bombay to a contract with Lancashire, 'Rocky' Engineer dismissed 824 batsmen (703 caught, 121 stumped) and fully deserved his big benefit cheque from Lancashire fans.

India's selectors supported his brash, flamboyant approach to keeping with an unprecedented move during the 1971 England tour. The Indians arrived with Pollamani Kirshnamurthy, who kept in all five Tests in the West Indies in 1970-71, and Syed Mutjaba Hussein Kirmani as their nominal keepers. Neither played in the Tests because Lancashire agreed to release Engineer from his county contract for the Tests.

Batting with flair and unorthodoxy, Engineer scored a career total of 13,436 first-class runs at 29.52, with 13 centuries, a performance well short of Ames' record but highly impressive considering he had 258 fewer games than Ames' 593. He made his highest score, 192, for the Rest of the World at Hobart in 1971-72, rescuing an injury-riddled outfit with his cheery nature and versatility. He opened the batting or went in near the tail and gloved the fireballs from Le Roux and Croft with the same competence he had for the spin of Bedi and Intikhab.

The artistic Kirmani, Engineer's long-time understudy, was a teenage prodigy who rose from the slums of Madras and Mysore to dismiss more Test batsmen than any other Indian keeper. He deputised for Engineer on the 1971 and 1974 England tours and in the 1975 World Cup competition, after gaining experience on an Indian schoolboy tour of England. He had to wait until his 27th year before making his Test debut against New Zealand at Auckland in 1975-76. His glovework passed a severe test handling Prasanna's off-spin. He did not figure in any of Prasanna's 11 dismissals, but was a constant threat up on the stumps to Prasanna, Chandrasekhar and Venkataraghavan.

Kirmani was rewarded in the second Test a week later in Christchurch when he equalled the then world record of six dismissals in an innings—five caught, one stumped. In the third Test, at Wellington, he had four victims in New Zealand's only innings and made 49 in a 116-run stand with Brijesh Patel.

He wore a wig through the late 1970s and, with team-mates teasing him with the nickname 'Kerry Packer', Kirmani kept going until his 37th year. He played for 11 years after Engineer retired and in 42 more Tests. He made his highest Test score, 102, against England at Bombay in 1984-85 in a record seventh wicket 235-run partnership with Ravi Shastri which led to India winning by eight wickets. He also hit 101 not out against Australia at Bombay in the sixth Test of the 1979-80 series

Syed Kirmani, one of India's great keepers, dives to his left to take a brilliant catch which dismissed David Gower at Old Trafford in a World Cup match.

which India won two–nil. Spectators giggled at his shining bald head in Australia in 1977–78 when he scored 411 runs at 41.10 with a best score of 59 not out, and kept wicket with brisk efficiency.

Kirmani's worst lapse in form came in the 1978–79 rubber against Pakistan and as a result he was omitted from the 1979 England tour. However, he bounced back in 1979–80 for another successful Australian tour. He had his finest series in 1981–82 against England when he did not concede a bye in three Tests in which England scored 1,964 runs.

Kiran More took over from Kirmani in 1986. A small, nuggety keeper from Baroda with the impressive speed of movement of Kirmani and Engineer, he served his apprenticeship as Kirmani's understody on the 1985–86 five-match Australian tour, when he made 35 not out against Victoria in his only appearance, and dismissed two batsmen.

Since he was given the Test job More has proved an admirable keeper facing spin and does his best work standing right up on the stumps, a keeper of strikingly different technique to the acrobatic Murray or the agile Pakistani Saleem Yousuf, whose job involved lots of sideways diving to reach wide snicks from positions well back from the stumps. Saleem Yousuf's hands have to withstand severe pounding from Wasim Akram and Waqar Younis. His relief comes in taking Pakistan's spinners, but they in turn make big demands on his concentration, which must remain sharp despite intense heat and howling mobs ready to hoot mistakes.

New Zealand keeper Ian David Stockley Smith reacted to noisy crowds with some spirited displays on the 1990–91 tour of Pakistan. Smith took over as New Zealand's first-choice keeper on the 1981–82 Australian tour and impressed experts in England in 1983. He followed Kiwi keepers Ken James (423 dismissals), Eric Tindall (119), Frank Mooney (213), Eric Petrie (231), 'Art' Dick (169), John Ward (257), Ian Colquhon (136), 'Jock' Edwards (142) and Warren Lees (235), who all had more than 100 first-class victims.

Lees had the difficult task of following Ken Wadsworth into the New Zealand Test team, but impressed on his first overseas trip in 1976–77 in Pakistan and India. Chasing 565, New Zealand were 5 for 104 against Pakistan at Karachi when Lees produced his first Test century, 152, sharing a 186-stand with Richard Hadlee. This was the innings in which Imran Khan became the first bowler to be banned from bowling for persistent intimidation after both umpires warned him against his surfeit of bouncers. Lees made valuable contributions to the 1979 New Zealand team's climb to the semi-finals of the World Cup as a player. His studious approach to big cricket earned him the job as coach to the New Zealand Test squad, and in the 1992 World Cup his innovative tactics, brilliantly executed by Martin

Alan Knott's great rival, Bob Taylor, avoiding flying bails against New Zealand at Trent Bridge in 1984. Taylor's catching for Derbyshire bowlers Brian Jackson and Harold Rhodes was similar to the Lillee-Marsh partnership.

New Zealand keeper Warren Lees, New Zealand's first choice keeper in the early 1980s, finds himself run out in the Test against England at The Oval as a Cowan throw hits the stumps.

Crowe, again took New Zealand to the semi-finals. Here New Zealand had cruel luck when Martin Crowe pulled a muscle and was forced to use a runner, only to be run-out when the runners confused their signals. To add to New Zealand's disappointment over losing their chance to reach the final by beating Pakistan Ian Smith announced his retirement. Smith finished with 176 dismissals (168 caught, 8 stumped) from 63 Tests and a career total of 456 first-class victims (417 caught, 36 stumped). His place in the New Zealand team was taken by Auckland-born Adam Parore, who began by dismissing five batsmen against England in the Auckland Test in 1991–92 and repeating that feat by dismissing five Sri Lankan batsmen in the Test at Colombo in 1992–93. This commendable start was interrupted when he was injured at practice while preparing for the second Test against Australia in New Zealand in March 1993, a ball from pace bowler Danny Morrison striking him in the eye. This forced the New Zealand selectors to recall Tony Blain, who had last played Test cricket in 1986, and install him as the New Zealand keeper.

15

The Packer Influence

The two-year Packer revolt brought profound changes to cricket at a time when schoolmasters across Australia were also reshaping their attitudes. Packer accelerated the development of one-day matches, at the expense of Sheffield Shield cricket, and teachers said they could no longer be burdened with coaching cricket and football teams as part of their employment.

District cricket clubs found they could not rely on frequent appearances by their Test players because of the packed limited-over and international tour schedule. Deprived of a flow of talent from the schools, grade clubs fielded teams of youngsters no longer inspired by playing alongside a Morris, an O'Reilly or a Grout. Standards slumped in the clubs, crowds declined for Shield matches and Test cricket itself appeared threatened.

In the first 10 years after the Packer dispute was settled, the Australian Cricket Board distributed more than $20 million to state associations, which in turn poured funds into their member clubs. There was little discernible sign at state training squad practices that the money produced better cricketers. Test players enjoyed higher pay but they often flopped on tour and lacked the exciting flair of the Bradmans, McCabes, Oldfields and others who overcame hardships in comparatively impoverished years.

To correct the problem and guarantee a regular supply of Test players, the ACB opened the Australian Cricket Academy in Adelaide in 1988. The idea was that the states should send their most promising youngsters for a year or more of intensive coaching. They spent at least five hours a day at practice nets under the John Creswell Stand at Adelaide Oval and were accommodated together at a Henley Beach dormitory, where they were also expected to continue studying for exams or prepare for a trade or professional career. The scheme costs more than $500,000 a year and is funded jointly by the federal government, the South Australian Cricket Association, the ACB and the Commonwealth Bank.

Victorian Jack Potter, who toured England in 1964 in the Australian team, was the first head coach. The first scholarship winners included two wicket-keepers: Darren Berry, born at Wonthaggi in Victoria, where he began with the local Rovers club before joining Fitzroy–Doncaster in Melbourne; and Peter Drinnen, recruited by the Queensland Cricket Association from Bundaberg after an exciting start in schools cricket. In 1990, record-busting keeper Rod Marsh took over as the academy's chief coach.

The academy opened in the same year that Gregory Charles Dyer from the Western Suburbs club in Sydney was sacked as Australia's keeper, following a controversial catch in the Melbourne Test which saw New Zealander Andrew Jones depart. Dyer appeared set for a long international career after dismissing 24 batsmen in six Tests and helping Australia win the World Cup in India. He was popular and competent with the bat and behind the stumps, a sportsmanlike figure with dark, thinning hair and a flourishing moustache, who had fitted into the Test team well.

Dyer dived forward to reach a snick from Jones

and when he thought he had reached it, held the ball in the air claiming a catch. Television replay showed the ball had bounced, but passed under Dyer's midriff as his body moved forward. The umpire gave Jones out, but when they studied the replays the New Zealanders were furious. New Zealand newspapers reflected the animosity that prevails in Australia–New Zealand matches by branding Dyer a cheat.

Dyer considered some of the New Zealand accusations libellous but played out the rest of the series against New Zealand and retained his job in the Test against Sri Lanka in Perth, believing the fuss would pass. At the end of the season he was stunned when Queenslander Ian Healy was preferred for Australia's tour of Pakistan.

At 29, Dyer concentrated on winning back his Test place as captain of New South Wales. However, he played only six more matches for New South Wales before the state selectors

Greg Dyer, the Sydney accountant dropped from the Australian team after a dismissal that brought charges of bad sportsmanship. Within a few weeks he was also dropped from the New South Wales side.

followed the Test panel and axed him. Officially, the end of Dyer's first-class career was blamed on loss of form but among students of the game the notion lingered that the selectors agreed with New Zealand on Dyer's ethics. For a man with 141 first-class dismissals (123 caught, 18 stumped) to be so brutally dumped appeared an injustice.

Dyer, a respected accountant, graduated to the New South Wales team from Australian Under 19 and Schoolboys teams and the New South Wales Colts. Steve Rixon, an energetic keeper in 13 Tests for Australia and 107 matches for the state, kept him out of the state team for a period but Dyer had an opportunity to return when Rixon was injured in 1983–84, and became a regular Shield player when Rixon joined the South African rebels in 1985–86. Rixon brought off many spectacular stumpings but endured frequent seasons as deputy to Rod Marsh.

Dyer enhanced his reputation when he stumped Queenslanders Andrew Courtice and Robbie Kerr in the 1985–86 Sheffield Shield final in Sydney. This display clinched a place in the Australian team that visited India in 1986 as understudy to Tim Zoehrer. Batting from a relaxed upright stance, Dyer scored his initial first-class century, 117, at Baroda against Delhi in a 175-run seventh-wicket stand with Dave Gilbert.

Dyer took Zoehrer's place for the third Test against England at Adelaide in 1986–87 and, despite early nervousness, gave an efficient display. Zoehrer held the job for the 1987 Australian visit to Sharjah, but when Australia failed to beat India, Pakistan or England on this trip, officials took a close look at Zoehrer's breaches of discipline. He did not improve his hold on the keeping job when he chased an opponent from the WACA in an abusive exchange, nor when he returned home early from New Zealand in 1985–86, claiming that he had sore eyes caused by volcanic ash.

Zoehrer was an intensely competitive young cricketer who reacted strongly to opposition sledging or spectators' jibes. He had come from a difficult upbringing in Armadale, Western Australia, and deserved sympathetic treatment from officials that unfortunately was not forthcoming. He made his debut for Western Australia in 1980–81 and, despite obvious gifts for keeping supported by consistent batting, did not secure a regular spot in the state team until 1984–85. He celebrated by dismissing 27 batsmen in seven matches, 25 caught and two stumped. He made his Test debut against New Zealand in Wellington on the 1985–86 tour.

In 1986–87 Zoehrer was fined $250 under the players' code of behaviour after the match between Western Australia and Tasmania. He appealed and Code of Behaviour commissioner Barry Gibbs upheld the fine and reprimanded Zoehrer. Since then Zoehrer has given Western Australia outstanding service despite a breach with the Perth club, who asked him to leave. He joined Midland Guildford.

Between seasons Zoehrer has had a happier time playing for Excelsior Twenty in Rotterdam as captain-coach. This venture allowed him to develop his skill as a leg-break and googly bowler and to lead Excelsior Twenty to their first premiership in 25 years. He is one of the few keepers to wear contact lenses, but in 1993 when

Tim Zoehrer, an intensely competitive cricketer who has had a few brushes with officialdom, shows the stumping style that took him to England in 1993 as Ian Healy's stand-in.

he won selection to tour England as Ian Healy's deputy he shared the honour of Australia's number-one keeper with Queenslander Peter Anderson.

Zoehrer's temperament has brought him under intense scrutiny among critics in Sydney, Melbourne, Adelaide, Hobart and Brisbane. When he was Australia's keeper, he was confronted in some of these places by spectators bearing banners advocating the selection of Greg Dyer, Michael Dimattina, Wayne Phillips and Richard Soule. Allan Border said he had to caution Zoehrer after a show of temper in a Sydney one-day match against the West Indies in February 1987.

The problems Zoehrer provided for team coach Bob Simpson were particularly unfortunate, as he appeared to have rescued the Test selectors from a long period of indecision over the keeping job following Marsh's retirement. Since Hanson Carter took over the job in December 1907, by bringing his slatted pads in his hearse to Sydney Cricket Ground, the main claimants for the job had won automatic approval and been allowed lengthy tenure to boost team spirit.

Marsh's departure saw selection of Roger Woolley, the first player chosen directly from the Tasmanian Shield side for Australia. In the role filled by the island's first captain John Marshall in 1851, and carried on by George Henry Gatehouse, Norman Dodds, Edward Arthur Pickett, Bruce Doolan and importations Cyril Parry, Len Maddocks (son of Ian) and Alan Knott, Woolley had given his state outstanding service since the 1977–78 season.

Woolley's heavy scoring with the bat gave him the chance to hold his place in the Australian team for an extended period. Indeed his innings of 88 in 1982–83 against New South Wales lifted Tasmania to 351, a total that gave Peter Clough and Michael Holding the opportunity to bowl Tasmania to a six-wicket win. In the return match Woolley made 111 not out, which lifted his aggregate for the season to 551 at 42.38. Behind the stumps he had made 42 dismissals, and his captaincy firmly established Tasmania as a force in Shield competition.

The all-round merit of Woolley's cricket gave him the edge over strong challenges from Steve Rixon, Wayne Phillips and Ray Phillips when the

Roger Woolley, the first player chosen directly from the Tasmanian team for Australia. He improved his Test chances with some consistent scoring with the bat.

Australian team for Sri Lanka was named. Woolley, born in Hobart and introduced to cricket at New Town High, made his Test debut at Kandy against Sri Lanka on 22 April 1983, excelling with a catch off Lillee and his gloving of spinners Tom Hogan and Bruce Yardley. His five catches helped Australia to a five-wicket win.

Back in Australia Woolley injured a hand, which upset his rise to permanent Test status, but he batted splendidly for 102 to set up another triumph for Tasmania over New South Wales. This innings also earned him Australia's keeping spot on the 1983–84 West Indian tour. He was the only specialist keeper on that tour but was replaced when he broke a finger by Wayne Phillips, from the Adelaide club, Sturt. Phillips

was preferred as keeper in four of the five Tests because of his superior batting, leaving Woolley bitter over his treatment by captain Kim Hughes.

'The tour of the West Indies was a waste of time for me,' Woolley said on his return home. 'I am really annoyed at some of the things Kim Hughes has said about me. An Australian captain should be behind his players, striving for team harmony. Hughes said that my breaking a finger in the second match against Guyana at Georgetown was a blessing in disguise. No captain should say that. It was very weak captaincy. I felt I was on the outer from the start and the injury did not help.'

The Australian Cricket Board did not offer Woolley a contract when the national team arrived home from the West Indies. Wayne Phillips got one but ultimately he, too, could justifiably feel he was unfairly treated, with his claims as an opening bat upset by his enforced keeping role. Free of Hughes' leadership, Woolley still believed he could force his way into the Australian side for England in 1985. When he failed to win selection, he quit keeping to concentrate on batting. He continued to bat impressively but the lack of bowling strength saw Tasmania slump to the bottom of the Shield table and he handed over the captaincy to David Boon.

Richard Eric Soule, Woolley's successor behind the stumps for Tasmania, proved a colourful personality. He had a beefy, roly-poly frame but moved to the ball smartly and his reflexes were surprisingly fast. He worked as a gardener in Launceston and took over as the Mowbray club's first XI keeper at the age of 15, quickly showing potential with his taking of the erratic West Indian speedster Franklyn Stephenson and the off-breaks of Lancashire professional Jack Simmons. Soule made his debut for Tasmania in 1983–84 at Hobart against Pakistan and became an automatic choice for his state. Selectors preferred him to the highly praised Victorian, Michael Gerard David Dimattina, for the 1984 Australian Under-19 team, and in 1987–88 he played for the Prime Minister's XI in Canberra against New Zealand. Soule has since been replaced in the Tasmanian team by Jim Holyman, who in turn lost his place to Mark Atkinson from Sydney's Western Suburbs who went south to further his big cricket ambitions.

Dimattina began his cricket with Marcellin College in Melbourne, developing later with the Ringwood club and in junior development classes organised by the Victorian Cricket Association. He played his initial match for Victoria in 1983–84 and in 1985–86 toured Zimbabwe with the Emerging Australian side. His keeping was consistent and stylish but he was less impressive with the bat in 69 appearances in the Victorian team. He dismissed 193 batsmen (172 caught, 21 stumped) and scored 1,516 runs at 21.36, top score his sole century (113) v. South Australia in Melbourne in 1988–89.

Dimattina was only 29 when selectors ended his first-class career and brought in Australian Cricket Academy graduate Darren Berry, apparently believing Berry could make a more valuable contribution to Victoria's innings than a man who had scored only three fifties. Berry had developed quickly in Victoria's Under 16 XI under coach Doug Rundle and had gone into the South Australian team for a season in 1989–90 after his Cricket Academy year. He returned to Melbourne when his father died and immediately settled in the Victorian team, holding some spectacular catches. At 20, he oozed promise, but competition for higher honours was tough.

In Queensland, for example, three skilled keepers duelled for the state XI job, Ian Healy, the plucky Australian team incumbent, long-legged Peter Anderson, and Peter Drinnen, a Bundaberg product recruited to the Australian Cricket Academy. Healy has been too successful to oust when he is available for Queensland, having secured his 100th victim in his 33rd Test in 1990–91 against India, although there are many sound judges in Queensland who consider Anderson a superior keeper.

Anderson, born in 1961, has been in and out of the Queensland team since 1983 when he established himself as Ray Phillips' understudy. He realised he had to wait for Phillips' retirement just as Grout, Maclean and Phillips had to be patient about their chances. In 1984, with Phillips still in the job, he considered moving to Western Australia to fill the gap left by Marsh's retirement, but a publicised transfer to the west by South Australia's Wayne Phillips frustrated that scheme.

Ray Phillips was the keeper who shed his pads for one-day matches, believing that they hindered his mobility. He wore hockey-style shin pads inside his trousers, a move Rodney Marsh had advocated but never put into practice.

Anderson finally made his debut for Queensland in a one-day match against Tasmania in Hobart in 1984, after Phillips had played in 58 successive Shield matches and 31 one-day matches. He had barely got used to the Queensland cap when he broke a finger in January 1987 in a Shield match against South Africa. This allowed Healy, who had challenged him for the most promising keeper's label since their teens, to play his first match for Queensland. But when the finger mended Anderson returned and made 25 dismissals with 21 catches and four stumpings in a gratifying initial Shield season.

Pressing his Australian team claims with a steady flow of runs in the middle order, Anderson had a further setback when he broke a thumb standing up to the stumps for Ian Botham in Perth in January 1988. Healy, born in the Brisbane suburb of Spring Hill in 1964 and nurtured by Brisbane's Northern Suburbs club, needed no second chance. He held the Queensland job for the rest of the season and when Anderson recovered selectors decided he lacked match practice.

Then in a shock selection Healy won a place in the Australian team to tour Pakistan in 1988–89 after only six first-class matches. Healy was the only keeper who made the tour. Relegated by a player three years his junior, Anderson contemplated retirement but instead opted to accept an offer to play in South Australia. 'If Healy is a better keeper than Anderson, he must be exceptional,' said South Australian captain David Hookes.

Anderson missed selection in the 1989 Australian team to England when Zoehrer went as Healy's deputy. This disappointment ended his desire to stay in Adelaide and he heeded his wife's pleas to return to their Brisbane home. On his return he found Drinnen established as Queensland's keeper and sporting 10 catches and an average of more than 50 from three Shield matches. Drinnen had been voted Country Cricketer of the Year after the 1986–87 season and had resisted invitations to play in South Australia after his year with the Australian Cricket Academy. Anderson had to content himself as player-coach for Easts in Brisbane.

Adrian Murrell's wonderful shot of West Indian keeper Jeffrey Dujon in action in the 1985 Pyjama Game final at Melbourne. Dujon thrilled Australians on all his three tours there.

Meanwhile Healy has had a season as Queensland's captain and become familiar in international cricket for his plucky middle-order batting and his acrobatic catches from nicks induced by Merv Hughes and Craig McDermott. He has dropped a few of these hot chances but he has also snared some gems moving wide on the leg side or towards first slip. His skill against spinners, the attribute that originally won him a place when Peter Sleep, Tim May and Peter Taylor were in the Australian team, brings out the best in him. His association with Shane Warne has yielded dramatic stumpings and established them as a threat to any international batsman.

After claiming his 100th Test victim by dismissing Kapil Dev in the third Test against India in 1991–92, Healy came under a similar cloud to Greg Dyer in the first Test against the West Indies in Brisbane in 1992–93. Brian Lara jumped down the pitch to drive Greg Matthews and missed. Healy fumbled the ball, which bounced in front of him. With Lara stranded by his inability to turn quickly in rubbers, Healy dived forward and cuffed the ball at the stumps. The bails fell and Lara was given out, but television replays showed the ball had passed outside the leg stump and that it was Healy's glove that dislodged the bails. The decision aroused widespread debate among millions of viewers but replays showed the umpire who had given the decision when his vision was obscured was to blame, not Healy's poor sportsmanship.

That West Indian tour showed how difficult it often is to replace outstanding Test keepers. Jeffrey Dujon, 38, took a rest after a long career during which he gave team-mates entertaining batting and some distinguished keeping, particularly in support of day-long fast bowling. Dujon, a product of Collyer's School in Kingston, Jamaica, entered first-class cricket in 1975 and made his international debut with tours of Zimbabwe and Australia in 1981–82. He made 104 not out against New South Wales in Sydney and played some dashing limited-over innings studded with strong drives and hooks. A lean, spare figure, he returned to Australia on Test tours in 1984–85 and 1988–89.

Dujon was still a significant force on Australia's 1990–91 West Indian tour and retired from Test cricket after touring England in the northern summer of 1991. He had played in 81 Tests, 23 against Australia and 23 against England, and dismissed 272 batsmen. Significantly in a team entirely dependent on pace bowlers, only five of his victims were stumped. Dujon made five centuries in his 3,321 runs at 31.93.

The West Indies brought David Williams and Junior Randolph Murray to Australia for the 1992–93 Tests against Australia. Early on the tour Murray lacked confidence following a couple of blunders, but by the end of the tour he had firmly established his place in the West Indies team with some superb catches. He is brimful of enthusiasm, blessed with a long reach in his windmill-like arms, whereas Williams is very small and a novice facing spin with the bat.

Healy has shown himself to be a splendid tourist, eager to join in the team drills set by coach Bob Simpson. He spends a lot of time out of the nets gathering the ball over one stump while team-mates practice their throwing. He has handled unusual conditions in Sri Lanka, India and New Zealand well.

The Sri Lankans have had difficulty settling on a regular keeper in their limited period in first-class cricket. Perhaps the best of them was Hettiarachige Mahes Goonatilleke, who proved quick and stylish on his first overseas tour in 1975–76 in India. He was born in Kandy and is a product of St Anthony's College, but was not chosen in one-day matches after appearing in five of Sri Lanka's early Tests. S.A.R. Silva, known as 'Amal', held the job for nine Tests and accounted for 33 batsmen. He was a very handy batsman, with two Test centuries to his credit—102 not out at Lord's against England in 1984 and 111 at Colombo in 1985–86 against India. Since Silva departed in 1988 Sri Lanka have used H.P. Tillekeratne (13 Tests), R.S. Kalvwitharne (two Tests) and A.M. de Silva (one Test) behind the stumps.

For a country with a tradition of long-serving keepers, England has picked a bewildering array of keepers for Tests in recent years. Paul Downton, son of a noted club cricketer in the Seven Oaks region who played eight first-class games for Kent in 1948 as wicket-keeper, followed Alan Knott into the Kent and England sides after graduating from Exeter University. He was an athletic keeper in the Rod Marsh mould, but he lost his place on

Ian Botham leaps in expectation but England keeper Paul Downton dropped this chance from Allan Border at Old Trafford in 1985.

the 1981 Australian tour of England when he dropped a vital catch in the Trent Bridge Test.

David Bairstow, a chunky redhead with infectious enthusiasm, came from a long line of Yorkshire keepers. He played for his county while still a schoolboy and appeared destined for as long a spell in the Yorkshire XI as Arthur Wood, who played first-class cricket for the 20 years from 1928 to 1948 and claimed he was always at his best in a crisis. Like Wood, who figured in the all-conquering Yorkshire sides of the 1930s, Bairstow had only four Tests.

Bairstow was flown to Australia as a replacement in 1978–79 when Roger Tolchard, the Devon-born Leicestershire all-rounder, was hurt. Bairstow lacked polish but he fitted well into the England limited-over sides because of his batting. He played in the Centenary Test against Australia at Lord's, but his untidiness finally caught up with him at Bridgetown against the West Indies in 1981. Dropped from the England team, he continued to score well in county cricket and in 1981 became the first Yorkshire keeper since Arthur Wood to score 1,000 runs in a season. He appeared later for Griqualand West in South Africa.

Since Ted Dexter took over as England's chief selector and guardian of the Test team's fortunes, England have experimented more with keepers who could be relied on to score heavily with the bat. Mickey Stewart, the high-scoring Surrey right-hand batsman of the 1960s who became the England team manager, has seen his son Alec handle this chore well. Alec Stewart is no Tallon or Knott, but in a beaten side in India and Sri Lanka in 1993 he made a favourable impression in his call for more discipline.

Keepers who gave their states outstanding service without attracting the Test selectors. *Top:* Victoria's Michael Dimattina, and West Australian Dennis Yagmich.

Jack Richards, a specialist keeper preferred in eight Tests to Alec Stewart, did well, with 20 dismissals. He scored 133 against Australia in Perth on the 1986–87 tour. The English keeper who appealed most to Australians was the artistic Jack Russell. He had fast hands, speedy feet and was especially impressive keeping to spinners John Emburey and the left-handed Phil Tufnell.

Rodney Marsh has seen some exciting keeping talent at the Australian Cricket Academy but in 1993 only one academy graduate keeper, Darren Berry, has won a permanent place in a state team. Peter Drinnen challenged for a time in Queensland but conceded to Peter Anderson, knowing Ian Healy would appear and probably take Anderson's place from time to time. Marsh's problem is that there are only six spots available in Sheffield Shield teams around Australia. His pupils have to remain patient, encouraged by the knowledge that Bert Oldfield, Don Tallon, Wally Grout, John Maclean, Steve Rixon, Len Maddocks and Gil Langley all had to wait for their chances to play Test cricket.

The keepers who deserve most sympathy, however, are those like South Australia's Tim Nielson and New South Wales captain Phil Emery, who do a fine job but are seldom mentioned in discussions about selections for Australian teams. Emery has handled the spin of Greg Matthews and the pace of Geoff Lawson and Wayne Holdsworth with tradesmanlike efficiency and often saved his side with the bat.

The challenge for first-class keepers remains strong. The job needs stamina, alertness, concentration and skilful hands. Modern equipment has taken most of the bruises and broken bones out of the task, but as Alan Knott said in his book *Alan Knott on Wicket-Keeping*, it provides unique satisfaction.

'A wicket-keeper can be bobbing up and down for five hours out of six, sometimes for two days, and possibly a third,' wrote Knott. 'He must be ready to dive to the wide ones, jump high when required, and be ready for a sprint to the stumps when he is standing back. It is hard work, but it is wonderfully rewarding, because you are never out of the game. No greater thrill existed for me than to take off, stretching every inch of the body, legs and arms, to claw a wide deflection into my gloves.'

Appendix I

Test Wicket-keeping Records

ROSS DUNDAS

MOST DISMISSALS IN A TEST CAREER

	Country	Tests	Caught	Stumped	Total
R.W. Marsh	Australia	97	343	12	355
P.J.L. Dujon[a]	West Indies	81	267	5	272
A.P.E. Knott	England	96	250	19	269
Wasim Bari	Pakistan	81	201	27	228
T.G. Evans	England	91	173	46	219
S.M.H. Kirmani	India	88	160	38	198
D.L. Murray	West Indies	62	181	8	189
A.T.W. Grout	Australia	51	163	24	187
I.D.S. Smith	New Zealand	63	168	8	176
R.W. Taylor	England	57	167	7	174
I.A. Healy	Australia	47	146	7	153
J.H.B. Waite	South Africa	50	124	17	141
K.S. More	India	47	106	28	134
W.A.S. Oldfield	Australia	54	78	52	130
J.M. Parks[a]	England	46	103	11	114
Salim Yousuf	Pakistan	32	91	13	104
G.R.A. Langley	Australia	26	83	15	98
L.E.G. Ames[a]	England	47	74	23	97
K.J. Wadsworth	New Zealand	33	92	4	96
Imtiaz Ahmed	Pakistan	41	77	16	93
A.F.A. Lilley	England	35	70	22	92
F.C.M. Alexander	West Indies	25	85	5	90
R.C. Russell	England	31	80	8	88
F.M. Engineer	India	46	66	16	82
P.R. Downton	England	30	70	5	75
H. Strudwick	England	28	60	12	72

Best for Sri Lanka

| S.A.R. Silva | Sri Lanka | 9 | 33 | 1 | 34 |

Best for Zimbabwe

| A. Flower | Zimbabwe | 3 | 6 | 1 | 7 |

[a]Includes two catches taken when fielding.

MOST DISMISSALS IN A TEST SERIES

	Venue	Series	Tests	Caught	Stumped	Total	Opponent
AUSTRALIA							
R.W. Marsh	Australia	1982–83	5	28	–	28	England
R.W. Marsh	Australia	1975–76	6	26	–	26	West Indies
I.A. Healy	Australia	1990–91	5	24	–	24	England
A.T.W. Grout	Australia	1960–61	5	20	3	23	West Indies
R.W. Marsh	England	1972	5	21	2	23	England
R.W. Marsh	England	1981	6	23	–	23	England
S.J. Rixon	Australia	1977–78	5	22	–	22	India
R.A. Saggers	South Africa	1949–50	5	13	8	21	South Africa
G.R.A. Langley	Australia	1951–52	5	16	5	21	West Indies
A.T.W. Grout	England	1961	5	20	1	21	England
R.W. Marsh	Australia	1983–84	5	21	–	21	Pakistan
D. Tallon	Australia	1946–47	5	16	4	20	England
G.R.A. Langley	West Indies	1954–55	4	16	4	20	West Indies
A.T.W. Grout	Australia	1958–59	5	17	3	20	England
H.B. Taber	South Africa	1966–67	5	19	1	20	South Africa
ENGLAND							
A.P.E. Knott	Australia	1970–71	7	21	3	24	Australia
A.P.E. Knott	Australia	1974–75	6	21	1	22	Australia
H. Strudwick	South Africa	1913–14	5	21	–	21	South Africa
T.G. Evans	South Africa	1956–57	5	20	–	20	South Africa
R.W. Taylor	Australia	1978–79	6	18	2	20	Australia
P.R. Downton	England	1985	6	19	1	20	Australia
SOUTH AFRICA							
J.H.B. Waite	South Africa	1961–62	5	23	3	26	New Zealand
D.T. Lindsay	South Africa	1966–67	5	24	–	24	Australia
J.H.B. Waite	South Africa	1953–54	5	16	7	23	New Zealand
WEST INDIES							
D.L. Murray	England	1963	5	22	2	24	England
F.C.M. Alexander	West Indies	1959–60	5	22	1	23	England
P.J.L. Dujon	West Indies	1990–91	5	23	–	23	Australia
P.J.L. Dujon	West Indies	1983–84	5	19	1	20	Australia
P.J.L. Dujon	England	1988	5	20	–	20	England
NEW ZEALAND							
A.E. Dick	South Africa	1961–62	5	21	2	23	South Africa
INDIA							
N.S. Tamhane	Pakistan	1954–55	5	12	7	19	Pakistan
S.M.H. Kirmani	India	1979–80	6	17	2	19	Pakistan
PAKISTAN							
Wasim Bari	Pakistan	1982–83	6	15	2	17	India
SRI LANKA							
S.A.R. Silva	Sri Lanka	1985–86	3	21	1	22	India

	Venue	Series	Tests	Caught	Stumped	Total	Opponent
ZIMBABWE							
A. Flower	Zimbabwe	1992–93	2	5	1	6	New Zealand

MOST DISMISSALS IN A TEST MATCH

	Venue	Series	Caught	Stumped	Total	Opponent
AUSTRALIA						
G.R.A. Langley	Lord's	1956	8	1	9	England
R.W. Marsh	Brisbane	1982–83	9	–	9	England
J.J. Kelly	Sydney	1901–02	8	–	8	England
G.R.A. Langley	Kingston	1954–55	8	–	8	West Indies
A.T.W. Grout	Lahore	1959–60	6	2	8	Pakistan
A.T.W. Grout	Lord's	1961	8	–	8	England
H.B. Taber	Johannesburg	1966–67	7	1	8	South Africa
R.W. Marsh	Melbourne	1975–76	8	–	8	West Indies
R.W. Marsh	Christchurch	1976–77	8	–	8	New Zealand
R.W. Marsh	Sydney	1980–81	7	1	8	India
R.W. Marsh	Adelaide	1982–83	8	–	8	England
I.A. Healy	Adelaide	1992–93	6	2	8	West Indies
ENGLAND						
R.W. Taylor	Bombay	1979–80	10	–	10	India
L.E.G. Ames	The Oval	1933	6	2	8	West Indies
J.M. Parks	Christchurch	1965–66	8	–	8	New Zealand
SOUTH AFRICA						
D.J. Richardson	Port Elizabeth	1992–93	9	–	9	India
D.T. Lindsay	Johannesburg	1966–67	8	–	8	Australia
WEST INDIES						
D.A. Murray	Melbourne	1981–82	9	–	9	Australia
NEW ZEALAND						
W.K. Lees	Wellington	1982–83	8	–	8	Sri Lanka
I.D.S. Smith	Hamilton	1990–91	8	–	8	Sri Lanka
INDIA						
K.S. More	Madras	1987–88	1	6	7	West Indies
K.S. More	Bombay	1992–93	5	2	7	England
PAKISTAN						
Wasim Bari	Leeds	1971	8	–	8	England
SRI LANKA						
S.A.R. Silva	Colombo	1985–86	9	–	9	India
S.A.R. Silva	Colombo	1985–86	8	1	9	India
ZIMBABWE						
A. Flower	Harare	1992–93	4	1	5	New Zealand

MOST DISMISSALS IN A TEST INNINGS

	Venue	Series	Caught	Stumped	Total	Opponent
AUSTRALIA						
A.T.W. Grout	Johannesburg	1957–58	6	–	6	South Africa
R.W. Marsh	Brisbane	1982–83	6	–	6	England
W.A.S. Oldfield	Melbourne	1924–25	4	1	5	England
G.R.A. Langley	Georgetown	1954–55	2	3	5	West Indies
G.R.A. Langley	Kingston	1954–55	5	–	5	West Indies
G.R.A. Langley	Lord's	1956	5	–	5	England
A.T.W. Grout	Durban	1957–58	4	1	5	South Africa
A.T.W. Grout	Lahore	1959–60	5	–	5	Pakistan
A.T.W. Grout	Brisbane	1960–61	4	1	5	West Indies
A.T.W. Grout	Lord's	1961	5	–	5	England
A.T.W. Grout	Sydney	1965–66	5	–	5	England
H.B. Taber	Johannesburg	1966–67	5	–	5	South Africa
H.B. Taber	Sydney	1968–69	5	–	5	West Indies
H.B. Taber	Port Elizabeth	1969–70	5	–	5	South Africa
R.W. Marsh	Manchester	1972	5	–	5	England
R.W. Marsh	Nottingham	1972	5	–	5	England
R.W. Marsh	Sydney	1973–74	5	–	5	New Zealand
R.W. Marsh	Christchurch	1973–74	5	–	5	New Zealand
R.W. Marsh	Melbourne	1975–76	5	–	5	West Indies
R.W. Marsh	Christchurch	1976–77	5	–	5	New Zealand
J.A. Maclean	Brisbane	1978–79	5	–	5	England
K.J. Wright	Melbourne	1978–79	5	–	5	Pakistan
R.W. Marsh	Brisbane	1979–80	5	–	5	West Indies
R.W. Marsh	Sydney	1980–81	5	–	5	India
R.W. Marsh	Perth	1981–82	5	–	5	Pakistan
R.W. Marsh	Perth	1983–84	5	–	5	Pakistan
R.W. Marsh	Sydney	1983–84	5	–	5	Pakistan
W.B. Phillips	Kingston	1983–84	5	–	5	West Indies
I.A. Healy	Adelaide	1989–90	5	–	5	Pakistan
I.A. Healy	Melbourne	1990–91	5	–	5	England
I.A. Healy	Adelaide	1990–91	5	–	5	England
ENGLAND						
R.W. Taylor	Bombay	1979–80	7	–	7	India
J.T. Murray	Lord's	1967	6	–	6	India
R.C. Russell	Melbourne	1990–91	6	–	6	Australia
J.G. Binks	Calcutta	1963–64	5	–	5	India
J.M. Parks	Sydney	1965–66	3	2	5	Australia
J.M. Parks	Christchurch	1965–66	5	–	5	New Zealand
A.P.E. Knott	Manchester	1974	4	1	5	India
R.W. Taylor	Nottingham	1978	5	–	5	New Zealand
R.W. Taylor	Brisbane	1978–79	5	–	5	Australia
C.J. Richards	Melbourne	1986–87	5	–	5	Australia
R.C. Russell	Bridgetown	1989–90	5	–	5	West Indies
SOUTH AFRICA						
D.T. Lindsay	Johannesburg	1966–67	6	–	6	Australia
D.J. Richardson	Port Elizabeth	1992–93	5	–	5	India

	Venue	Series	Caught	Stumped	Total	Opponent
WEST INDIES						
F.C.M. Alexander	Bridgetown	1959–60	5	–	5	England
D.L. Murray	Leeds	1976	5	–	5	England
D.L. Murray	Georgetown	1976–77	5	–	5	Pakistan
D.A. Murray	Delhi	1978–79	5	–	5	India
D.A. Murray	Melbourne	1981–82	5	–	5	Australia
P.J.L. Dujon	Kingston	1982–83	5	–	5	India
P.J.L. Dujon	Bridgetown	1985–86	5	–	5	England
P.J.L. Dujon	St John's	1990–91	5	–	5	Australia
D. Williams	Brisbane	1992–93	5	–	5	Australia
NEW ZEALAND						
I.D.S. Smith	Hamilton	1990–91	7	–	7	Sri Lanka
R.I. Harford	Wellington	1967–68	5	–	5	India
K.J. Wadsworth	Auckland	1972–73	5	–	5	Pakistan
W.K. Lees	Wellington	1982–83	5	–	5	Sri Lanka
I.D.S. Smith	Auckland	1983–84	4	1	5	England
I.D.S. Smith	Auckland	1990–91	5	–	5	Sri Lanka
A.C. Parore	Auckland	1991–92	5	–	5	England
A.C. Parore	Colombo	1992–93	5	–	5	Sri Lanka
INDIA						
S.M.H. Kirmani	Christchurch	1975–76	5	1	6	New Zealand
B.K. Kunderan	Bombay	1961–62	3	2	5	England
S.M.H. Kirmani	Faisalabad	1982–83	5	–	5	Pakistan
K.S. More	Madras	1987–88	–	5	5	West Indies
PAKISTAN						
Wasim Bari	Auckland	1978–79	7	–	7	New Zealand
Imtiaz Ahmed	Lahore	1959–60	4	1	5	Australia
Wasim Bari	Leeds	1971	5	–	5	England
Salim Yousuf	Karachi	1985–86	5	–	5	Sri Lanka
Salim Yousuf	Faisalabad	1990–91	5	–	5	New Zealand
SRI LANKA						
S.A.R. Silva	Colombo	1985–86	6	–	6	India
S.A.R. Silva	Colombo	1985–86	5	–	5	India
H.P. Tillekeratne	Hamilton	1990–91	5	–	5	New Zealand
ZIMBABWE						
A. Flower	Harare	1992–93	4	–	4	New Zealand

NO BYES CONCEDED IN A TOTAL OF 500 TEST RUNS

	Venue	Series	Total	Team	Opponent
H.P. Tillekeratne	Wellington	1990–91	4–671	Sri Lanka	New Zealand
T.G. Evans	Sydney	1946–47	8d–659	England	Australia
S.M.H. Kirmani	Faisalabad	1982–83	652	India	Pakistan
J.L. Hendriks	Sydney	1968–69	619	West Indies	Australia
I.D.S. Smith	Auckland	1988–89	5d–616	New Zealand	Pakistan
R.C. Russell	Leeds	1989	7d–601	England	Australia
W.W. Wade	Cape Town	1938–39	9d–559	South Africa	England
J.J. Kelly	Sydney	1897–98	551	Australia	England
A.P.E. Knott	Lord's	1973	9d–551	England	New Zealand
Imtiaz Ahmed	Birmingham	1962	5d–544	Pakistan	England
T.M. Findlay	Georgetown	1971–72	3d–543	West Indies	New Zealand
I.A. Healy	Bridgetown	1990–91	9d–536	Australia	West Indies
A.P.E. Knott	The Oval	1975	9d–532	England	Australia
D.T. Lindsay	Johannesburg	1964–65	531	South Africa	England
S.M.H. Kirmani	Adelaide	1980–81	528	India	Australia
R.C. Russell	Lord's	1989	528	England	Australia
A.P.E. Knott	Port-of-Spain	1967–68	7d–526	England	West Indies
W.A.S. Oldfield	Brisbane	1928–29	521	Australia	England
J.H.B. Waite	Melbourne	1952–53	520	South Africa	Australia
P.J.L. Dujon	Adelaide	1988–89	515	West Indies	Australia
R.G. de Alwis	Kandy	1982–83	4d–514	Sri Lanka	Australia
C.J. Richards	Adelaide	1986–87	5d–514	England	Australia
B.N. French	Wellington	1987–88	6d–512	England	New Zealand
J.L. Hendriks	Melbourne	1968–69	510	West Indies	Australia
W.B. Phillips	Bridgetown	1983–84	509	Australia	West Indies
K.J. Wadsworth	Dunedin	1972–73	6d–507	New Zealand	Pakistan
S.M.H. Kirmani	Faisalabad	1978–79	8d–503	India	Pakistan

MOST BYES CONCEDED IN AN INNINGS

	Venue	Series	Byes	Team	Opponent
F.E. Woolley	The Oval	1934	37	England	Australia
J.T. Murray	Bombay	1961–62	33	England	India
J.M. Parks	Kingston	1967–68	33	England	West Indies

AUSTRALIAN TEST WICKET-KEEPERS

	Debut	Matches	Innings[a]	N.O.	Runs	H.S.	50	100	Average	Innings kept wicket	Caught	Stumped	Total
B.A. Barnett	1938	4	8	1	195	57	1	–	27.86	6	3	2	5
J.M. Blackham	1876–77	35	62	11	800	74	4	–	15.69	56	36	24	60
F.J. Burton	1886–87	2	4	2	4	2	–	–	2.00	1	1	1	2
W. Carkeek	1912	6	5	2	16	6	–	–	5.33	8	6	–	6
H. Carter	1907–08	29	47	9	873	72	4	–	22.97	58	44	21	65
G.C. Dyer	1986–87	6	6	–	131	60	1	–	21.83	11	22	2	24
A.T.W. Grout	1957–58	51	67	8	890	74	3	–	15.08	97	163	24	187
I.A. Healy	1988–89	47	71	2	1,434	71	7	–	21.73	86	146	7	153
B.N. Jarman	1959–60	19	30	3	400	78	2	–	14.81	35	50	4	54
A.H. Jarvis	1884–85	11	21	3	303	82	1	–	16.83	15	9	8	17
J.J. Kelly	1896	36	56	17	664	46	–	–	17.03	67	43	20	63
G. Langley	1951–52	26	37	12	374	53	1	–	14.96	50	83	15	98
H.S.B. Love	1932–33	1	2	–	8	5	–	–	4.00	1	3	–	3
J.A. Maclean	1978–79	4	8	1	79	33	–	–	11.29	7	18	–	18
L.V. Maddocks	1954–55	7	12	2	177	69	1	–	17.70	10	18	1	19
R.W. Marsh	1970–71	97	150	13	3,633	132	16	3	26.52	181	343	12	355
W.L. Murdoch	1876–77	18	33	5	896	211	1	2	32.00	1	18	1	19
W.A.S. Oldfield	1920–21	54	80	17	1,427	65	4	–	22.65	96	78	52	130
W.B. Phillips	1983–84	27	48	2	1,485	159	7	2	32.28	27	43	–	43
S.J. Rixon	1977–78	13	24	3	394	54	2	–	18.76	23	42	5	47
R.A. Saggers	1948	6	5	2	30	14	–	–	10.00	10	16	8	24
H.B. Taber	1966–67	16	27	5	353	48	–	–	16.05	29	56	4	60
D. Tallon	1945–46	21	26	3	394	92	2	–	17.13	41	50	8	58
R.D. Woolley	1982–83	2	2	–	21	13	–	–	10.50	2	7	–	7
K.J. Wright	1978–79	10	18	5	219	55	1	–	16.85	15	31	4	35
T.J. Zoehrer	1985–86	10	14	2	246	52	1	–	20.50	17	18	1	19

[a]Innings shown is for batting, not the number of innings in which the player kept wicket. Ian Healy, for example, kept wicket in 86 innings but batted 71 times in Tests to the end of the 1992–93 season.

BYES ALLOWED BY AUSTRALIAN TEST WICKET-KEEPERS – PER RUNS SCORED

	Tests	Innings kept	Byes	Runs	Byes per 100 runs
S.J. Rixon	13	23	50	7,092	0.71
I.A. Healy	47	86	184	24,410	0.75
H.B. Taber	16	29	73	8,649	0.84
G.C. Dyer	6	11	26	2,934	0.88
W.B. Phillips	27	27	98	9,000	1.09
L.V. Maddocks	7	10	33	2,907	1.14
H.S.B. Love	1	1	2	162	1.23
W.L. Murdoch	18	1	3	232	1.29
R.W. Marsh	97	181	639	47,607	1.34
B.A. Barnett	4	6	36	2,643	1.36
B.N. Jarman	19	35	139	10,121	1.37
K.J. Wright	10	15	68	4,793	1.42
H. Carter	28	58	221	14,344	1.54
A.T.W. Grout	51	97	416	25,653	1.62
W.A.S. Oldfield	54	96	433	26,065	1.66
G.R.A. Langley	26	50	205	11,994	1.71
T.J. Zoehrer	10	17	84	4,847	1.73
R.A. Saggers	6	10	41	2,356	1.74
J.J. Kelly	36	67	287	15,648	1.83
J.A. Maclean	4	7	40	1,507	2.65
R.D. Woolley	2	2	19	703	2.70
A.H. Jarvis	11	15	96	3,053	3.14
D. Tallon	21	41	289	8,710	3.32
J.M. Blackham	35	56	402	11,804	3.41
W. Carkeek	6	8	97	1,793	5.41
F.J. Burton	2	1	12	154	7.79

BYES ALLOWED BY AUSTRALIAN TEST WICKET-KEEPERS – PER BALLS BOWLED

	Tests	Innings kept	Byes	Balls	Byes per 100 balls
I.A. Healy	47	86	184	51,039	0.36
H.B. Taber	16	29	73	19,664	0.37
S.J. Rixon	13	23	50	13,641	0.37
G.C. Dyer	6	11	26	6,686	0.38
H.S.B. Love	1	1	2	478	0.42
L.V. Maddocks	7	10	33	7,497	0.44
W.L. Murdoch	18	1	3	613	0.49
B.N. Jarman	19	35	139	24,957	0.56
W.B. Phillips	27	27	98	16,709	0.59
R.W. Marsh	97	181	639	102,315	0.62
A.T.W. Grout	51	97	416	65,972	0.63
K.J. Wright	10	15	68	10,262	0.66
W.A.S. Oldfield	54	96	433	65,346	0.66
B.A. Barnett	4	6	36	5,291	0.68
R.A. Saggers	6	10	41	6,044	0.68
G.R.A. Langley	26	50	205	30,339	0.68
H. Carter	28	58	221	30,814	0.72
J.J. Kelly	36	67	287	34,828	0.82
J.A. Maclean	4	7	40	4,543	0.88
T.J. Zoehrer	10	17	84	9,366	0.90
D. Tallon	21	41	289	23,501	1.23
A.H. Jarvis	11	15	96	7,545	1.27
J.M. Blackham	35	56	402	27,933	1.44
R.D. Woolley	2	2	19	1,266	1.50
F.J. Burton	2	1	12	561	2.14
W. Carkeek	6	8	97	4,122	2.35

Appendix II
English Wicket-keeping Records

LEADING ENGLISH WICKET-KEEPERS' CAREER RECORDS

	Career	Caught	Stumped	Total dismissals
L.E.G. Ames (Kent)	1926–51	703	418	1,121
K.V. Andrew (Northamptonshire)	1952–66	723	181	904
D.L. Bairstow (Yorkshire)	1970–90	961	138	1,099
J.G. Binks (Yorkshire)	1955–75	895	176	1,071
R. Booth (Yorkshire, Worcestershire)	1951–70	949	177	1,126
G. Brown (Hampshire)	1908–33	568	78	646
H.R. Butt (Sussex)	1890–1912	953	275	1,228
W.L. Cornford (Sussex)	1921–47	675	342	1,017
A. Dolphin (Yorkshire)	1905–27	608	273	881
P.R. Downton (Kent, Middlesex)	1977–91	690	89	778
G. Duckworth (Lancashire)	1923–47	754	341	1,095
D.E. East (Essex)	1981–90	480	53	533
F.M. Engineer (Lancashire)	1959–76	703	121	824
T.G. Evans (Kent)	1939–67	816	250	1,066
W. Farrimond (Lancashire)	1924–45	255	177	332
B.N. French (Nottinghamshire)	1976–1992	731	91	822
F.H. Huish (Kent)	1895–1914	933	377	1,310
D. Hunter (Yorkshire)	1888–1909	914	351	1,265
K.C. James (Northamptonshire)	1923–47	311	112	423
E.W. Jones (Glamorgan)	1961–83	840	93	933
A.P.E. Knott (Kent)	1964–83	1,129	131	1,260
W.H.V. Levett (Kent)	1930–47	283	195	478
A.F.A. Lilley (Warwick, London County)	1884–1911	717	194	911
A. Long (Surrey)	1960–75	921	124	1,045
A.J.W. McIntyre	1938–63	639	156	795
D.L. Murray (Cambridge University, Nottinghamshire, Warwickshire)	1960–81	741	108	849
J.T. Murray (Middlesex)	1952–75	1,270	257	1,527
T.W. Oates (Nottinghamshire, London County)	1897–1925	758	235	993
J.M. Parks (Sussex, Somerset)	1949–76	1,088	93	1,181
R.J. Parks (Hampshire)	1980–92	638	72	710
R. Pilling (Lancashire)	1877–89	461	206	667
C.J. Richards (Surrey)	1976–88	603	72	675
A.C. Smith (Warwickshire, Oxford University)	1958–74	715	61	776
E.J. Smith (Warwickshire)	1904–30	722	156	878
R.T. Spooner (Warwickshire)	1948–59	589	178	767
W. Storer (Derbyshire, London County)	1887–1905	376	55	431
G.B. Street (Sussex)	1909–23	308	121	429
H. Strudwick (Surrey)	1902–27	1,242	254	1,496
B. Taylor (Essex)	1949–73	1,081	283	1,294
R.W. Taylor (Derbyshire) [a]	1961–83	1,473	176	1,649
H. Yarnold (Worcestershire)	1938–55	463	231	694

[a] R.W. Taylor played 639 first-class matches to achieve this world record of 1,527 dismissals, whereas Australia's Rodney Marsh played 244 matches for his 810 dismissals.

MOST DISMISSALS IN AN INNINGS FOR EACH COUNTY

	Wicket-keeper	Venue	Season	Caught	Stumped	Total	Opponent
Derbyshire	R.W. Taylor	Derby	1966	7	–	7	Glamorgan
	R.W. Taylor	Chesterfield	1975	7	–	7	Yorkshire
Essex	D.E. East	Taunton	1985	8	–	8	Somerset
Glamorgan	E.W. Jones	Cambridge	1970	6	1	7	Cambridge Uni
	C.P. Metson	Chesterfield	1991	7	–	7	Derbyshire
Gloucestershire	H. Smith	Bristol	1923	3	3	6	Sussex
	A.E. Wilson	Portsmouth	1953	6	–	6	Hampshire
	B.J. Meyer	Taunton	1962	6	–	6	Somerset
Hampshire	G. Ubsdell	Southampton	1865	1	5	6	Surrey
	B.S.V. Timms	Portsmouth	1964	4	2	6	Leicestershire
	G.R. Stephenson	Lord's	1976	5	1	6	Middlesex
	R.J. Parks	Portsmouth	1981	6	–	6	Derbyshire
	R.J. Parks	Colchester	1984	6	–	6	Essex
	R.J. Parks	Southampton	1986	5	1	6	Nottinghamshire
	A.N. Aymes	Oxford	1989	6	–	6	Oxford University
Kent	S.A. Marsh	Lord's	1991	8	–	8	Middlesex
Lancashire	W. Farrimond	Manchester	1930	6	1	7	Kent
	W.K. Hegg	Chesterfield	1989	7	–	7	Derbyshire
Leicestershire	P. Corrall	Hove	1936	4	2	6	Sussex
	P. Corrall	Leicester	1949	3	3	6	Middlesex
	R.W. Tolchard	Leeds	1973	6	–	6	Yorkshire
	R.W. Tolchard	Southampton	1980	6	–	6	Hampshire
	P.A. Nixon	Hinckley	1990	5	1	6	Glamorgan
Middlesex	W.F.F. Price	Lord's	1937	7	–	7	Yorkshire
Northamptonshire	K.V. Andrew	Manchester	1962	7	–	7	Lancashire
Nottinghamshire	T.W. Oates	Nottingham	1906	6	–	6	Middlesex
	T.W. Oates	Leicester	1907	6	–	6	Leicestershire
	B. Lilley	Taunton	1932	6	–	6	Somerset
	E.A. Meads	Ilkeston	1948	5	1	6	Derbyshire
	E.A. Meads	Nottingham	1949	5	1	6	Kent
	G. Millman	Nottingham	1959	6	–	6	Northamptonshire
	B.N. French	Nottingham	1982	6	–	6	Essex
	B.N. French	Taunton	1984	6	–	6	Somerset
	B.N. French	Nottingham	1985	6	–	6	Derbyshire
	B.N. French	Birmingham	1992	6	–	6	Warwickshire
Somerset	H.W. Stephenson	Bath	1962	5	1	6	Glamorgan
	G. Clayton	Kidderminster	1965	6	–	6	Worcestershire
	D.J.S. Taylor	Taunton	1981	6	–	6	Essex
	D.J.S. Taylor	Bath	1982	6	–	6	Hampshire
Surrey	A. Long	Hove	1964	7	–	7	Sussex
Sussex	H. Phillips	The Oval	1872	3	3	6	Surrey
	H.R. Butt	Bristol	1899	6	–	6	Gloucestershire
	H.R. Butt	Hove	1901	6	–	6	Hampshire
	H.R. Butt	Hove	1909	6	–	6	Leicestershire
	A.A. Shaw	Hove	1927	3	3	6	Cambridge Uni
	R.T. Webb	Hove	1955	3	3	6	Nottinghamshire
	J.M. Parks	Dudley	1959	6	–	6	Worcestershire
	R.T. Webb	Hove	1960	6	–	6	Somerset
	M.G. Griffith	Clacton	1964	6	–	6	Essex
Warwickshire	E.J. Smith	Birmingham	1926	4	3	7	Derbyshire
Worcestershire	H. Yarnold	Glasgow	1951	1	6	7	Scotland
Yorkshire	D.L. Bairstow	Scarborough	1982	7	–	7	Derbyshire

MOST DISMISSALS IN A MATCH FOR EACH COUNTY

	Wicket-keeper	Venue	Season	Caught	Stumped	Total	Opponent
Derbyshire	H. Elliott	Manchester	1935	8	2	10	Lancashire
	R.W. Taylor	Chesterfield	1963	10	–	10	Hampshire
Essex	K.L. Gibson	Leyton	1911	7	2	9	Derbyshire
	D.E. East	Hove	1983	9	–	9	Sussex
Glamorgan	H.G. Davies	Swansea	1935	6	2	8	South Africa
	E.W. Jones	Birmingham	1970	8	–	8	Warwickshire
	E.W. Jones	Cardiff	1982	8	–	8	Essex
	C.P. Metson	Taunton	1991	7	1	8	Somerset
Gloucestershire	A.E. Wilson	Portsmouth	1953	10	–	10	Hampshire
Hampshire	R.J. Parks	Portsmouth	1981	10	–	10	Derbyshire
	A.N. Aymes	Oxford	1989	10	–	10	Oxford University
Kent	F.H. Huish	The Oval	1911	1	9	10	Surrey
	J.C. Hubble	Cheltenham	1923	9	1	10	Gloucestershire
Lancashire	W.K. Hegg	Chesterfield	1930	11	–	11	Derbyshire
Leicestershire	P. Corrall	Hove	1936	7	3	10	Sussex
Middlesex	M. Turner	Prince's	1875	6	3	9	Nottinghamshire
	J.T. Murray	Lord's	1965	8	1	9	Hampshire
Northamptonshire	L.A. Johnson	Worthing	1963	10	–	10	Sussex
	L.A. Johnson	Birmingham	1965	8	2	10	Warwickshire
Nottinghamshire	T.W. Oates	Nottingham	1906	9	1	10	Middlesex
	B.N. French	Oxford	1984	7	3	10	Oxford University
	C.W. Scott	Derby	1988	10	–	10	Derbyshire
Somerset	A.E. Newton	Lord's	1901	6	3	9	Middlesex
	H.W. Stephenson	Taunton	1963	8	1	9	Yorkshire
Surrey	E. Pooley	The Oval	1868	8	4	12	Sussex
Sussex	H. Phillips	The Oval	1872	5	5	10	Surrey
Warwickshire	E.B. Lewis	Birmingham	1949	8	1	9	Oxford University
Worcestershire	H. Yarnold	Worcester	1949	5	4	9	Hampshire
	S.J. Rhodes	Kidderminster	1988	9	–	9	Sussex
Yorkshire	D.L. Bairstow	Scarborough	1982	11	–	11	Derbyshire

MOST DISMISSALS IN A SEASON FOR EACH COUNTY

	Wicket-keeper	Season	Caught	Stumped	Total
Derbyshire	H. Elliott	1935	69	21	90
	B. Taylor	1962	79	10	89
Glamorgan	E.W. Jones	1970	85	9	94
Gloucestershire	J.H. Board	1895	52	23	75
	B.J. Meyer	1962	59	16	75
Hampshire	L. Harrison	1959	76	7	83
Kent	L.E.G. Ames	1929	71	45	116
Lancashire	G. Duckworth	1928	69	28	97
Leicestershire	J. Firth	1952	65	20	85
Middlesex	J.T. Murray	1960	92	7	99
Northamptonshire	K.V. Andrew	1962	84	6	90
Nottinghamshire	B.N. French	1984	76	11	87
Somerset	H.W. Stephenson	1954	50	36	86
Surrey	A. Long	1964	74	17	91
Sussex	G.B. Street	1923	69	26	95
Warwickshire	G.W. Humpage	1985	76	4	80
Worcestershire	H. Yarnold	1949	60	44	104
Yorkshire	J.G. Binks	1960	96	11	107

INDEX

Abberley, Neal, 145
Adamson, L.A., 53
Adcock, Neil, 115
AIF XI, 62, 64–6, 85
Alcock, Charles, 37
Alexander, Franz C.M., 100, 164–5, 168
Alexander, George, 33, 35
Alexander, Gerry, 118
Allan, David W., 100
Allan, Frank, 9, 11
Allen, David, 121
Allen, 'Gubby', 77–8, 81, 83–4
Allsopp, Arthur, 122, 135
Altham, Harry, 23
Amarnath, Lala, 99
Ambler, Albert M., 65, 79–80, 83
Ames, Leslie, 72–8, 81, 83–4, 86, 103–4, 142, 164, 166, 172, 175
Amir Elahi, 106
Amiss, Dennis, 145
Anderson, Peter W., 157, 159, 163
Andrew, Keith V., 129–30, 144, 172–3, 175
Andrews, Jack, 104
Andrews, Tommy, 79
Archer, Ken, 111, 113
Armitage, Tom, 12
Armstrong, Warwick, 47, 65–7
Ashes, 36, 87
Asif Iqbal, 145
Atkinson, Mark N., 158
Australia
    test records for, 164–7, 170–1
    v America, 51
    v England, 12–17, 19, 23–7, 29–33, 35, 37–8, 43–8, 51–3, 56–7, 60–1, 66–8, 70–2, 75, 77–88, 91, 94, 96–7, 99, 102–4, 114–15, 117–19, 124, 127–9, 137, 142, 146–7, 151, 162–3, 166
    v India 106, 117, 122, 140, 151–2, 156
    v New Zealand, 35, 61, 95, 114, 124, 137, 154, 157
    v Pakistan, 106–7, 110, 117–18, 140, 159
    v The Rest **1898–99**, 46
    v Rest of the World **1971–72**, 131, 135, 151
    v South Africa, 40, 52, 65, 68, 82, 84, 86–7, 99, 108, 114–15, 122, 124
    v Sri Lanka, 156, 158
    v West Indies, 89, 97, 99–101, 114, 118–19, 122, 124–6, 137, 157–8, 161
    v Zimbabwe, 159
    see also AIF XI; byes; dismissals; intercolonial matches; World Series Cricket
Australian Board of Control, 52
Australian Cricket Academy, 155, 159, 163
Australian Cricket Board, 62, 155, 158
Aymes, A.N., 173–4

Bacher, Ali, 125
Badcock, Clayvell (Jack), 80
Bailey, Trevor, 115, 144
Bairstow, David L., 162, 172–4
Baker, E.A., 172–3
Balaskas, Xenophon C., 82
Bancroft, Claude K., 68
Bannerman, Alick, 14, 35–6, 106
Bannerman, Charles, 10, 12, 14–15
Barbour, Dr Eric, 62
Barlow, Eddie, 125
Barnes, Sidney, 57–8, 88, 103, 106
Barnett, Benjamin A., 78–9, 83–8, 91, 94, 170–2
Barrett, Dr John, 38
Barrow, Ivan, 89
Batchelor, Denzil, 104
Beauclerk, Lord Frederick, 22
Beaumont, John, 26
Becker, Gordon C., 122, 132, 135
Bedser, Alec, 87, 102–4, 109–10
Benaud, Richie, 107, 109, 115, 118–19, 121, 135
Bennett, Francis, 122
Bensted, Eric, 94
Berry, Darren S., 155, 159, 163
Bevan, John, 43
Binks, James G., 124, 129, 144, 167, 173, 175
Binns, Alfred P., 100
Blackham, Frederick, 9
Blackham, John M., 8, 9–19, 24, 26–7, 31–2, 35–8, 42, 44–5, 47, 55–6, 59, 73, 88, 136, 170–2
Blain, Tony, 154
Bligh, Hon. I., 22, 24, 36–7
Blythe, Colin, 75
Board, John H., 30, 58, 175
Bodyline series, 72, 78, 80–1, 83
Bolton, John, 53
Bonnor, George, 16, 26
Boon, David, 158
Booth, Roy, 144, 172
Border, Allan, 157
Bosanquet, Bernard, 46, 57
Botham, Ian, 137, 159, 162
Bowden, Monty, 39
Bowley, Tom, 26
Box, Tom, 20–1, 23
Boyle, Harry, 17, 32, 35–6
Bradman, Donald, 77–9, 81–2, 86, 91, 94, 97, 99, 103, 112, 119, 122, 137
Braund, Len, 57
Brearley, Mike, 140, 145
Brearley, Walter, 46
Brennan, Don, 124, 144
Briggs, Johnny, 18, 39
Bright, Ray, 137
Brown, Bill, 81, 94–5, 113

Brown, Charles, 21
Brown, David, 121
Brown, Freddie, 129
Brown, George, 70, 172
Brown, J.T., 56
Brown, 'Snuffie', 71
Bryant, Richard, 37, 44
Buggins, Bruce L., 122–3
Burge, Peter, 114
Burke, Jimmy, 115
Burn, Ken, 37–8, 45
Burton, Frederick J., 26–7, 44, 170–1
Bush, James A., 11, 30
Butt, Harry, 27, 29, 172–3
byes
    allowed in Australian tests
        per balls bowled, 171
        per runs scored, 171
    most conceded in an innings, 169
    none conceded in a total of 500 test runs, 169

Cadbury, Richard, 55
Caffyn, William, 14
Callacher, Jack, 44
Cameron, Horace, 70–1, 81–2, 87
Campbell, Gordon, 53
Carew, Joey, 135
Carew, Patrick J., 51
Carkeek, William (Barlow), 47–8, 51–3, 83
Carmody, Keith, 95, 122
Carter, Hanson, 48, 50–2, 53, 61, 64–8, 73, 77, 83, 157, 170–2
Catt, Tony, 144
Chadwick, Derek, 125
Challenor, George, 70
Chapman, Percy, 64, 68, 70, 76–7
Chappell, Greg, 132, 141
Chappell, Ian, 120, 125–6, 135, 137, 148
Cheetham, Jack, 108, 113
Chilvers, Hughie, 84
Christiani, Cyril M., 89
Christiani, Robert J., 89
Clayton, G., 173
Close, Brian, 144
Clough, Peter, 157
Cohen, Vic, 18
Collins, Herbie, 62, 64, 70
Colquhon, Ian, 152
Compton, Leslie, 94, 102, 104, 128
Coningham, Arthur, 18
Constantine, Learie, 68, 70–1
Constantine, Lebrun, 68
Conway, John, 9, 10, 15, 32
Cooper, B.B., 172
Cooper, Lew D., 135
Cooper, William, 14, 24
Coppin, George, 10
Cornford, Walter L., 83, 89, 172
Corrall, Percy, 104, 173–4
Coulthard, George, 33
county cricket records, 13, 173–5

Courtice, Andrew, 156
Craig, Ian, 100, 109, 115
Croft, Colin, 151
Crouch, George, 53
Crowe, Martin, 154

Daniel, Wayne, 151
Darling, Joe, 12, 40, 45
Darling, Len, 81
Davidson, Alan, 115–17, 131, 137
Davidson, Hugh L., 81
Davidson, Rex, 130
Davies, H.G., 174
Dawkes, George, 104
de Alwis, R.G., 169
de Silva, A.M., 161
Deane, Sid, 37, 53
Delves, Richard, 53
Denness, Mike, 151
Denton, David, 59
Depeiza, Clairemonte, 100
Dev, Kapil, 161
Dewhurst, George, 68
Dexter, Ted, 118, 129, 162
Dick, A.E., 152, 165
Dimattina, Michael, 157–9, 163
dismissals
    English county, 172–5
    test match, 164–8
Docker, Cyril, 62
Dodds, Norman, 157
Dolphin, Arthur, 26, 66, 172
Donkin, Ralph, 12
D'Oliviera, Basil, 145
Donnan, Harry, 47
Doolan, Bruce, 157
Douglas, Johnny, 60–1, 65
Downton, Paul R., 161–2, 164–5, 172
Drinnen, Peter, 155, 159, 163
Ducker, John R., 130
Duckworth, George, 70–2, 77, 81, 83, 99, 104, 172, 175
Duff, Reggie, 27, 47, 75
Dujon, P.J.L. (Jeffrey), 160–61, 164–5, 168–9
Dwyer, E.A., 97
Dyer, Gregory C., 155–7, 161
Dymock, Geoff, 140

East, D.E., 172–4
Easton, Frank A., 81, 87
Ebeling, Hans, 104
Edrich, Bill, 88, 104
Edrich, Geoff, 91
Edwards, 'Jock', 152
Edwards, Richard, 135
Edwards, Ross, 130, 143
Elliott, Harry, 71, 77, 174–5
Ellis, Jack L., 61, 65–6, 78–80
Ellis, Matthew, 53
Emburey, John, 163
Emery, Phil A., 163
Endean, William R., 108–9
Engineer, Farokh M., 117, 125, 151, 164, 172

England
  country records for, 13, 173-5
  test records for, 164-7
  v America, 23
  v Australia 12-19, 23-7, 29-33,
    35, 37-8, 43-8, 51-3, 56-7,
    60-1, 66-8, 70-2, 75, 77-8,
    91, 94, 96-7, 99, 102-4,
    114-15, 117-19, 124, 127-9,
    137-8, 142, 146-7, 151, 156,
    162-3, 166
  v India, 27, 78-9, 106, 109-10,
    117, 124, 129, 151-2, 162
  v New South Wales, 10, 33, 135
  v New Zealand, 77, 83, 89,
    102-3, 110, 127, 148, 154
  v Pakistan, 106-7, 110, 129,
    144-6
  v Queensland, 92
  v South Africa, 26, 29-30,
    39-40, 58, 60, 70-1, 77, 81-3,
    87, 97, 102, 108
  v South Australia, 57
  v Sri Lanka, 127, 161-2
  v Tasmania, 57
  v Victoria, 10, 31, 66
  v West Indies, 30, 68, 70-1, 77,
    83, 89, 91, 99-101, 104-5, 109,
    126-7, 145-6, 162
  see also AIF XI; byes;
    dismissals
Evans, Edwin, 31, 37
Evans, T.G. (Godfrey), 73, 75, 93,
  101, 103-6, 109, 118, 124, 136,
  142, 144, 164-5, 169, 172
Evans, William T., 53, 87, 94
Evers, Harold, 53, 66, 122

Fairfax, Alan, 104
Fallowfield, Les, 87
Farquhar, John, 87-8, 111
Farrimond, William, 58, 83,
  172-3
Favell, Les, 118
Fazal Mahmood, 107
Ferguson, Bill, 51
Ferris, Jacky, 39, 44
Fillary, Ted, 144
Findlay, T.M., 169
Fingleton, Jack, 122
Firth, J., 175
Fleetwood-Smith, 'Chuck', 79, 82,
  84, 87-8
Flower, A., 164, 166, 168
Flynn, Brian, 115
Ford, Douglas A., 123-4, 172-3,
  175-6
Foster, Frank, 55, 57-60
Francis, George, 68, 70-1
Freeman, Alfred P., 75-8
French, Bruce N., 137, 169, 172-5
Fry, Charles, 38, 60

Gale, Terry, 132
Gamsy, Dennis, 125
Garner, Joel, 151
Garrett, Tom, 10, 25, 37
Gatehouse, George, 157
Gay, Leslie, 27
Geary, George, 81
Gee, Dan, 45
Gentlemen v Players, 22-3, 25-7,
  29, 38, 40, 56
Gibb, Paul A., 102, 109, 144
Gibbs, Barry, 157
Gibbs, Lance, 101
Gibson, K.L., 174
Giffen, George, 15, 18, 43-6
Gilbert, Dave, 156

Gilbert, Eddie, 92
Gilligan, Arthur, 68, 83
Gilmour, Garry, 138
Gleeson, John, 125, 137
Goddard, David, 132
Goddard, Trevor, 125
Goonatilleke, Hettiarachige M.,
  161
Grace, E.M., 33, 35
Grace, G.F. (Fred), 33, 35
Grace, W.G., 14, 17-19, 25, 27,
  32-3, 35-6, 40-1, 56
Graham, Harry, 12
Graveney, Tom, 115
Greenwood, Luke, 19
Gregory, Dave, 10, 12, 14, 24, 33,
  37
Gregory, Jack, 62, 64-6, 71, 85
Gregory, Ned, 10
Gregory, Syd, 47, 53
Griffith, Charlie, 101, 119, 135
Griffith, Herman, 70, 71
Griffith, M.G., 173
Griffith, S.C. (Billy), 102, 104-5
Grimmett, Clarrie, 70, 77, 79, 82,
  85, 91, 137
Grout, Arthur T.W. (Wally), 95,
  111-19, 121, 124, 128-30, 137,
  144, 163-7, 170-1
Guillen, Simpson C., 99-100
Gunn, Terry, 144

Hadlee, Richard, 137, 152
Hall, Richard, 36-7, 44
Hall, Wes, 100-1, 118, 135
Halliwell, Ernest A., 39-40
Halliwell, R. Bissett, 39
Hammond, John, 22
Hammond, Wally, 69, 76-7, 81,
  94, 102
Hampshire, John, 137, 144
Hanif Mohammad, 106-7
Harford, I., 168
Harris, Gordon, 66
Harris, Lord, 23, 33, 43, 58, 73
Harrison, L., 174
Harry, Jack, 37
Harvey, George, 53
Harvey, Neil, 109, 114-15
Hassett, Lindsay, 87, 95, 97, 103,
  109
Hastings, Tom, 44, 53
Hawke, Lord, 29, 58
Hawke, Neil, 118-19
Hayman, Francis, 21
Hazlitt, Gervys, 53
Headley, George, 89
Healy, Ian A., 64, 118, 156-7, 159,
  161, 163-7, 169
Hegg, W.K., 173-4
Hendren, 'Patsy', 85
Hendrick, Mike, 114
Hendriks, Jackie L., 100-1, 119,
  125, 169
Herron, Keith, 124
Hewson, Robert, 122
Higgs, Ken, 145
Hill, Alan, 75
Hill, Clem, 12, 29, 35, 47, 51-2,
  57, 60-1
Hill, Jack, 109
Hindlekar, Dattoram D., 89, 106
Hobbs, Jack, 61, 65, 68, 70, 83,
  85-6, 89
Hodder, Alfred, 96
Hodges, John, 11
Hogan, Tom, 158
Holding, Michael, 151, 157
Holdsworth, Wayne, 163

Hole, Graeme, 109
Holmes, Errol, 127
Holyman, Jim M., 158
Hone, Charles, 24
Hone, Leland, 23-4
Hone, Nathaniel, 24
Hooker, Halford, 79, 104
Hookes, David, 159
Horan, Tom, 9, 15-16
Hordern, 'Ranji', 52
Hornby, A.N., 33
Howard, Tom, 46
Howell, Bill, 40, 65
Hubble, John C., 58, 73, 75-7,
  104, 174
Hughes, Kim, 158
Hughes, Merv, 161
Huish, Frederick H., 27, 59, 75,
  77, 172, 174
Humpage, G.W., 175
Humphreys, Walter, 27
Humphries, Joe, 58
Hunt, Bill, 84
Hunte, Errol A.C., 89
Hunter, David, 25-6, 172
Hunter, Joe, 25
Hurn, Brian, 119
Hutcheon, Jack, 84
Hutton, Len, 87, 94-5, 108

Ibadulla, Billy, 145
Illingworth, Ray, 110, 126, 146-7
Imran Khan, 151-2
Imtiaz Ahmed, 106-7, 113, 164,
  169
India
  test records for, 164-6, 168
  v Australia, 106, 117, 122, 140,
    151-2, 156
  v England, 27, 78, 89, 106,
    109-10, 117, 124, 129, 151-2,
    162
  v New Zealand, 151-2
  v Pakistan, 106-7, 152
  v Sri Lanka, 161
  v West Indies, 100-1, 151
Inkster, Gordon B., 65-6, 83
intercolonial matches, 10, 15-17,
  31, 35, 43-4, 47
Intikhab Alam, 135, 151
Inverarity, John, 135
Iredale, Frank, 15, 56
Irvine, Jock, 135

Jackson, Archie, 81
Jackson, Brian, 124
Jackson, Vic, 86
James, C.L.R., 68
James, Cecil J., 88-9
James, K.C., 172
James, Ken, 152
Jantke, Jack, 114
Jardine, Douglas, 78, 81
Jarman, Barrington N., 111,
  114-15, 117-19, 121, 124, 130,
  135, 170-1
Jarvis, Alfred, 44
Jarvis, Arthur H., 15-16, 37, 43-5,
  51, 170-1
Jarvis, Harwood, 44
Jenner, Herbert, 23
Jennings, Claude, 53
John, George, 68
Johns, Alfred E., 46-7, 172
Johnson, Ian, 94, 96, 100, 106,
  113-14
Johnson, L.A., 187
Johnston, Bill, 96
Johnston, W.J., 97

Jones, A.O., 51
Jones, Andrew, 155-6
Jones, E.W., 172-5
Jones, Ernie, 12, 18, 43-5
Jones, Sam, 15, 36-7
Jordan, Ray C., 119, 130, 135
Joshi, Padmanabh, 117
Jupp, Henry, 12

Kadir, Abdul, 106-7
Kallicharan, Alvin, 147
Kalvwitharne, R.S., 161
Kanhai, Rohan, 100, 118
Kardar, A.H., 106
Kelleway, Charles, 62, 66, 68, 79,
  106
Kelly, James J., 42, 45-7, 55, 166,
  169-71
Kelly, Joe, 29, 40, 56, 83
Kelly, Thomas J.D., 13
Kendall, Tom, 12
Kerr, Robbie, 156
Kessey, Gwilym (Glyn), 95, 122
Khan Mohammad, 107
Kilner, Roy, 66
Kippax, Allan, 79
Kirmani, Syed M.H., 151-2,
  164-5, 165, 168-9
Kirshnamurthy, Pollamani, 151
Kline, Lindsay, 115, 117, 118
Knight, Barry, 119
Knott, Alan P.E., 110, 118, 124,
  126, 131, 136, 138, 142-8, 151,
  157, 163-5, 167, 169, 172
Kortright, Charles, 29, 45
Kotze, Johannes J., 40, 59
Kroger, Jack, 78
Kunderan, Budhisager K., 117,
  168

Lacy, Howard, 66
Laidler, Ernie, 87
Laker, Jim, 103, 108-10, 117, 144
Lambert, Ossie S., 124, 130
Lambert, William, 22
Lampard, Albert, 53, 62, 65
Lane, John, 53
Langley, Gilbert R.A., 66, 95-9,
  109, 113-14, 164-7, 170-1
Lara, Brian, 161
Larwood, Harold, 71, 77-8, 80,
  83, 86
Laver, Frank, 57
Lawrence, Charles, 14
Lawry, Bill, 121, 124-6, 129, 137
Lawson, Geoff, 163
Le Roux, Garth, 151
Learmond, George, 68
Leary, Stuart, 144
Lee, Ian, 81, 91, 95
Lees, Warren, 136, 152, 154, 166,
  168
Legall, Ralph A., 100
Lemmon, David, 23
Levett, W. (Hopper), 83, 129, 172
Levy, Roy, 92, 94
Lewis, E.B., 174
Lewis, Richard, 30
Leyland, Maurice, 88
Lillee, Dennis, 132, 136-7, 141,
  151
Lilley, Arthur F.A., 14, 29-30, 46,
  48, 51, 54-9, 73, 164, 172
Lilley, B., 173
Lillywhite, James, 10, 13, 26, 31-2
Lillywhite, William, 21
Lindsay, D.T., 165-7, 169
Lindsay, John, 125
Lillywhite, James, 10, 13, 26, 31-2

Lillywhite, William, 21
Lindsay, D.T., 165-7, 169
Lindsay, John, 125
Lindwall, Ray, 94, 96, 109, 118
Livsey, Walter, 76
Lloyd, Clive, 101, 146
Lock, Tony, 109-10, 117, 122, 128, 137
Lockwood, William, 26, 57
Lockyer, Tom, 11-13, 23, 26
Lohmann, George, 26, 39
Long, A., 172-3, 175
Long, Ted, 62
Love, Hampden S.B., 61-2, 65, 80-1
Lovelock, Ossie I., 91, 122
Loveridge, Walter, 53
Lowry, Tom, 89
Loxton, Sam, 96
Lyon, Malcolm, 58
Lyons, Jack, 12, 18
Lyttelton, Alfred, 24-5, 33-4, 36, 55

McAlister, Percy, 52, 60
Macartney, Charlie, 53, 62, 70
McCabe, Stan, 86
McCarthy, Jack, 112
McCauley, Bede, 86
McCool, Colin, 95-6, 99
McCormick, Ernie, 88
McCosker, Rick, 137
McDermott, Craig, 161
McDonald, Colin, 106, 109, 115
McDonald, Dr Ian H., 106, 118
McDonald, Ted, 66, 71
McDonnell, Percy, 17, 35, 37, 44
McGlew, Jackie, 108
MacGregor, Gregor, 27-8, 38, 55
McIntyre, Arthur J.W., 109-10, 172
Mackay, 'Slasher', 114-15, 117
Mackay, 'Sunny Jim', 47
McKenzie, Alick, 45
McKenzie, Graham, 101
Mackinnon, Francis, 73
MacLaren, Archie, 56, 67, 80
Maclean, John A., 126-7, 130, 132, 140, 163, 167, 170-1
McLeod, Bob, 15
McLeod, Charles, 18-19, 47
McWatt, Clifford A., 100
Maddocks, Ian L., 114
Maddocks, Len V., 114, 157, 163
Maddocks, Richard, 114
Mailey, Arthur, 51, 61, 65, 68, 70, 122
Mallet, Ashley, 125, 148
Mann, Tony, 135, 137
Marsh, Graham, 131-2
Marsh, Rodney W., 126, 130-8, 140-1, 148, 155-6, 164-7, 170-1
Marsh, S.A., 173
Marshall, George, 17
Marshall, John, 10, 157
Martineau, G.D., 20
Massie, Bob, 132
Massie, Hugh, 13, 15, 24, 36
Matthews, Greg, 161, 163
Matthews, Thomas, 53
May, Peter, 127
Mead, Phil, 60
Meads, E.A., 173
Meckiff, Ian, 110, 115, 117
Mendonca, Ivor L., 100-1
Metson, C.P., 173-4
Meuleman, Ken, 103
Meyer, B.J., 173, 175
Midwinter, Billy, 9, 11, 13-14, 24, 32

Milburn, Colin, 135
Millman, Geoff, 129, 173
Milton, Sir William, 39
Mitchell, Bruce, 82
Monfries, John E., 47
Mooney, Frank, 152
Moore, William, 122
More, Kiran S., 152, 164, 166, 168
Morris, Arthur, 102-3, 109
Morrison, Danny, 154
Moule, Bill, 35
Moyes, Johnnie, 52, 62
Moyle, Charles, 53
Munro, John K.E., 106, 122-3
Murdoch, Gilbert, 31, 41
Murdoch, William, 10-11, 13-14, 29, 31-3, 35-41, 43-4, 170-1
Murray, Deryck L., 100-1, 118, 143, 164-9, 172
Murray, John T., 48, 62, 124, 127-9, 145, 172, 174-5
Murray, Junior R., 161
Murrell, Harry, 64
Mushtaq, Mohammad, 106

Nascimento, Cecil, 68
Nashad, Ali, 106
Navle, Janardhan G., 89
New South Wales
  v AIF team, 65
  v England, 10, 33, 135
  v New Zealand, 61
  v Queensland, 91
  v South Australia, 43, 80, 86, 121, 124
  v Tasmania, 157
  v Victoria, 10, 15-17, 31, 35-7, 47
New Zealand
  test records for, 164-6, 168
  v Australia, 35, 61, 95, 114, 124, 137, 154, 157
  v England, 77, 83, 89, 102-3, 110, 127, 148, 154
  v India, 151-2
  v New South Wales, 61
  v Pakistan, 152, 154
  v Sri Lanka, 154
  v Victoria, 79
  v West Indies, 100
Newland, Phillip, 47, 51
Newton, Arthur E., 89, 174
Nielson, Tim J., 163
Nixon, P.A., 173
Noble, Monty, 45, 51, 57, 80
Noel, John, 43
Norton, Jack, 115
Nourse, Dudley, 108
Nunes, Robert K., 68, 7
Nyren, John, 10, 21-2

Oates, Tom W., 60, 172-4
O'Brien, Leo, 81
O'Connor, Leo, 53, 65, 87-8
O'Halloran, Jim, 47
O'Hanlon, W.J., 37, 44
O'Keefe, Kerry, 137
Oldfield, William (Bert), 53, 61-71, 73, 77-8, 80, 82-8, 92, 97, 104, 118, 121, 136-7, 147-8, 163-4, 167, 169-71
O'Reilly, Bill, 60, 81-2, 84, 86-7, 94
O'Shea, Tom, 92
Oxenham, Ron, 101

Packer, Kerry, see World Series Cricket

Pakistan
  test records for, 164-6, 168
  v Australia, 106-7, 110, 117-18, 140, 159
  v England, 106-7, 110, 129, 144-6
  v India, 106-7, 152
  v New Zealand, 152, 154
  v Tasmania, 158
  v West Indies, 107
  v Western Australia, 137
Pallett, H.J., 55
Palmer, Joey, 15, 24-5, 33, 44
Park, Dr Roy, 62
Parks, Henry, 127
Parks, James, 118, 126-7, 129, 145, 164, 166-7, 169, 172-3
Parks, James snr, 127
Parks, Robert J., 127, 173-4
Parore, Adam C., 154, 168
Parry, Cyril, 80, 83, 157
Paynter, Eddie, 60, 88
Pearce, Tom, 121
Peel, Bobby, 19
Pellew, 'Nip', 62
Petrie, Eric, 152
Philipson, Hylton, 27
Phillips, Harry, 23
Phillips, Henry, 23, 173-4
Phillips, Ray P., 157, 159
Phillips, Wayne B., 150, 157-9, 167, 169-71
Pickett, Edward A., 157
Piggott, —, 68
Pilling, Richard, 13, 24, 172
Pinder, George, 25
Players v Gentlemen, 22-3, 25-7, 29, 38, 40, 56
Plumb, Tom, 23
Pollard, Reg, 103
Pollock, Graeme, 125, 135
Pollock, Peter, 125, 135
Ponsford, Bill, 77, 79
Pooley, Edward, 12-13, 23, 26, 48, 91, 124, 174
Pope, Rowley, 67
Potter, Jack, 155
Povey, Arthur, 75
Price, Wilfred F.F., 84, 173
Pritchard, Dave, 79
Proctor, Mike, 125, 151
Pryke, Dick, 53
Pullar, Geoff, 121
Pyke, Frank, 132

Queensland
  v AIF team, 65
  v England, 92
  v New South Wales, 91
  v South Africa, 159
  v South Australia, 94
  v Victoria, 94
Quin, Stan O., 78, 81

Ramadhin, Sonny, 99
Ranjitsinhji, K.S., 38
Ratcliffe, Andrew T., 61, 65
Raymer, Mick, 115
Read, J.M., 44
Read, Walter, 26, 39
records
  non-test
    England, 172-5
  test, 164-71
  see also byes; dismissals
Reedman, Jack, 19
Reeves, William, 53
Reid, Alex, 100
Rhodes, Harold, 124
Rhodes, S.J., 174

Rhodes, Wilfred, 66
Richards, Barry, 125
Richards, C.J., 167, 169, 172
Richards, Jack, 163
Richardson, D.J., 166-7
Richardson, Tom, 26, 46
Richardson, Vic, 80-2, 96, 122
Rigg, Keith, 91
Ring, Doug, 96, 106
Rixon, Steve J., 138-40, 156-7, 163, 165, 170-1
Roach, Clifford, 89
Roberts, Ron, 124
Robins, Walter, 88
Robinson, Ray, 48, 50-1, 64, 82, 87, 97, 99, 103-4
Robinson, Richie D., 130, 143, 149
Rorke, Gordon, 118
Routledge, Tom, 39
Rowan, Athol, 108
Rowan, Eric, 108
Rundell, Percy, 66
Rundle, Doug, 159
Russell, Charles, 68
Russell, R.C. (Jack), 163-4, 167, 169
Ryder, Jack, 66, 79-80, 104, 113-14

Sadiq Mohammad, 106
Saeed Ahmed, 106
Saggers, Roy A., 94-7, 165
Saleem Yousuf, 152, 164, 168
Sanders, Leyland, 111
Sandham, Andy, 89
Saunders, Jack, 40, 47, 57
Saunders, Warren, 122
Scott, C.W., 174
Scott, Dr Henry, 17
Scott, Tommy, 71
Sealy, James E.D., 89, 91
Searle, Jimmy, 44
Seddon, Dudley, 119
Selby, John, 12-13
Sen, Probir, 106
Sharjah, 156
Sharpe, John, 26
Sharpe, Phil, 144
Shastri, Ravi, 151
Shaw, A.A., 173
Shaw, Alfred, 13, 25-6, 32, 35
Sheehan, Paul, 135, 137
Sheffield, James, 58
Sheffield Shield competition, 44, 88, 91, 106, 111, 122, 156, 163
Sheppard, David, 118
Sherwell, Percy, 52
Sherwin, John, 55
Shrewsbury, Arthur, 16, 25-6, 37, 43-4, 56, 58
Sides, Frank, 101
Sidwell, Tom, 58, 76
Siggs, Doug, 112
Silk, Dennis, 128
Silva, S.A.R., 161, 164-6, 168
Simmons, Jack, 158
Simpson, Bob, 119, 124, 140, 157, 161
Sims, Alfred, 53
Sinclair, Geoff, 132
Sismey, Stanley G., 87, 95
Sleep, Peter, 161
Smith, Alan C., 129, 172
Smith, Charles A., 26, 39
Smith, Ernest J., 55, 58-61, 173
Smith, Frederick W., 39
Smith, Harry, 71, 173
Smith, Ian D., 152, 154, 164, 166, 168-9